The Investing Primer

A Comprehensive Guide for the
Aspiring Investor

Mitchel Myers

The Investing Primer by Mitchel Myers

ISBN: 978-1-973-55717-3

Contents

II Accounting, Essential Formulas, and Financial Analysis

4 The Anatomy of a 10-K/10-Q   **33**

5 Accounting Basics   **37**

IV   Valuation and Financial Modeling   111

About the Author

Mitchel Lee Myers is a passionate believer in and adherent to the proven principles of value investing and has a deep desire to help others interested in truly understanding the art and science of it. After studying computer science and finance at MIT, Mr. Myers set out to actively learn and gain experience in a range of investing approaches and philosophies. These efforts included stints at Goldman Sachs, Barclays, and notable hedge funds such as EcoR1 and Working Capital. Mr. Myers also worked on leading edge machine/deep learning and data science research for finance and investing/trading applications at both MIT Sloan School of Management and at Eureka Software.

In addition to his industry exposure and research, Mr. Myers voraciously analyzed and surveyed the leading publications on investment philosophies and basics including topics like accounting, valuation, and financial analysis. Mr. Myers was also selected to join Global Platinum Securities, a student run long/short hedge fund. Through this intensive exploration process, Mr. Myers discovered some critical challenges to and even a lack of adequate help for individuals wanting to be exposed to high quality information on value investing. Ultimately, this led Mr. Myers to write The Investing Primer for the purpose of educating aspiring investors.

Acknowledgments

This book was only possible due to the input and support of many individuals. Their contributions, though different in nature, were essential to the writing of this book. None shall be highlighted to the exclusion of others.

Introduction

The realm of investing captivates millions of people from all ages and backgrounds. Investing is enjoyable and stimulating, and provides the potential for significant monetary gain. However, it is tempting to focus on just that: monetary gain. When contemplating an initial foray into investing, one must remember nothing great comes easy, especially investing returns. Many investing books flaunt "get-rich-quick" schemes to allure readers. This is no such book. This book is intended to educate the reader on the nuts and bolts of professional investing.

An electrical engineer must learn the basics of electricity before designing a processor, and a structural engineer must learn the basics of materials and mechanics before designing a building. In the same vein, an investor must learn the building blocks of the industry in order to hope for a reasonable economic gain outside of luck. This book serves as a primer on the building blocks of investing.

Is investing identical to learning an engineering profession, then? Far from it. Whereas engineering disciplines are grounded in the laws of physical reality, investing attempts to assess the ever-elusive future. Investing success is also subject to the foibles and whims of people, including oneself. Engineering is purely a science. The answer is usually right or wrong. In investing, the correct answer is less clear. There's an art to investing.

To achieve long-term investing success, an investor must be equipped with the technical building blocks and a philosophical framework for navigating the uncertainty and behavioral components of investing. This book also presents such a philosophical framework, called value investing, that will arm the diligent reader with knowledge and know-how for navigating the financial markets.

To the knowledge of the author, there are no books that accomplish what this book aims to convey in one work. In fact, there are few books, if any, that arm the novice investor with an understanding of the core technical concepts of investing, while also discussing both the common qualitative characteristics of great investments, and a practical philosophical framework through which to implement this knowledge. Most books under the realm of corporate finance and investing have one of three critical flaws: 1) an exclusive focus on technical concepts, 2) an exclusive focus on philosophical concepts, or 3) an assumption that the reader understands the very basics of investing and finance. The objective of The Investing Primer is to fill the apparent void in investing literature by covering basic financial and investing concepts, advanced technical concepts, qualitative analysis, and a proven philosophical framework in a single, concise resource. Ultimately, the engaged reader will have a much deeper knowledge of investing and the ability to utilize this knowledge for significant economic gain. The topics covered in this book are:

- Part I: Investing Essentials and Acquiring Information

- Part II: Accounting, Essential Formulas, and Financial Analysis

- Part III: Debt and Capital Structure

- Part IV: Valuation and Financial Modeling

- Part V: Fundamental Analysis

- Part VI: Value Investing

- Part VII: Private Equity

- Part VIII: Advanced/Selected Topics

Part I

Investing Essentials and Acquiring Information

1

Investing Basics

1.1 The Basics of Investing

In the dictionary, the verb invest means: "to expend money with the expectation of achieving a profit or material result by putting it into financial schemes, shares, or property, or by using it to develop a commercial venture." From this definition, there are many important facts about investing that can be inferred. First, there are multiple parties involved in investing. There is a party that has money and a party in need of money to develop a product, service, etc. The party(s) with money currently are called investors or capital providers (where capital is essentially a word for money). Generally, the party that needs money to develop a product, or service is a company.

What are the motives of the investor? The investor expends cash or capital in the current time period, in exchange for some form of compensation, generally a financial claim to the future cash flows of the company to which the investor is providing capital. This financial claim takes two main forms: debt and equity. Each of these financial claims have unique attributes that will be discussed extensively in later chapters.

But, why does the investor want to acquire the debt or equity of a firm? What is in it for him? The investor is seeking a *return* on his investment in the debt or equity of the firm. In fact, put succinctly, the objective of investment is to *maximize total after-tax return* while *minimizing risk*. Risk is defined as the permanent loss of capital.

Shortly, we will review the basics of debt and equity to develop a more concrete understanding of the objective of investment. First, we must again consider the company.

What are the motives of the company that is receiving capital? Generally, the company intends to use the funds to invest in and grow the business. This could take several forms, such as buying new equipment (computers, machinery, etc), hiring new employees, growing a salesforce, or improving marketing initiatives. Ultimately, the main objective of the company is to increase its value using the funds provided by investors, which is quite similar to the investor's goal of maximizing his or her total after-tax return while minimizing risk. For now, we will focus on the return aspect of investing, but later on, an entire chapter will be devoted to understanding and qualifying risk.

First, let us define the two basics components of return: 1) cash flow paid from the company to the investor (this cash flow is called interest expense in the case of debt, and dividends in the case of equity), and 2) price appreciation of the financial claim (this price appreciation is called a capital gain). In traditional debt investment, the main source/focus of return is paid cash flow. In traditional equity investment, the main source/focus of return is price appreciation of the financial claim.

To briefly cover what debt is, consider a loan from an investor to a business for $100 with a 1 year maturity and a 5% interest rate. The $100 is called the face value or principal amount of the loan and represents the upfront investment made by the investor. This amount must be paid back to the investor after the maturity period elapses, in this case, after 1 year. On top of paying back the face value after 1 year, the company must also pay 5% interest on the debt. The cash or interest payment from the company to the investor equals face value * interest rate. A total of $5 in this example. Therefore, at the end of a year, the investor will have made $5 more dollars than he started with, or a 5% return on his initial $100 investment. In this case, notice that the return itself came exclusively from cash flow paid from the company to the investor (interest expense) and not from price appreciation of the debt.

To netter understand price appreciation, let us consider an equity investment. Purchasing equity is the same as purchasing stock in a company. Unlike debt, equity provides the investor with an ownership stake in the underlying company. As the company grows in value, so should the value of the equity stake in the underlying company. If an investor buys a stock for $100 and later sells it for $120, the investors return is 20%. What if the company pays a $5 dividend (a dividend is a cash payment to the stock holders of the company) to the equity holders *and* the stock rises in value from \$100 to \$120? In this case, the investor's return would be 25%.

Having provided basic examples of how debt and equity returns work, let us bring the discussion full circle with a formal definition of returns before moving on to more terminology definitions:

$$\% \text{ Return } = \frac{P_1 + C_1}{P_0} - 1$$

Here, P_0 is the amount of money paid or invested upfront. P_1 is the amount received upon exiting or selling the investment. And C_1 is the amount of cash paid out (whether in the form of interest expense or dividends) by the company to the investor during the time the investment is held (the holding period).

A collection of several investments is called a portfolio. A "portfolio company" is a company that an investors is currently invested in. The weight of a given investment in the portfolio equals (Value of Investment) / (Total Portfolio Size). Therefore, if an investor is invested in Stock A worth \$60 and Stock B worth \$40, then the Total Portfolio Size is \$100. Therefore, the "weight" of Stock A in the portfolio is 60%. To determine the return an investor receives from a given investment in the portfolio, we must multiply the % Return of Specific Investment by the Weight of the Specific Investment in the Portfolio or: % Return Relative to Entire Portfolio = (% Return of the Specific Investment)*(Weight of the Specific Investment). In the preceding example, if Stock A returned 10%, then the % Return Relative to the Entire Portfolio (which is more important) is 6%.

Now that we've established what a portfolio is, it is important to introduce diversification, the concept that making several different and diverse types of investments rather than just one or two can help reduce the variability (volatility) in value of an overall portfolio. Volatility is how much and how quickly the value of an investment or portfolio changes and is commonly used as a measure of the risk of a portfolio.

Remembering that the objective of the investor is to maximize *after-tax* total return while minimizing risk, let us briefly discuss how investments are taxed. The time between when an investment is bought and then sold is called the holding period. If the holding period of the investment is less than one year *and* the % Return of the investment is positive, the return is taxed at the standard income tax rate for the individual. If the holding period of the investment is greater than one year *and* the % Return of the investment is positive, the return is taxed at the long-term capital gains rate, which is 15% for most individuals.

Both equity and debt are also called securities. A security is a fungible, negotiable financial instrument that holds some type of monetary value. At this point, it is valuable to discuss the market(s) in which securities are traded. There are two main types: the primary market and the secondary market. The primary market refers to the market where securities are *created/issued.* The secondary market is the market where securities are *traded* among investors. Therefore, the proverbial *stock market* refers to the secondary market in which company equity is traded. The defining characteristic of the secondary market is that investors trade among themselves. That is, in the secondary market, investors trade previously issued securities *without the issuing companies involvement.* In contrast, the primary market is where new stocks and bonds are sold to investors for the first time and how companies raising debt or equity actually receive capital. You can think of the primary market as the market where an initial public offering (IPO) takes place. Simply put, an IPO occurs when a private company sells stocks or ownership stakes to the public for the first time. The securities are purchased directly from the issuing company.

Compound interest is the powerful wealth creating effect from generating sequential, positive investment returns for several years in a row. Want to really understand the wealth power of compounding interest? Consider the following thought experiment: the stock market has returned an average of 10% since 1926. So, if you were to take some money and invest it in the stock market today, what would that be worth 50 years from now? A mere $100 would be worth $11,739! What if you were able to become intelligent in investing and finance and increase your return to a market-beating level of 12% a year? That $100 would then be worth an astounding $28,900.

What defines a good return? To discuss this, we must introduce the concept of an index. An index is a hypothetical portfolio of securities that represents a particular market or market segment. For example, the S&P 500 is a common benchmark/index for the American stock market. This is commonly referred to as "the market". The S&P has returned about 10% a year on average for the past 90 years. So an investor who averages a return above the market over a long period of time is generally considered skilled. However, "beating the market" is notoriously difficult, so many advisers suggest simply buying an index and enjoying whatever return it gains from year to year. While that's a fine investment tactic, this book focuses on strategies and principles to try and beat the market.

To be "bullish" on a security or company means you are optimistic regarding the future prospects or price appreciation potential of that security. To be "bearish" means the opposite.

Lastly, to go "long" on a security means that the portfolio will profit from a rise in market value of the security. To "short" a security means that the portfolio will profit from a fall in market value of the security. To go long, an investor simply buys the security. The process of going short is more complicated and one we will come back to later.

The "Investment thesis" or "thesis" are the core rationales that support an investor going long or short on a security. The work an investor or research analyst puts in to develop a thesis is called "diligence" or "due-diligence." When an investor has direct conversations with individuals during the research process, such as management, this is called "primary diligence." All other research is called "secondary diligence."

1.2 A Company

The astute reader has observed something important in the preceding discussion: the returns of the investor are determined largely by the ability of portfolio companies to maintain and improve their worth. Therefore, it is essential that the diligent investor understand a company's competitive dynamics, financial situation, potential, and industry prior to investment. Focusing on these low-level, microeconomic aspects of a specific company is called bottom-up or fundamentals based investing. The opposite, or a top-down approach, focuses on macroeconomic trends and dynamics to make investment decisions. The author believes that the microeconomics of a business are easier to assess than macroeconomics of an entire economy. Thus much more attention will be given to the fundamental analysis of companies in the subsequent chapters.

Since we will focus on analyzing and understanding companies, it is valuable to establish the goals of a company, determine all its stakeholders, understand how it is controlled, and determine the incentives and goals of both the company and its controlling entities.

The goal of a company, generally speaking, is to maximize shareholder wealth and the monetary value of the company. Later, we will discuss why the monetary value of a company is equal to value of future cash flows produced by the company. Therefore, the goal of a rational company should be to maximize long term cash flow, though, we will see that this is often not the case.

We define a stakeholder as any group that has an interest in preserving the vitality of a firm. With this definition, several stakeholders come to mind: employees (the individuals who work at the firm), the government (which takes a portion of excess cash flow in the form of taxes), the suppliers (the firms or individuals who help produce the products of the firm), the customers (the firms or individuals who purchase the products of the firm), the creditors (the investors who have lent money to the firm), the shareholders (the investors who have an equity claim on the firm), the management team (the group of individuals who lead a company's strategic and financial direction), and the board of directors (the shareholder elected group of individuals who selects the members of the management team).

Therefore, a company is primarily controlled by its shareholders, who elect the board of directors, which then decides on the management team. In practice, management teams tend to be fairly "sticky" and last for a long time. The management team is broken up into many key individuals, such as the Chief Executive Officer (CEO) and the Chief Financial Officer (CFO). Per the prior discussion in this section, the goal of the management teams should be to maximize long-term shareholder wealth. However, sometimes this is not the case, since many management team focus on the short-term stock price of the company. Notice though, that the focus is generally always on shareholders, rather than the creditors, the other investors in the company. This is largely because creditors are not actual owners of the underlying business.

Ownership of a company is divided into shares. When you buy stock of a company, you are buying shares. If there are 100 shares outstanding, and you own 5, then you own 5% of the company. Each share has a price. This is the price that you see quoted in places like Yahoo Finance and Google Finance. Typically, companies have millions of shares outstanding, so purchasing any one share represents a fractional ownership of the business. The total value of a company's equity, or its market capitalization, is equal to the (Number of Shares Outstanding) * (Share Price).

Every publicly traded company has a ticker, which is an abbreviated name used for identifying the company. For example, the ticker of Apple is AAPL. Tickers are expressed in all capitalized letters.

1.3 Introduction to Value Investing

An investor must not walk blindly into the world of investment. It's a world that's incredibly complex and difficult, both technically and emotionally. With this in mind, an investor must be equipped with a sound investment philosophy, supported by empirical research and logical reasoning. The author, after a reasonable exploration of the world of investing, believes value investing to be superior to alternative philosophies. A long list of famous and incredibly successful investors have employed the value investing strategy, including Warren Buffett, Howard Marks, Benjamin Graham, and Seth Klarman. When implemented correctly and with an appropriate temperament, the efficacy of value investing has been duly proven.

At its core, value investing seeks to buy a \$1 for less than a \$1. Value investors believe that a company's market price (the price listed on the stock market) and its intrinsic value (the actual worth of the company) are two very different concepts. Price is what you pay, intrinsic value is what you get. Through deep, fundamental analysis, value investors seek to identify stocks and debt securities that have a market price well below the securities' intrinsic value. The wider the discrepancy between price and intrinsic value, the greater the *margin of safety* for the investment. The basic concepts and philosophy of value investing will be explored much more extensively in Part VI. Some value investors also invest in special situations that provide asymmetric risk/reward opportunities, such as distressed investing or biotechnology. However, these more advanced, technical topics are discussed in Part VIII.

2

Key Participants in the Investing World

2.1 Investment Banks

In most areas of life, there are intermediaries that play an essential role in facilitating the flow of money and products. For example, real estate agents facilitate the connection between a seller of a home and a buyer of a home. An investment bank is basically a financial intermediary that provides auxiliary and support services for companies, investors, and their various transactions. The basic business lines of most large investment banks are:

- **Investment Banking Business** - The investment banking business of an investment bankhas two main functions: intermediate on financing transactions and coordinate on mergers and acquisitions. Both of these functions are defined below:

  - Financing Transactions -

    A capital markets financing is basically when companies try to raise money from investors in the form of debt or equity. This process was explained in detail in the Investing Primer. An investment bank's capital markets division connects companies trying to raise capital with potential investors/providers of capital. The company raising debt or equity with the help of an investment bank is called the issuer. Raising new debt or equity is also called issuing debt or issuing equity.

    A capital markets financing is usually underwritten by investment banks, meaning that the investment bank first purchases the securities (debt or equity) from the company raising capital. Then the investment bank tries to sell the securities to interested investors. This

11

underwriting process is a primary offering (as defined in the Investing Primer) since new securities are created for the first time by this process. This underwriting process, for example, is how new shares are transferred to the public in an initial public offering (IPO). Subsequent equity raises are called follow-on offerings. After the securities are created in the primary market, and sold to investors, the securities begin to trade in the secondary market. The capital markets group also helps define what the terms of the financing should be (i.e. the price that equity is sold at, or the interest rate on the debt, etc.). With some exceptions, a capital markets financing must be registered with the Securities Exchange Commission (SEC), which is the governing body over securities that regulates and enforces the laws regarding capital markets and transactions.

When performing a capital markets transaction, an investment bank must make several important considerations. Will investors actually want to purchase the securities? How will the capital markets transactions impact the earnings of the company? Does the company need to raise capital right now? Should the capital be raised through debt or equity? We will work to understand these considerations more in subsequent chapters.

The investment bank is generally compensated for its help through a percent of the total raising amount. For example, if the issuer raises $100M in equity, generally the investment bank will receive 2-6% of that $100M as a fee. The fee percent varies with the type of security issued and the complexity of the capital raise.

— Mergers and Acquisitions -

The other important function of the investment banking business of an investment bank is the Mergers and Acquisitions role. In this role, the investment bank serves as an intermediary between buyers and sellers of companies. In this case, the investment bank could be an intermediary between a company buying another company, or an investor buying a company.

Mergers and acquisitions (M&A) arise when a change of ownership transaction occurs or a business combination occurs. This includes mergers (combining two companies), acquisitions (acquiring a company), divestitures (selling a business unit), and joint ventures (sharing ownership of a specific project with another company). The goal of M&A is to increase shareholder value and reduce shareholder risk, though this is not always the result. At the core of M&A is the buying and selling of corporate assets to achieve one or more strategic objectives. Therefore, a company must have a strategic rationale for completing an acquisition.

Investment bankers play a key role in initiating (determining and contacting companies that might want to acquire or be acquired), valuing (determining how much money it should cost to acquire the company), and executing (actually closing the deal). A key component in determining whether a specific M&A transaction is justifiable is whether synergies exist between the two businesses that might allow them to perform better in a combination. For providing these support services, the investment bank charges a fee as a percent of the total deal value (typically 2-8%).

To value and assess companies and transactions, investment banks employ five main techniques: discounted cash flow analysis, comparable companies analysis, precedent transactions analysis, leveraged buyout models, and merger models. All of these techniques will be covered in this book except merger models which are not as useful from an investing perspective.

- **Sales and Trading Business -** Investment banks conduct two types of trading: client-related trading and proprietary trading. Most investment banks focus on client-related trading, since recent regulation changes have made proprietary trading difficult within an investment bank.

  An investment bank's client-related trading business, also called market making, is comprised of traders, sales professionals, and research analysts.

  Traders are responsible for buying securities from investors trying to sell. Traders then aim to resell those securities to other investing clients. As such, the main function of client-related trading is to provide *liquidity* to investor clients. Liquidity is the degree to which an asset or security can be quickly bought or sold in the market without affecting the asset's price. Therefore, the main role of traders is to allow investor clients to easily, quickly, and cheaply exit positions. In exchange for the benefits of liquidity, investors pay the investment bank a commission on each trade. A secondary motive of client-related traders is to actually resell the securities they buy at a higher price. The commissions received for providing liquidity to investor clients are the main source of revenue/money for the sales and trading division. Since traders are buying and selling securities, they also manage a portfolio of securities. However, the objective of a traders' portfolio is less to generate return and more to minimize risk.

Beyond commissions, market makers/traders also make money by "capturing" the bid-ask spread. The "bid" is the current maximum price at which people will buy a given security. The "ask" is the current minimum price at which people will sell a given security. The bid-ask spread is the difference between the bid and the ask. For example, if the bid is $1 and the ask is $1.10, the bid-ask spread is $0.10. Therefore, if the market maker buys at the bid of $1 and is then able to resell securities at the ask of $1.10, they have "captured" the bid-ask spread and generated a $0.10 profit.

Sales professionals serve as a bridge between traders and investor clients. Whereas the traders are focused on developing trading prices, understanding market dynamics, and managing a portfolio, sales professionals are focused on communication with the investor clients on behalf of the traders. When an investing client wishes to purchase a security, their sales representative will quote an offer price determined by the trader.

The prime brokerage business is a subset of the sales and trading business and focuses on hedge fund clients who borrow securities and cash to support their investment business. Hedge funds will be discussed in detail later on in this chapter.

The sales and trading division is broken up into three main groups: 1) equities which focuses on trading stock, 2) fixed income, currencies, and commodities (FICC) which focuses on trading interest rate products (debt), currencies (like the US dollar and the Euro), and commodities (like oil or pork bellies), and 3) derivatives (complex financial instruments that are beyond the scope of this book).

Research analysts provide investor clients with research

on the markets and specific securities. While the investment bank is not directly compensated for this research, the hope is that investor clients will be impressed with the research and then trade through the sales and trading division, allowing the investment bank to generate a profit from the commission received on the trading activity. This investment bank produced research research is called sell-side, as opposed to buy-side, research. A more concrete discussion of the two will be had later.

Proprietary traders are non-client related traders who trade solely to generate a return for the investment bank. Basically, the proprietary trading business is similar to the business conducted by hedge funds, which will be elaborated on later in this chapter.

- **Asset Management Business -** The asset management business refers to the professional management of investment funds for individuals, families, and institutions. Investments include stocks, bonds, alternative assets (such as hedge funds, private equity funds, and real estate), commodities, and indexes. Asset managers specialize in different asset classes, and management fees are paid based on the asset class.

  Asset management products are offered through separately managed investment vehicles such as mutual funds, which are basically investment funds one can invest in through the stock market. The large investment banks manage dozens of mutual funds for a variety of asset classes. Historical mutual fund performance is key to selecting a mutual fund to invest in.

  Most major investment banks have large hedge funds housed within their asset management division. A hedge fund is a much less regulated version of a mutual fund. It charges higher fees than a mutual fund and is a private investment vehicle rather than a public investment vehicle (available on the stock market).

  Within the asset management business of an investment bank, there is another branch called wealth management. Wealth management refers to advisors who provide investment advice to select individuals, families, and high-net-worth clients.

Examples of large investment banks are: J.P. Morgan, Morgan Stanley, Goldman Sachs, Credit Suisse, and Bank of America

Merrill Lynch. These large investment banks are called "bulge-bracket" investment banks. However, dozens of smaller investment banks exist focusing on smaller clients and a narrower range of services. These smaller investment banks are called boutiques. Boutiques generally focus on producing high quality research and advisory/intermediary services for specific industries (such as technology) or market niches (such as special situations or distressed/bankrupt companies).

2.2   Hedge Funds

In the United States, the SEC has stated that the term hedge fund has no precise legal or universally accepted definition. Generally, a hedge fund refers to a private investment vehicle that manages a client's money and then invests that money to generate a return. A hedge fund is much more flexible than a mutual fund. Most market participants agree that hedge funds have the following characteristics: 1) almost complete flexibility in relation to investments, including both long and short positions (this depends on the hedge fund's mandate), 2) the ability to borrow money in an effort to enhance returns, 3) minimal regulation, 4) illiquid since an investor's ability to get his or her money back after investing in a hedge fund is restricted through lock-up agreements, 5) investors in hedge funds include only wealthy individuals and institutions, and 6) fees that reward managers for performance.

But how is a hedge fund actually structured and why do they exist? Imagine the following scenario: individual A has a lot of money but is poor at investing or believe they can find someone who can generate a better return. Individual B, on the other hand, has a lot of investing skill (with hope). So, individual A and B come together in a partnership, specifically in what is called a limited partnership, forming a hedge fund. Individual A has a high-net-worth and a lot of money to invest in the partnership. Let's say $50M. So individual A, seeking a return on that money, invests in individual B's hedge fund and gives him the $50M to invest with. In this scenario, individual A is called a "limited partner" since he is simply providing capital for individual B, the "general partner" to invest with on his behalf. Limited partner(s) (LPs) are essentially the clients/investors in the fund of the general partner(s) (GPs). The general partner is the investment manager. In the preceding scenario, individual B now has money that he can employ his investing skill with, and individual A is putting his money to work through a vehicle that with hope produces money.

So how are the different parties compensated? A typical fee structure for a hedge fund includes both a "management fee" and a "performance fee." In contrast, a typical mutual fund does not charge a performance fee, only a management fee. The standard hedge fund management fee is 2%. The standard hedge fund performance fee is 20% of the generated returns. The performance fee is also called "carried interest". In the industry, this fee structure is called "2 and 20." To give a concrete example of this fee structure at work, consider a hedge fund that has raised $100M dollars from limited partners. This hedge fund is said to have $100M in assets under management (AUM). So, the general partners receive $2M (2% of AUM) per year as a management fee. This fee is used to pay operating expenses (such as hiring research analysts), legal expenses, consulting fees, and technology fees. Beyond that, the general partners are also heavily incentivized to generate a great return with the capital they deploy because of the carried interest. If the fund is able to produce a 25% return in a year, then the fund has produced a $25M increase in AUM. As mentioned prior, the general partners receive 20% of the return they generate. In our example, the general partners receive an additional $5M (20% of $25M). The rest of the return, $20M in this case, goes to the limited partners. A high "water mark" relates to the payment of performance fees: hedge fund managers typically receive performance fees only when the value of the fund exceeds the highest AUM it has previously achieved. Some hedge funds also agree to a hurdle rate, whereby the fund receives a performance fee only if the fund's annual return exceeds a benchmark rate, such as 5%. The lock-up period is how long limited partners leave their capital with the general partners. The typical lock-up period is 1-5 years.

Hedge funds target absolute returns, which are investment returns that don't depend on the performance of broad markets and the economy. However, implementing this in practice is very difficult. For example, a hedge fund could short many equities in anticipation of a market downturn, which, if predicted correctly, results in positive returns for the fund while the rest of the markets and economy are struggling. Hedge funds are largely free from regulation because they invite investment only from sophisticated institutional investors and high-net-worth individuals.

Hedge funds frequently borrow additional money to invest with. This is called creating or using "leverage". If a hedge fund borrows money that has an interest rate of 5%, and then is able to produce a 10% return on that borrowed money, the result is a net profit. This works great, until the returns are bad, in which case the use of leverage can be threaten the vitality of the fund.

There are also hedge funds that invest in other hedge funds. These are called fund of funds. The fee structure and objective of maximizing return are identical between a fund of funds and a normal hedge fund, but their strategy for doing this is obviously very different. A hedge fund generally focuses on liquid, public securities such as stocks and bonds (or more complex financial instruments like options and other derivatives). In contrast, a fund of funds focuses on illiquid investments in other hedge funds.

While all hedge funds follow the same corporate structure, there are six main types of hedge funds strategies used to generate returns: arbitrage, event-driven, equity-based, credit-based, macro, and generalist. Arbitrage strategies and event-driven strategies are beyond the scope of this discussion.

Equity-based strategies are the most famous, since they focus on investing in the stocks of publicly traded companies. A fund that goes long or short equities is called a long/short hedge fund. Equity long/short managers generally employ a fundamentals, bottom-up based investing process. The other common equity strategy is long-only equity. This strategy is common to hedge funds, mutual funds, and other investors (such as individuals). Equity investing requires stock-picking skill that is fairly uncommon considering the number of hedge funds that fail (80% of all hedge funds fail in the first year).

Credit-based hedge funds invest in the debt of companies, usually public debt, and go either long or short. This will be explained more in later chapters.

For macro strategies, the hedge fund is focused on anticipating price movements in global interest rates, exchange rates, inflation, and other macroeconomic indicators and measures.

In a generalist strategy, the company has an open mandate and can try to invest using any of the previously described strategies. However, getting limited partners to agree to an open mandate for the fund can be difficult and impair the ability of the general partners to raise capital. A generalist strategy can also refer to an equity long/short hedge fund that invests in companies of all industries (rather than a specific industry).

2.3 Private Equity Funds

Private equity (PE) funds are structured similarly to hedge funds and have an almost identical fee structure (2 and 20). The main difference between public equity and private equity funds is that PE funds invest in illiquid, long-term, private investments. These investments can last for several years (4-10 years) and can be difficult to exit. There are three main types of PE funds:

- **Leveraged buyout** (LBO) refers to the purchase of all or most of a company or business unit by using equity from a small group of investors in combination with a significant amount of debt. This will be covered extensively in future chapters.

- **Growth capital** typically refers to minority (non-controlling, <50% of the equity) equity investments in mature, private companies. These companies generally need capital to expand or restructure operations, pay for an acquisition, or enter a new market, without a change of control of the company.

- **Venture capital** refers to equity investments in earlier stage, non-public companies to fund the launch, provide early development, or bankroll the expansion of a business.

Although PE can be considered to include all three of these investment activities, it is common for private equity to be the principal descriptor for LBO activity. Venture capital and growth equity are each considered a separate investment strategy, although some large private equity firms participate in all three areas. Investment firms that engage in LBO activity are called private equity firms. These firms are also called buyout firms or financial sponsors. The term financial sponsors come from the role a private equity firm has as the "sponsor", or provider, of the equity component in an LBO. They are also the orchestrator of all aspects of the LBO transaction including negotiating the purchase price and, with investment banker assistance, securing debt financing to complete the purchase. A lot could be said about the LBO activity of private equity firms alone, but this is a very involved and technical process that will be covered more extensively in later chapters.

2.4   Other Key Financial Players

2.4.1   Exchanges

An exchange is a marketplace where securities and other financial instruments are traded. The main purpose of an exchange is to guarantee fair and orderly trading. Exchanges also disseminate information about the securities they trade. Exchanges give companies, governments, and other entities an avenue to sell securities to the public. Examples of notable exchanges are the New York Stock Exchange (NYSE) and the NASDAQ.

2.4.2   Credit Rating Agencies

When companies raise debt, there are obviously interest payments and face value repayments associated with that debt. It is the job of the Credit Rating Agencies to ascribe a "rating" to the company that assesses the likelihood of a company to meet their interest and principal payments. A broad range of ratings exist, with AAA being the best, and D being the worst. Any debt with a rating of BBB or above is called "investment grade" and is considered less risky. Any debt with a rating of below BBB is called "junk grade" and is considered high risk. The top three credit rating agencies are: Moody's, Standard & Poor's, and Fitch Ratings.

2.4.3   Pension Funds

Pension funds are large institutions that manage pooled contributions of money from pension plans setup by employers, unions, or other organizations to provide retirement benefits for employees or other members. Pension funds are the largest investment blocks in most countries and dominate the stock markets where they fund. Pension funds frequently play a role as a limited partner in hedge funds or private equity funds.

2.4.4   Insurance Companies

To illustrate the role of insurance companies in the financial markets, consider a simple life insurance plan, in which an individual pays $5 to a life insurance company in year 0. Fifty years later, the individual dies and the insurance company has to pay out a life insurance claim of $50. However, this insurance company did not have to pay out the claim for 50 years! During this time, the insurance company can do whatever they want with that $5. In fact, most insurance companies invest that money (called float) and try to generate a return on it. Going back to the preceding example, if the insurance company can generate a 10% return for all of those 50 years before they pay out the $50 claim, then the $5 will be worth $587! After paying out the $50 claim in year 50, the insurance company will have made a $537 profit.

By investing float in this way, insurance companies represent another type of institutional investor. insurance companies regularly play a role as a limited partner in hedge funds and private equity funds.

2.4.5 Commercial Banks

Commercial banks generally provide loans to consumers (everyday people) and secured loans to companies. The role of commercial banks will be covered more extensively in future chapters, but it is worth noting early that there are other institutions that provide credit beyond hedge funds. In fact, commercial banks make up a significant portion of lending activity.

2.4.6 Endowments

Endowments are institutional investors that invest on behalf of universities. The returns generated by an endowment help to fund the schools research, growth, and maintenance initiatives. Endowments regularly play a role as a limited partner in hedge funds and private equity funds.

2.5 Buy-side Versus Sell-side

Buy-side and sell-side are common terms thrown around in the financial community. Buy-side refers to the financial institutions and the sub-functions of financial institutions that are actually investing in and purchasing securities. This includes: hedge funds, private equity funds, insurance companies, endowments, pension funds, and some portions of the asset management division of an investment bank. The sell-side generally refers to the sub-functions of investment banks that provide services to the Buy-side and the investor community. This includes: the Investment Banking division, the Sales and Trading division (including Research),

some portions of the Asset management Division of an investment
bank, and most functions of a boutique investment bank.

3

Finding Information

3.1 Introduction

We have defined the goal of investing, identified some key players in the world of finance, and established the concept of value investing. But how do we actually sift through the universe of potential investments and gather information on companies to make more informed investment decisions? The objective of this chapter is to begin to understand the various sources of information on companies and industries, and to understand the language that companies use to communicate financial information about themselves to the world and potential investors.

3.2 Financial Documents

As mentioned previously, the Securities Exchange Commission (SEC) is the United States governing body that enforces and maintains laws related to securities, financial transactions, and investment firms. There are several documents public companies must file with the SEC detailing their financial position and business operations for potential investors. These documents are commonly referred to as the company's financial documents. There are several types of financial documents that will be described below:

- **10-K** - A firm's 10-K is also called an annual report. This is generally the most important financial document filed by a public firm. The report gives a comprehensive summary of a company's financial performance and business operations. This document is prepared and released by a company once a year. It is important to note that companies operate under "fiscal years" rather than "calendar years". This means that a company's year, for the sake of releasing financial documents, could start in any month, where calendar years start in January. Typically, 10-Ks are very dense documents, running 80-100 pages. However, many great investors spend most of their time reading through dozens of 10-Ks to find information that other investors have missed or overlooked. Warren Buffett is famous for employing this strategy.

Most notably, 10-Ks (and 10-Qs) contain the "Consolidated financial statements" which is the formal report of the companies financial position, using the standards of accounting. This is why accounting is important to understand. It is the language through which companies communicate their financial situation to investors. The anatomy of a 10-K and 10-Q will be covered much more extensively next chapter.

- **10-Q** - A firm's 10-Q is also called a quarterly report. This is another very important document that a company files three times a year (because during the fourth quarter of the fiscal year a 10-K will be filed instead of a 10-Q). A 10-Q updates investors on the financial situation and operations of a company regarding the preceding quarter.

- **8-K** - The SEC requires that companies update their shareholders with material information regarding their operations or financial situation. A form 8-K is a very broad form used to immediately notify (rather than waiting for a 10-Q or a 10-K filing) investors of specific events, outside the normal course of business that may be important company shareholders. For example, a company might file an 8-K if it plans to acquire another company, or if it hires a new CEO.

- **S-1** - When a company goes public and sells its shares to the public markets for the first time in an IPO, the company must file a form S-1 in advance of the IPO date. A form S-1 is a very detailed document, similar to a 10-K, that updates and informs potential investors of the financial situation and operations of a business.

- **13-F** - A 13-F is a special type of form filed with the SEC. However, a 13-F is not filed by companies. Instead, a 13-F is filed by hedge funds. Hedge funds with an AUM over $100M are required to file a 13-F once per quarter. The form discloses their total AUM and all of their portfolio holdings and weights. Because of this disclosure, some investment/trading strategies hinge solely on buying securities that famous hedge funds have purchased.

There are many places that financial documents can be found on the internet. https://www.bamsec.com/ is the website used by the developers of this program.

3.3 Earnings Transcripts

When a company files a 10-K or 10-Q, they also hold an earnings call for investors. This is a conference call in which the company's management team provides a detailed review of their recent results and operations. It is also an opportunity for analysts to ask the company's management team questions. Following an earnings call, several websites publish a transcript of the call and its discussion. These calls/transcripts are an important source of information about a company. A great place to find historical earnings call transcripts is the website Seeking Alpha.

3.4 Investor Presentations

All public companies have an Investor Relations section on their website. In this part of the website, an investor can find a lot of information about a public company. Notably, there are usually PowerPoint presentations (called a deck) that present a lot of useful information about the company. To find these presentations, navigate to the Investor Relations section of a public company of interest and look for a subsection containing presentations and reports.

3.5 Management Conversations

A common way to gather information on a public company is to have a conversation with the management team. These usually can be scheduled directly or through the investor relations team of a company. Generally, it is difficult to get a conversation with management if you are not affiliated with an institutional investment organization like a hedge fund. management conversations can be useful because they allow the investor to explore specifics about the company and ask specific questions, but, one must approach most management conversations with a grain of salt since management is often incentivized to make their business and prospects sound better than economic reality.

3.6   Sell-side Research

As discussed in Chapter 2, investment banks produce stock research reports. These research reports are collectively referred to as sell-side research or sell-side analyst reports. All sell-side stock analysts give buy or sell recommendations regarding the stocks they cover. Sell-side analysts also make forecasts for the future earnings prospects of the companies they cover. The aggregate or average earnings estimate of the sell-side community for a given stock is called the "earnings consensus" or "consensus earnings estimate" or just "consensus". If the actual reported earnings of a company (as revealed by the release of a 10-K or 10-Q) are higher than consensus, then an "earnings beat" has occurred. If the reported earnings are lower, then an "earnings miss" has occurred. Sell-side research can be a good way to learn about a company and its operations, but, like management calls, the information and estimates of a sell-side research report must often be taken with a grain of salt. This is because most sell-side research analysts are not compensated based on whether or not their predictions are correct. In fact, sometimes the company they are covering actually pays the sell-side analyst or investment bank to cover their security, creating an incentive to give positive or bullish recommendations. A good resource for sell-side research reports is Thomson-One.

3.7   Industry Reports

An industry is a classification that refers to groups of companies that have a similar primary business activity. Two examples of industries are auto manufacturers or grocery stores. These are broad classifications or descriptions of the operations of a group of businesses. A sector is an even broader term for a group of similar companies than industry. Some examples of sectors are healthcare, consumer, and financial sectors. Several companies produce research reports for entire industries and sectors. These can be very helpful for understanding industry average levels of profitability and sales. It is very helpful to understand how a company is performing relative to "peers" (other companies in its industry), since outperformance could help indicate that the business is "good" or has competitive advantages. industry reports are also helpful for understanding the drivers of growth and profitability for the company and its industry. Free, high-quality industry reports are harder to find.

3.8   Public Market Data

Finding information on current stock market prices and the trading history of a stock is simple. There are dozens of outlets that provide this information. Two popular resources are Yahoo Finance and Google Finance. However, sophisticated investors use a platform called Bloomberg, which is expensive. Bloomberg has a huge amount of financial information and data on most companies, especially public, and industries which allows for detailed financial analysis to be performed. The vast amount of financial data available on Bloomberg is helpful, but in some cases, it can be overwhelming and become the sole focus of analysis, resulting in analysis paralysis. It is important to remember that the true determinants of a great investment are usually the price paid up-front and qualitative factors, like competitive advantages and brand power. When focusing on Bloomberg financial data, it is easy for an investor to get lost in the weeds.

3.9   Current Events

For keeping up with current events, the industry standard resources are: Wall Street Journal and Barron's. The Wall Street Journal has business, economic, and financial news on everything under the sun. Barron's focuses on potential security investments, particularly in the United States. Both WSJ and Barron's have a subscription fee.

3.10   Information on Private Companies

For private companies, most of the preceding documents are not available. However, when a private equity firm or private credit investor approaches a private company, if the private company is interested in a deal or transaction, then the private company will often give the investor access to a "data room". Usually, to get access to a data room, an investor must sign a non-disclosure agreement (NDA). An NDA requires that the investor not discuss the confidential and private material contained in the data room with other

individuals. Generally, a data room contains very detailed information about a company, including customer level financial data, detailed financial statements, employee agreements, legal documents,
and more. The granularity of information in a data room is usually
much more significant than that in publicly available documents.

A useful resource for understanding the financing history of
private and public companies is https://crunchbase.com/. The financial supporters of a company are important to understand, and
this resource can give insight into the financial backing of a company or its competitors.

Investment banks also prepare a special, extensive document
called a confidential information memorandum (CIM) to educate
potential investors on a company that wants to be bought. This
document is very detailed, and a core component of the private
equity and private credit due-diligence process.

3.11   Additional Resources

Despite the seemingly secondary nature of an "Additional
Resources" section, the importance of finding alternative sources
of information on potential investments cannot be understated.
Particularly in public markets, investors generally seek an "edge".
Since all public investors have access to the same documents discussed previously, an investor must rely on superior intuition to
generate an edge. Superior intuition is very rare. Therefore, perhaps a more reliable source of an edge is an information advantage.
By diving deeper into a company, its operations, its customers, its
suppliers, and its competitors, an investor can acquire additional
information and (hopefully) insight into a business. However, more
information is not always better. This is why it is important to ask
the right questions. Quality is greater than quantity. This being
said, what are some other sources of information that might help
an investor acquire an information edge?

3.11.1   Customer Calls

All successful businesses depend on customers that actual
buy their products. This is an essential point that must not be
forgotten. Customer calls can be a valuable way to understand
several pieces about a company: does the product add value to
the customer? What is the user experience associated with the
product? Is the product of high quality? Does the customer expect

to purchase from the company again? What are the customers other options? Why did the customer choose this product over alternatives? Answers to all of these questions can be very helpful to understanding a business.

3.11.2 Supplier Calls

Businesses also depend on suppliers. It is important to understand a businesses relationship with their suppliers. If a supplier is essential to the operations of a given business, then the supplier has a lot of bargaining power. This could be a threat to the longevity of a business. This is why understanding the dynamic between a business and its suppliers is key. Further, interesting information can be revealed through a conversation with suppliers, such as an increase in ordering activity from the business in question. This might indicate that the company is ramping up production for an anticipated increase in sales.

3.11.3 Competitor Diligence

Exploring the financial history and operating characteristics of a business' competitors through the public resources discussed in this chapter and through additional calls can provide deep insight into the competitive dynamics of an industry. It helps to understand, from all the businesses in an industry, what each individual company believes in their competitive advantage. If this diligence is performed systematically, patterns might begin to emerge, allowing a deeper understanding of the business, or, perhaps, outliers and differentiating factors will emerge, which could be a key supporting argument for an investment thesis.

3.11.4 Employee or Ex-Employee Calls

Company culture is a key determinant of the success of a business. Understanding why a given employee works where they do, or why they left a company of interest, can give deep insight into the elusive concept of company culture. Further, conversations with employees can reveal whether the employees understand the business they work at well, and whether they are interested in adding value to their organization, an important discovery.

3.11.5   Consultants and Industry Experts

Many firms on Wall Street hire professional consultants to develop a deep understanding of industries and companies. For example, a company like Bain & Company might be hired to develop customer surveys and industry diagnostics for a company of interest. Other services, like Gerson Lehrman Group (GLG), connect investors with experts on a topic that is difficult to gather information, such as natural resources. These types of consulting services are usually expensive, but can be helpful for rounding out an investment thesis and solidifying or contradicting previously carried beliefs about a company in preliminary diligence.

3.11.6   Blogs, Forums, and Social Media

There are dozens of informative and high quality investing blogs and forums that discuss current events, investment philosophy, and potential investments. These resources are an under-utilized and under-appreciated source of information for investors. However, there is a lot of bad content as well, so one must thoroughly vet a blog or forum before trusting its content. Lastly, if you follow the right people, Twitter can be a great source of information and news for investors.

3.11.7   Alternative Data

Alternative data is a budding area that sophisticated investors are utilizing to acquire an information edge. Alternative data relates to developing or acquiring obscure data sources and data sets to gain deeper insight into companies. Examples include: purchasing credit card transaction data and web scraping the web sites of a company of interest or its competitors. Often times, the analysis of alternative data is co-mingled with the use of novel machine learning and statistical techniques that allow large amounts of data to be broken into quantifiable, and (hopefully) helpful insights. The true power of alternative data comes from data sets that provide insight into the fundamentals and qualitative characteristics of a business.

Part II

Accounting, Essential Formulas, and Financial Analysis

4

The Anatomy of a 10-K/10-Q

4.1 Introduction

As described in the previous chapter, a 10-K is the annual document a public company files with the SEC. A 10-Q is the quarterly document a public company files with the SEC. These are critical sources of information for understanding a public business and how it makes money. While usually quite long, these documents are also full of fluff. The main sections of importance are discussed here, including: Business Overview, Risks, Financial Statements, and Management's Discussion and Analysis (MD&A). This chapter will be much more valuable to readers who actually go to https://www.bamsec.com/ to open and explore a 10-K or 10-Q.

4.2 Business Overview

This is where a business tells you what they do. Before performing any broad or deep analysis, it is essential to understand what the company does and how they make money. This section will contain significant company information, such as recent sales, the company's history, a breakdown of sales between different product lines, a listing of different brands, recent developments, strategic initiatives, distribution practices, and an overview of the industry, competition, and foreign operations.

4.3 Risks

The risks section contains a lot of fluff. The company is required to disclose all possible risks that might affect the business.

So naturally there is a lot of legalese present in this section. However, the risks section is worth scanning for anything that stands out. You could spot an abnormal risk here that indicates something unique or material that threatens a business' competitive position.

4.4   Financial Statements

The financial statements section contains the "Consolidated Financial Statements" of a business for the relevant reporting period and recent history. There are three main financial statements in this section: the income statement, the balance sheet, and the cash flow statement. It is standard practice for businesses to present financial statements that adhere to generally accepted accounting principles (GAAP). This accounting standard is the "language of business". The financial statements section is extremely important. It reveals the amount of money the company has earned in recent history, the assets of the company, the liabilities of the company, and where the company is allocating cash. Understanding and analyzing financial statements is also discussed extensively in the remaining chapters of Part II.

4.5   Management's Discussion and Analysis

The MD&A section of a company's annual report provides an overview of the previous year's operations and the company's financial performance. Here management also discusses the upcoming year, future objectives, strategic initiatives, and new projects. This is an important section for reviewing the company's financial results and the performance/objectives of management.

4.6   Other Important Areas and Analysis

4.6.1   Cover Page

The cover page of a 10-K or 10-Q contains an important piece of information: the number of "common shares" the company has outstanding. Multiplying this figure by the share price of the company produces the non-diluted market capitalization. It is important to note that there are more potential shares beyond the "common shares" that could be created from a variety of sources such as convertible debt, warrants, and management options. These sources are beyond the scope of the current discussion, but will be covered in later chapters. These extra potential shares are called "diluting shares." The common term for "common shares" + "diluting shares" is "fully diluted shares outstanding" (FDSO). When time allows, calculating market cap based off of FDSO is preferred.

4.6.2 Legal Proceedings

The legal proceedings section details any outstanding lawsuits the company has. This is an important risk to note. Depending on the scenario, lawsuits can severely threaten a company.

4.6.3 Properties

The properties section provides a detailed overview of the real estate and buildings owned by the company. This can help give an idea of the company's geographic distribution.

4.6.4 Executive Compensation

This important section gives insight into how management is compensated. The compensation of the board of directors and management is important because these governing bodies of a corporation will normally pursue strategies and financial actions that produce the greatest financial returns for themselves. For example, management compensation might depend on the price appreciation of the company's stock.

4.6.5 Language Changes

A helpful analysis is to compare differences between different 10-Ks and 10-Qs over the life of a company. This analysis reveals the changing perception that a company has of its own business, and can magnify material changes in a business' estimates of its own prospects. This analysis also highlights material changes to the risks section, which allows investors to spot new potentially threatening occurrences early.

5

Accounting Basics

5.1 What is accounting?

Accounting is the method of processing and communicating financial information about companies. Some people refer to accounting as the "language of business". There are several parties interested in the accounting information of firms: investors (both creditors and shareholders), management, regulators, suppliers, competitors, and customers.

The financial statements, which are created by the "accountants" of a company, can be found in the 10-K or 10-Q of a public company. For private companies, the same accounting standards apply, but generally the granularity of information in private company financial statements is higher.

In the United States, companies prepare their financial statements in accordance with general accepted accounting principles (GAAP), a set of guidelines governing the reporting of financial information. The organization that sets GAAP standards is the Financial Accounting Standards Board (FASB).

The three main financial statements contained within a 10-K and 10-Q are: the income statement, the balance sheet, and the cash flow statement. The income statement records the total amount of money the company received and spent over the fiscal period. The balance sheet is a *snapshot* of what the company owns versus what the company owes. The cash flow statement focuses specifically on changes in cash, which has a lot of nuance and will be discussed later.

Accounting is important to know because it allows an investor to analyze several important pieces of information about a company: its financial health, its cash flow generating poten-

tial, and its overall strategy. Beyond this, accounting and financial
statement analysis is core to financial ratio analysis, financial modeling, valuation, and leveraged buyout modeling. All of these topics
will be covered in later chapters.

With all of that in mind, it is easy to see why a solid grasp
of accounting practices and principals is essential. A quick note on
formatting: in financial statements, parentheses around a number
indicates it is negative. For example, ($50) is the same as -$50.

5.2   The Income Statement

The income statement records what a company has earned
and spent over a fiscal period or period of time (quarter, year-
to-date, or year). For example, in the example income statement
below, the dollar figures presented represent transactions over the
entire fiscal year. The rows of any financial statement are called
"line items". For example, the "Sales" row is a line item. To
determine the sales over the fiscal year of 2017, an analyst would
go across the row of interest (Sales) and down the column of the
fiscal period of interest (2017). In this case, the total Sales recorded
over the fiscal year 2017 is $1200. For the remainder of this section,
we will review the maining of each line item of this basic income
statement. To illustrate the function of each line item, we will
use a simple lemonade stand as an example. While this discussion
focuses on understanding the essential and major line items that
appear on every income statement, it is important to realize line
items beyond t hose in this example can exist.

Income Statement			
Year	**2017**	**2016**	**2015**
Revenue	$1200	$1100	$1000
Cost of Goods Sold	$500	$400	$300
Gross Profit	$700	$700	$700
SG&A	$350	$325	$300
Operating Profit	$350	$375	$400
Interest Expense	$80	$90	$100
Profit Before Tax	$270	$285	$300
Tax Expense	$108	$114	$120
Net Income	$162	$171	$180

5.2.1 Revenue

Revenue is the total money that a firm takes in before expenses. Revenue is also called sales or the top line since it is the top line of the income statement. Let us assume our lemonade stand sells 500 cups of lemonade for $2 each in 2015. The sales in this case are $1000. Notice that this figure represents the total amount of money that came in before any expenses associated with the revenue were subtracted.

5.2.2 Cost of Goods Sold

Cost of goods sold (COGS) is the money directly associated with producing the revenue. This usually includes material costs and labor directly associated with producing the product. Going back to the lemonade stand, lets assume that the cups, lemons, sugar, and water associated with producing a single cup of lemonade costs $0.60. This means that the total COGS of selling 500 cups of lemonade was $300 in 2015.

5.2.3 Gross Profit

Gross profit is simply revenue minus COGS. In the case of the lemonade stand, revenue was $1000 and COGS was $300 in 2015. Therefore, gross profit was $700.

$$\text{Gross Profit} = \text{Revenue - COGS}$$

5.2.4 Selling, General, and Administrative

Obviously, the lemonade stand could have several other expenses beyond COGS. Let us assume that the owner of the lemonade stand is really trying to grow the business, so he or she hires a sales and marketing team to advertise and spread the word. This costs $100 a year. Furthermore, the owner also has to hire an individual to actually work at the lemonade stand. This costs $100. There are other miscellaneous expenses that are core to the operations of the lemonade stand, such as paying the owner a salary, another $100 cost. Therefore, the total selling, general, and administrative expense (SG&A) adds up to $300.

5.2.5   Operating Profit

The combination of COGS and SG&A are called operating expenses (OpEx). In short, these expenses are core to the *operations* of a business. Interest and tax expenses, on the other hand, are expenses that are non-core to the actual money-producing operations of the business. These non-operating expenses will be covered shortly. Revenue minus operating expenses equals operating profit. Operating profit is also called earnings before interest and tax (EBIT).

Operating Profit (EBIT) = Revenue - COGS - SG&A
OR
Operating Profit (EBIT) = Revenue - Operating Expenses

5.2.6   Interest Expense

To recap, interest expenses are the payments to the debt holders or creditors of a company. In 2015, the interest expense of the lemonade stand was $100. It is important to note that the interest expense depends on the *financing* decisions of the company. For example, since the lemonade stand has a non-negligible interest expense, it is evident the company raised debt at some point in its history that it has yet to pay back.

5.2.7   Profit Before Tax

Profit before tax is operating profit minus interest expense. The profit before tax of the lemonade stand in 2015 was $300. The formulas are below:

Profit Before Tax = Revenue - COGS - SG&A - Interest
OR
Profit Before Tax = Operating Profit - Interest

5.2.8   Tax Expense

This is the expense paid to the government. The standard corporate tax rate is 35%. However, because of the way tax accounting works (which is different than GAAP) sometimes the *effective tax rate* of a company can be different than 35%. This discrepancy between GAAP and tax accounting is a complex topic that is not essential to understand at this point. However, it is easy to calculate the effective tax rate of a company using its income statement and the following formula:

Effective Tax Rate = Tax Expense / Profit Before Tax

The lemonade stand paid $120 in tax expense, therefore; therefore, the effective tax rate in 2015 was 40%.

5.2.9 Net Income

Bottom line, earnings, and net profit are all other names for net income which represents the total earnings of the company after all expenses are paid. Net income *is* not how much *cash* the company made. This will make more sense when the cash flow statement is discussed later in the chapter.

5.2.10 Missing Items?

There are a few significant items in the lemonade stand example that are not included in the income statement. Notably, we have not yet considered the original purchase of the actual stand. This is because the income statement shows stakeholders the amount of money made by the *standard, recurring business operations* of the company. Since businesses save up money for a long time before investing in long-term assets like a lemonade stand, the purchase of the lemonade stand is not considered part of the standard, recurring operations of the business. Instead, the purchase of these long-term assets is classified as a capital expenditure (CapEx). This appears on the cash flow statement rather than the income statement. Otherwise, the income statement would have significant negative numbers when a large capital expenditure occurs, which might confuse investors.

This raises the question, how are capital expenditures expressed in the income statement? The answer is depreciation. Accountants try to capture the economic reality of a depreciating building or long-term asset (such as aging machinery) by depreciating long-term assets over the period of the asset's useful life. These depreciation expenses are usually embedded in COGS or SG&A on the income statement, but they can always be found on the cash flow statement. Suppose a long-term asset was purchased for $500 in 2015. Now, suppose the useful life of that long-term asset is 10 years. Let us also assume the long-term asset is worth

$0 at the end of its useful life (this is called residual value). The standard way to calculate the depreciation expense embedded in the COGS and SG&A of the income statement in this scenario is with the following formula:

$$\text{Depreciation Expense} = (\text{Purchase Price - Residual Value}) \, / \, \text{Useful Life}$$

Using the numbers from the example described in the previous paragraph, the depreciation expense is $50.

5.3   The Balance Sheet

The balance sheet records a *snapshot* of the things a company *has* versus the things the company *owes*. Assets are the things a company has. Liabilities are the things a company owes. The difference is called shareholder's equity. It is essential to realize that the balance sheet captures the value of a given line item at a specific *point in time* rather than over the course of a fiscal period (such as the income statement). In the example balance sheet below, the $200 in the Cash & Equivalents line item in 2017 is the precise amount of cash the company has at the end of 2017. This is why the balance sheet is a snapshot.

The Balance Sheet Equation (BSE) is crucial. Its formula is below:

$$\text{Assets} = \text{Liabilities} + \text{Book Value Shareholder's Equity}$$

This equation must "balance" for the balance sheet to be accurate. In the example balance sheet below, the reader can observe that the BSE is satisfied since the value of total assets equals the value of liabilities and equity in all time periods.

The BSE is a nifty formula, but how exactly do we guarantee that the equation is continuously satisfied? The answer is a concept called journal entries or balance sheet entries. Journal entries capture how transactions affect balance sheet line items. All transactions essential have a counter-action that forces the balance sheet equation to balance. For example, if a building is purchased for $100, then property, plant, and equipment (PPE) increases by $100, and cash & equivalents decreases by $100. Therefore, the net change in assets is $0. This means that the change in assets, $0, precisely equals the change in liabilities and equity, $0. If the BSE was satisfied before this transaction, then the journal entry guarantees that this transaction will not violate the BSE. Essentially, a journal entry for a given transaction guarantees that:

$$\Delta(\text{Assets}) = \Delta(\text{Liabilities} + \text{Book Value Shareholder's Equity})$$

Therefore, if the previous equation holds for all transactions, then the BSE is guaranteed to be satisfied. It is normal for this concept to be confusing, especially since most college accounting courses focus exclusively on the various BSE-satisfying journal entries.. But to fully understand a company's financial statements, an investor will eventually want to understand the different journal entries for various transactions. This is not essential to reading the three income statements and will not be covered in this book, though.

Balance Sheet			
Year	2017	2016	2015
Assets			
Cash	$200	$175	$150
Accounts Receivable	$120	$110	$100
Inventory	$100	$90	$80
Current Assets	$420	$375	$330
PPE	$600	$550	$500
Goodwill	$90	$95	$100
Other Assets	$10	$10	$10
Total Assets	$1120	$1030	$940
Liabilities			
Accounts Payable	$80	$70	$60
Deferred Revenue	$50	$40	$30
Current Liabilities	$130	$110	$90
Long-term Debt	$357	$449	$550
Other Liabilities	$50	$50	$50
Total Liabilities	$537	$609	$690
Equity			
Common Stock	$100	$100	$100
Additional Paid-in Capital	$50	$50	$50
Retained Earnings	$433	$271	$100
Total Equity	$583	$421	$250

Liabilities and Equity	$1120	$1030	$940

5.3.1   Assets

As mentioned previously, assets are things the company has or owns. Current assets are assets that are cash or are expected to be cash in the next year. Long-term assets are all other assets. Example current assets on a balance sheet are: cash, accounts receivable, and inventory. Other common current assets that are not included in the example are cash-equivalents/marketable securities and prepaid expenses. The long-term assets included in the example balance sheet are property, plant, and equipment (PPE), goodwill, and other assets. Intangible assets are another common long-term asset not included in our example.

Cash

Cash is actual money on hand. This is the most liquid asset. This makes sense, because liquidity is how quickly an asset can be turned into cash. So naturally, cash itself would be the most liquid asset.

Cash-equivalents/Marketable Securities

This current asset includes any security (such as stock in another company) that can be liquidated or sold quickly. This is essentially the same thing as cash since it can be converted to cash quickly.

Accounts Receivable

When a company extends credit to a customer, this goes into accounts receivable. For example, going back to the lemonade stand, if the owner sells $100 worth of lemonade, but does not immediately get paid in cash, then the owner has sold the lemonade on credit. Therefore, the customers who purchased that lemonade owe the owner $100. Since the customers are expected to pay the owner back soon, this increases accounts receivable and is a current asset – it should soon convert to cash.

Inventory

Inventory includes the *short-term* goods and supplies used to operate the business. In the lemonade stand example, the cups, lemons, and prepared lemonade are all part of inventory since they are short-term goods/supplies core to the operations of the business. To give a different example, the unsold merchandise on the shelves of a retail store is part of inventory.

Prepaid Expenses

Prepaid expenses are an asset because, once purchased, the company owns the right to receive a given service at a specific time. For example, if at the beginning of the year the owner of the lemonade stand spends $10 for insurance that lasts a year, then the owner has effectively "prepaid" his insurance expense for the next year. Therefore, $10 is added to prepaid expenses. Halfway through the year, the prepaid expense line item will be worth only $5, since the service related to that prepaid expense is effectively half-complete.

Property, Plants, and Equipment (PPE)

Property, plant, and equipment (PPE) includes the *long-term and physical* assets core to the operations of a business. This might include: land, machinery, trucks, buildings, and computer equipment. In the lemonade stand example, the PPE is the stand itself. As a reminder, the initial purchase of PPE is called a capital expenditure (this appears on the cash flow statement) and the gradual wear-and-tear of PPE overtime is called depreciation (this also appears on the cash flow statement).

Intangible Assets

Whereas PPE captures long-term, *physical* assets, the intangible assets line item captures the value of *non-physical* assets, such as patents, brand names, or customer relationships. These are difficult to ascribe a value to, and the accountants of the firm usually decide the value of these assets. Furthermore, while physical assets are depreciated, intangible assets are amortized. The same principles underlying depreciation apply to amortization.

Goodwill

Goodwill is a type of intangible asset. There is a lot going on in this line item, but, basically, when a company acquires another company for more than the other company is worth on its balance sheet (shareholder's equity), the acquiring company adds goodwill to its balance sheet. Goodwill is supposed to capture the intangible assets that would justify the acquirer paying more than book value for the acquired company.

Other Assets

Other assets is a catch-all category for any assets not captured in the preceding line items.

5.3.2 Liabilities

As mentioned previously, liabilities are things the company owes. Current liabilities are liabilities expected to be paid out in cash in the next year. Long-term liabilities are all other liabilities, namely long-term debt. The current liabilities in the example balance sheet are accounts payable and deferred revenue. The long-term liabilities are long-term debt and other liabilities.

Accounts Payable

Accounts payable captures money owed to suppliers. For example, remember that the owner of the lemonade stand must buy cups and lemons to make lemonade. An important supplier would be the company or individual that sells the cups and lemons to the lemonade stand. Suppose the owner of the lemonade stand does not have cash on hand but still needs to buy cups and lemons for his business. The stand's supplier could extend credit to the stand for purchasing cups and lemons under the assumption the mini-loan will be repaid shortly. In this scenario, the amount of money the stand owes its supplier would go in accounts payable. When the stand pays back the supplier, the accounts payable entry goes away.

Deferred Revenue

Deferred revenue is the opposite of prepaid expenses. In this case, the company has received money for a service that it must provide to a customer. Suppose a customer comes to the lemonade stand and is willing to pay $24 in cash at the beginning of the year to have one cup of lemonade per month over the next year (essentially, a one-year, monthly subscription to the lemonade stand). This $24 is a deferred revenue liability of the lemonade stand since the stand now *owes* the customer the service of providing him a cup of lemonade once per month. One month into the year, assuming the stand does actually provide the customer with his first cup of lemonade, the value of deferred revenue will be $22.

Long-term Debt

As described in Chapter 1, the two main ways investors invest in a company is through debt and equity. Put differently, a company can finance its operations through two mechanisms: debt and equity. The long-term debt line item captures the debt owed to investors. Specifically, long-term debt refers to interest-bearing debt (i.e. debt that has an interest rate associated with it). Some debts, such as accounts payable (often times) and deferred revenue, do not require the company to pay interest to the creditors. This is a key difference between long-term debt and the other debts on the balance sheet. A *lot* can be said about debt and this line item alone, which is why all of Part III is devoted to explaining debt and the concept of capital structure, (the mix of debt and equity a firm uses to finance operations).

Other Liabilities

Other liabilities is a catch-all category for any liabilities not captured in the preceding line items.

5.3.3 Equity

The book value (the value in the accounting statements) of equity is the difference between assets and liabilities. This makes sense, because, theoretically, the value of owning a company should be the difference between what the company owns and owes. The most important equity account is retained earnings, which represents the cumulative value of earnings reinvested in the business. To be precise, the formula for retained earnings is:

$$\text{Retained Earnings}_{t+1} = \text{Retained Earnings}_t + \text{Net Income -}$$
$$\text{Dividends}$$

In the preceding formula, net income comes from the bottom of the income statement. Dividends is the money paid out to investors, which can be found on the cash flow statement. Retained Earnings$_t$ is the preceding periods retained earnings value. From this formula, we can see that the current value of retained earnings is the accumulated value of reinvestments (money left after all expenses are paid) in the business.

The other equity accounts, such as common stock and additional paid-in capital, are important to understand when performing a deep dive into understanding a company, but are not essential to understand in the basics of accounting. As such, the other equity accounts will not be discussed in this book. However, for the avid reader, further exploration of this topic would have merit.

5.3.4   Book Value Versus Market Value

The preceding discussion on the book value of equity might be confusing, because it is hard to reconcile the difference between the value of equity suggested by the accounting statements (book value) and the value of the equity in the stock market (market cap). The book value of equity and the market value of equity are regularly very different.

Why is this the case? One reason for this is that long-term assets that are purchased, such as the lemonade stand itself, are recorded in the balance sheet at historical cost (the price paid for the asset). Let's say this value is $500 in 2015. However, since its purchase in 2015, a lot of people have been buying lemonade stands and the price to buy a lemonade stand has increased to $1000 in 2017. Therefore, the market value of the lemonade stand itself is $1000, but the book value of the lemonade stand itself is still $500 (booked at historical cost). Because of this, the market value of equity would generally increase relative to the book value of equity from 2015 to 2017. This is because the market cares more about the current and prospective monetary value of the assets and liabilities, which is not necessarily reflected in the book value, as exhibited by the previous example. There are other reasons for the discrepancy between the book value and market value of equity, such as inflation and prospective earnings potential. This being said, the key takeaway is that the market value of equity is generally more important and reliable than the book value of equity, since it more accurately reflects the economic reality of the company.

5.4 The Cash Flow Statement

5.4.1 The Need for the Cash Flow Statement

So we have an income statement. Many readers are likely wondering then what's the purpose of the cash flow statement? The reason: a concept called accrual accounting.

We've already been introduced to the concept of accrual accounting through the previous examples of accounts receivable, accounts payable, prepaid expenses, and deferred revenue. Under accrual accounting, sales and expenses flow through the income statement in a manner consistent with underlying economic reality, *not* the exchange of cash.

Remember when our lemonade stand owner sold to a customer on credit? Well the customer who purchased that lemonade owes the owner $100. Since the customer is expected to pay the owner back soon, this increases accounts receivable. In this case, despite the fact that cash was *not yet exchanged*, revenue or sales is recorded on the top line of the income statement. Therefore, a discrepancy between the eventual value of net income arises. The same reasoning applies to several different types of transactions, such as changes in accounts receivable, accounts payable, prepaid expenses, and deferred revenue.

Beyond this, there are non-cash charges that affect the income statement, but do not affect cash. For example, consider the case of depreciation (discussed previously). When depreciation flows through the income statement (by being embedded in COGS and SG&A), it reduces net income. However, the owner of the lemonade stand does not *pay* anyone with cash to depreciate his lemonade stand, it just happens overtime. For this reason, depreciation is considered a *non-cash expense* – an expense that flows through the income statement but does not actually affect the cash flow of the business. There are several other types of non-cash expenses, such as impairments, stock option expenses, and restructuring charges. It is not essential to memorize all the non-cash expenses and their causes, but it is important to realize that non-cash expenses do exist and further amplify the discrepancy between net income and cash flow.

Before we dive into the actual construction of the cash flow statement, it is important to note that the cash flow statement is

the only financial statement that can be reconstructed solely from
the income statement and balance sheet.

Cash Flow Statement		
Year	2017	2016
Cash Flow from Operating Activities		
Net Income	$162	$171
Depreciation	$55	$50
Amortization	$5	$5
Non-cash Adjustments:		
Impairment Loss	$0	$50
Stock Option Expense	$0	$0
Other Non-cash Expenses	-$92	-$151
Changes in Current Assets and Liabilities:		
Accounts Receivable	-$10	-$10
Inventory	-$10	-$10
Accounts Payable	$10	$10
Accrued Expenses	$10	$10
Cash Flow from Operating Activities	$130	$125
Cash Flow from Investing Activities		
Capital Expenditures	-$105	-$100
Acquisitions	$0	$0
Proceeds from the Sale of PPE	$0	$0
Cash Flow from Investing Activities	-$105	-$100
Cash Flow from Financing Activities		
Payment of Dividends	$0	$0
Repurchase of Shares	$0	$0
Issuance of Equity	$0	$0
Payment of Debt	$0	$0
Issuance of Debt	$0	$0
Cash Flow from Financing Activities	$0	$0
Net Change in Cash and Equivalents	$25	$25

Cash at the Beginning of Year		$175	$150
Cash at the End of Year		$200	$175

5.4.2 Cash Flow from Operating Activities

Cash flow from operating activities (CFO) is the cash flow produced from the core, day-to-day operations of the business. As pictured above, the calculation of CFO starts with net income (the bottom line of the income statement), and adds back non-cash expenses (such as depreciation and amortization, impairments, and stock options).

Now, before continuing with the calculation of CFO, we must define two important concepts: working capital and sources/uses of funds:

Working Capital = Current Assets - Current Liabilities

Working capital is the net amount of capital tied up in the day-to-day operations of the business, hence why it includes only current assets and liabilities. Sources/uses of funds, on the other hand, has four key rules:

1. An increase of an asset is a *use* of cash (decreases cash)

2. A decrease of an asset is a *source* of cash (increases cash)

3. An increase of a liability is a *source* of cash (increases cash)

4. A decrease of a liability is a *use* of cash (decreases cash)

But why are these the four rules of sources/uses? First, let us consider a specific asset: inventory. If the value of inventory increases, the amount of goods we are trying to sell has increased. This means we have spent or *used* cash to increase inventory. By the opposite reasoning, a decrease in inventory means we have actually sold some of the goods we are trying to sell. As a result, a decrease in inventory is a *source* or increase of cash. Now, let us consider a specific liability: deferred revenue. When deferred revenue increases, this means we have been paid cash *now* for a service that we must provide later. Therefore, the increase in deferred revenue (a liability) is a *source* or increase of cash. By the opposite reasoning, a decrease in deferred revenue means we have performed the service we owe to the customer, but have not received any cash for it (since the customer paid upfront). This means the decrease in deferred revenue is a *use* or decrease of cash.

By combining the concepts of working capital and sources/uses, we can conclude the following derivation must be true:

$$\Delta \text{ in Current liabilities (CL)} = CL_{t+1} - CL_t \text{ (1)}$$

$$\Delta \text{ in Cash from CL} = \Delta \text{ in CL (2)}$$

$$\Delta \text{ in Cash from CL} = CL_{t+1} - CL_t \text{ (3)}$$

$$\Delta \text{ in Current Assets (CA)} = CA_{t+1} - CA_t \text{ (4)}$$

$$\Delta \text{ in Cash from CA} = -(\Delta \text{ in CA) (5)}$$

$$\Delta \text{ in Cash from CA} = -(CA_{t+1} - CA_t) \text{ (6)}$$

$$\Delta \text{ in working capital (WC)} = WC_{t+1} - WC_t \text{ (7)}$$

$$\Delta \text{ in WC} = (CA_{t+1} - CL_{t+1}) - (CA_t - CL_t) \text{ (8)}$$

$$\Delta \text{ in Cash from WC} = \Delta \text{ in Cash from CA} + \Delta \text{ in Cash from CL (9)}$$

$$\Delta \text{ in Cash from WC} = -(CA_{t+1} - CA_t) + (CL_{t+1} - CL_t) \text{ (10)}$$

$$\Delta \text{ in Cash from WC} = -CA_{t+1} + CA_t + CL_{t+1} - CL_t \text{ (11)}$$

$$\Delta \text{ in Cash from WC} = -(CA_{t+1} - CL_{t+1}) + (CA_t - CL_t) \text{ (12)}$$

$$\Delta \text{ in Cash from WC} = -((CA_{t+1} - CL_{t+1}) - (CA_t - CL_t)) \text{ (13)}$$

$$\Delta \text{ in Cash from Working Capital} = -(\Delta \text{ in Working Capital) (14)}$$

Formula (14) from above is the key insight from this derivation. This will be helpful to remember for Chapter 6. We can see that in the example cash flow statement that formulas (3) and (6) are used to calculate the change in cash due to changes in current assets and current liabilities. Therefore, the formula for CFO can be written as:

$$CFO = \text{Net Income} + \text{Depreciation} + \text{Amortization} +/- \text{Other}$$

$$\text{Non-cash Expenses} - (\Delta \text{ in WC})$$
$$\text{OR}$$
$$\text{CFO} = \text{Net Income} + \text{Depreciation} + \text{Amortization} +/- \text{Other}$$
$$\text{Non-cash Expenses} - (\Delta \text{ in CA}) + (\Delta \text{ in CL})$$

5.4.3 Cash Flow from Investing Activities

Fortunately, cash flow from investing activities (CFI) is much simpler than CFO. CFI relates to cash flow associated with investing and divesting (selling) in the long-term assets or PPE of the company. This might include: capital expenditures (already discussed), acquisitions, or proceeds from selling PPE. Generally, the most important component of CFI is capital expenditures. Therefore the formula for CFI is:

$$\text{CFI} = - \text{ (Capital Expenditures)} - \text{ (Cash Spent on Acquisitions)}$$
$$+ \text{ (Proceeds from Selling PPE)} + \text{ (Net Proceeds from Cash}$$
$$\text{Transactions of Other Non-current Assets)}$$

5.4.4 Cash Flow from Financing Activities

Cash flow from financing activities (CFF) includes all cash flows related to the issuance or repurchase of debt and equity. It also includes dividends paid to equity holders. Naturally, CFF includes the discretionary cash flows related to the financing (debt and equity) of the company. The formula for CFF is:

$$\text{CFF} = \text{ (Cash Inflow from Equity Issuance)} - \text{ (Cash Outflow}$$
$$\text{from Repurchase of Equity)} + \text{ (Cash Inflow from Debt Raise)} -$$
$$\text{ (Cash Outflow from Debt Payback)} - \text{ (Cash Outflow from}$$
$$\text{Dividend Payments)}$$

5.4.5 Net Change in Cash

By summing the cash flows for each type of activity (operating, investing, and financing), the result is the net change in cash. To get the current years cash balance (on the balance sheet), one must add the previous year's cash balance (on the balance sheet) to the net change in cash. The formulas for these concepts are below:

$$\text{Net } \Delta \text{ in Cash} = \text{CFO} + \text{CFI} + \text{CFF}$$

$$\text{Cash}_{t+1} = \text{Cash}_t + \text{Net } \Delta \text{ in Cash}$$

5.5 Strengths and Weaknesses of the Financial Statements

5.5.1 Income Statement

The biggest strength of the income statement is that it is easily understood by investors. Another strength is that it amortizes capital expenditures and other one-time charges over the life of the asset through depreciation and amortization. This highlights the core "earnings power" of the business.

The weakness of the income statement is that it can be manipulated by accountants due to depreciation and accrual accounting. Thinking back to the formula for determining depreciation, the accountant usually determines both the useful life and residual value of a long-term asset. Therefore, the accountant and the company can manipulate the income statement to some extent.

This introduces an important concept: accounting is not a perfect system. It has flaws. This is why it is so important to understand the incentives of the management team. If the company has an incentive to exaggerate their earnings, then the investor must approach accounting numbers with a sense of skepticism, especially numbers that can be manipulated, such as depreciation and the accrual accounts. There are dozens of books written on this topic alone, so we are just scratching the surface with this tangent. That being said, it is an important concept to be aware of.

5.5.2 Balance Sheet

The balance sheet's main strength is that it shows the financial health of the company. The weaknesses are: assets are booked at cost, as discussed; the book value of equity is not very useful, and goodwill and intangible assets are ascribed specific numerical values when the actual value of most intangible assets is very uncertain. Furthermore, the worth of some companies largely centers on intangible assets, so the book value of their assets might materially understate their actual worth.

5.5.3 Cash Flow Statement

The strength of the cash flow statement is that it actually shows investors how much money the company made from various sources. There is a common phrase in investing: "cash is king". The nature of the cash flow statement eliminates a lot of the problems with the manipulation of the income statement. The main weakness of the cash flow statement is that there is some gray area regarding what is an operating, investing, or financing cash flow.

5.6 Linking the Financial Statements

By now, you have probably noticed that the financial statements are not completely independent. The different relationships between the statements are defined here. Some of these have already been mentioned. The various relationships are:

- Net income on the income statement is the top line of the cash flow statement

- $Cash_{t+1} = Cash_t +$ Net change in cash on the cash flow statement

- To get to cash flow from operations on the cash flow statement, change in working capital from the balance sheet is subtracted

- PPE_{t+1} (current PPE on the balance sheet) = PPE_t (old PPE on the balance sheet) + Capital Expenditures (from the cash flow statement) - Depreciation (from the cash flow statement)

- Retained Earnings$_{t+1}$ (current retained earnings on the balance sheet) = Retained Earnings$_t$ (old retained earnings on the balance sheet) + Net Income (from the income statement) - dividends (from the cash flow statement)

5.7 Notes to the Financial Statements

The notes to the financial statements (or footnotes) provide additional information regarding the company's operations and financial information. These footnotes are essential to understanding a company at a deeper level. For example, consider the long-term debt line item on the balance sheet. This line item gives very little information regarding the details of the long-term debt, such as the maturity, the interest rate, etc. Additional information can be found in the footnote (located far below the financial statements in a 10-K or 10-Q) related to long-term debt. There are usually footnotes for several more complex line items, such as long-term debt and stock options.

6

Cash Flow and Earnings Metrics

6.1   Introduction

By now you have probably realized there are several metrics for determining a company's earnings and cash flow. Each metric has its strengths and weaknesses. This chapter will review these metrics and discuss the pros and cons of each.

6.2   Cash Flow from Operating Activities

Cash flow from operating activities (CFO) was discussed extensively in Chapter 5. As a reminder, CFO is the cash generated from the core operations of the business. It does not include cash generated or spent on long-term investments (investing activities) or financing decisions (financing activities). The main advantage of CFO is that it focuses on the cash generative ability of the core business, rather than the "earnings" or net income of a company, which we know can be manipulated via non-cash charges and accrual accounting techniques. The main weakness of CFO (and other cash flow formulas) is that it takes a relatively long time to calculate. Another weakness: CFO does not capture cash related to a company's investing or financing activities. As a reminder, the formula for CFO is:

$$\text{CFO} = \text{Net Income} + \text{Depreciation} + \text{Amortization} +/- \text{Other Non-cash Expenses} - (\Delta \text{ in Working Capital})$$

6.3   Net Income

Net income is also called the bottom line, earnings, or profits of a business. This is the amount of money available to shareholders of a company's stock. This money can either be reinvested in the business or paid out as dividends. Net income represents the "earnings" (remember that there is a difference between earnings and cash flow) of the business after all expenses (operating expenses, investing expenses, and financing expenses) are paid. It is handing because it is found directly on the income statement, making it easy to reference. The main weakness of net income are that it can be manipulated by non-cash charges, depreciation, and other one-time expenses. As such, net income does not represent actual cash flow to the firm. The formula for net income is:

Net Income = Sales - COGS - SG&A - Interest Expense - Taxes

6.4   EBIT

Pronounced "ee-bit" on the income statement, EBIT (earnings before interest and taxes) is also called operating profit or operating income. This is calculated by subtracting operating expenses (COGS and SG&A) from revenue. A strength of EBIT is that it is a shorthand proxy for CFO. Using EBIT in place of CFO assumes that working capital did not change from one year to the next, which is often, depending on the company, a fair assumption times a fair assumption. However, as a measurer, EBIT is considered inferior to EBITDA and free cash flow, which are covered next.

6.5   EBITDA

Pronounced "ee-bit-da," EBITDA (earnings before interest, tax, depreciation, and amortization) is calculated by taking EBIT (from the income statement) and adding back depreciation and amortization (from the cash flow statement). EBITDA is a widely used metric, particularly in credit/debt analysis and private equity. EBITDA is a proxy for the cash flow of a business since it takes EBIT (the operating profit of a business) and adds back the non-cash expenses of depreciation and amortization (D&A). Further, EBITDA is easier to calculate than CFO or the other cash flow formulas. The main strength of EBITDA is that it represents that earnings power of the business, independent of the depreciation of capital expenditures (which is a proxy for the management teams strategy), tax rates, and financing decisions (interest payments). That being said, EBITDA is still a shorthand calculation and free cash flow (whether levered or unlevered) is generally the superior measure of the actual cash produced by a business.

6.6 Unlevered Free Cash Flow

Unlevered free cash flow (UFCF) is the cash generated by all of the firm's operations, including management strategy (captured by capital expenditures in the investing activities section of the cash flow statement). The concept of unlevered free cash flow is very important. As mentioned previously, cash is considered "king" in the investing community. Furthermore, when we cover the essentials of valuation in Part IV of this book, we will see that this formula (with a slight variation) is core to the most popular method of company valuation: the discounted cash flow method. The full formula for unlevered free cash flow is:

$$\text{UFCF} = \text{EBITDA - Capital Expenditures - } (\Delta \text{ in Working Capital) - Taxes}$$

Notice this is very similar to CFO. The only difference is that unlevered free cash flow adds back interest expense and subtracts capital expenditures. The downside of UFCF is that it takes longer to calculate than other metrics like EBITDA.

6.7 Levered Free Cash Flow

Levered free cash flow is identical to unlevered free cash flow apart from one difference: levered free cash flow subtracts interest expense. There are several ways to calculate levered free cash flow (LFCF):

$$\text{LFCF} = \text{Net Income + D\&A - } (\Delta \text{ in Working Capital) - Capital Expenditures}$$

$$\text{LFCF} = \text{CFO - Capital Expenditures}$$

$$\text{LFCF} = \text{EBITDA - Interest - Taxes - } (\Delta \text{ in Working Capital) - Capital Expenditures}$$

Levered free cash flow is the total amount of cash flow available for discretionary spending by management. Levered free cash flow subtracts interest expense on debt, so it only represents the cash flow available to equity investors (and not debt investors, since their claim to the cash flows of the firm is only interest expense). For this reason, LFCF is also called free cash flow to equity. Therefore, UFCF is simply free cash flow to equity + interest expense (where interest expense can be thought of as the cash flow claim that debt investors have on the company). Consequently, UFCF is also called free cash flow to the firm, since UFCF includes both the cash flows to equity and the cash flows to debt holders.

6.8   Navigating the Different Cash Flow Metrics

Clearly, there are a lot of metrics for simply understanding a company's overall cash or earnings. the amount of cash or earnings a company is making. The following diagram may prove helpful to remembering the differences (note: this diagram does not show all the possible connections, but it does show the critical ones):

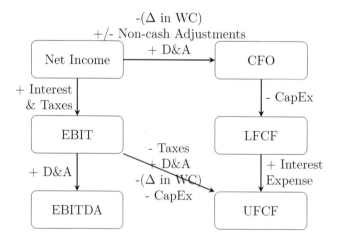

7

Equity Versus Firmwide Metrics

7.1 Introduction

Remember how firms are composed of both debt and equity financing? The mix of debt and equity a firm utilizes is called capital structure, which is a big focus of Part III of this book. In this chapter, we will explore the concept of equity value versus enterprise value, two different ways of approaching what a company/firm is "worth," based on whether just equity investors or both equity investors and credit investors are considered. Furthermore, we will introduce the concept of equity and firmwide metrics, which follow a similar line of reasoning as the topic of equity value versus enterprise value.

7.2 Equity Value Versus Enterprise Value

Also called market cap, equity value is simply the number of shares outstanding multiplied by the share price. This is the value of the claim that *equity* holders have in the company. But what does this fail to consider? Notably, market cap does not consider *debt* holders' claim on the company. Therefore, another metric is needed to captures the total value of claims: enterprise value.

Enterprise value measures a company's total value, independent of capital structure decisions. A firmwide metric, enterprise value is also thought of as the value of the total firm. In contrast, equity value (market cap) is an equity metric. Enterprise value can also be thought of as the value it would take to acquire a company, since the buyer of the company would have to buy out both the debt and equity of the target company. The formal formula for enterprise value is:

Enterprise Value (EV) = Market Cap + Long-term Debt - Cash
+ Minority Interest + Preferred Equity + Unfunded Pension
Liabilities

This formula appears complicated, but it helps to think of minority interest, preferred equity, and unfunded pension liabilities as special types of debt. Most companies do not even have minority interest, preferred equity, and unfunded pension liabilities. Furthermore, cash is subtracted since it is essentially anti-debt. Money that a company has (cash) is the opposite of money owed (debt). Therefore, a shorthand formula regularly used to calculate enterprise value is:

Enterprise Value (EV) = Market Cap + Long-term Debt - Cash

7.3 Equity Multiples versus Firmwide Multiples

In the previous chapter, the various cash flow and earnings metrics were discussed. We laso discussed equity metrics for measuring equity value (market cap) and firmwide metrics for measuring firm value (enterprise value). In a similar vein, there are equity metrics for measuring earnings to equity and firmwide metrics for measuring earnings to the entire firm. Basically, a firmwide earnings metric is any metric that includes interest expense (since it includes the earnings/cash flow claim of both the equity and debt holders). This includes: EBIT, EBITDA, and UFCF. An equity earnings metric is any metric that excludes interest expense (and therefore only includes the earnings/cash flow claim of the equity and debt holders). This includes: net income and LFCF.

Now, the concept of valuation multiples must be introduced. In short, a valuation multiple is simply the ratio of equity value or enterprise value to some underlying earnings metric. One extremely common example is the price-to-earnings ratio or the P/E ratio (pronounced "pee-ee" ratio). Here is an example. Let us say the market cap of a company is $100, and the net income of the company is $10 – then the P/E is 10. The inverse of the P/E ratio, or E/P, is called earnings yield. The formula for P/E ratio is:

P/E = Market Cap / Net Income
OR

P/E = Price per Share / Earnings Per Share

Valuation ratios, such as the P/E ratio, give an idea of how "expensive" a stock is relative to its own earnings. Valuation ratios also give an idea of how expensive a stock is relative to competitors and its own price history. There are several other valuation ratios beyond the P/E ratio. When utilizing valuation ratios, it is essential to use an equity value metric (market cap) with an equity earnings metric (net income or LFCF). Similarly, one must use a firmwide value metric (EV) with a firmwide earnings metric (EBIT, EBITDA, or UFCF). Therefore, the valid valuation ratios are:

- Enterprise Value / EBITDA

- Enterprise Value / EBIT

- Enterprise Value / UFCF

- Enterprise Value / Sales

- Market Cap / Net Income

- Market Cap / LFCF

UFCF / Enterprise Value is called unlevered free cash flow yield. LFCF / P is called levered free cash flow yield. Generally, a lower valuation ratio or higher yield indicates a stock is "cheaper" relative to its earnings or cash flow. There are two main factors that influence a valuation ratio (this is perhaps an over simplification, but still a helpful framework): 1) the stability of the earnings stream and 2) the growth prospects for the earnings stream.

Valuation ratios are very industry dependent. Valuation ratios tend to be very low for a low-growth industry facing obsolescence. For a high growth industry with a lot of growth potential, valuation ratios tend to be very high. Companies with high valuation ratios are often called growth stocks. Companies with low valuation ratios are often called value stocks.

8

Financial Ratio Analysis

8.1 Introduction

Financial ratio analysis is a way to quantitatively assess a company's financial statements. Financial ratio analysis is core to fundamental analysis. Ratio analysis allows the investor to better evaluate the income statement, the balance sheet, the cash flow statement, and other relationships between statements. A single financial ratio in isolation is not that helpful. It is more helpful to compare ratios relative to 1) historical levels and 2) competitor levels. By using a relative ratio analysis in this way, the investor can gain valuable context and understanding regarding trends, patterns, and comparisons. There are several types of ratios in ratio analysis: profit margins, liquidity ratios, solvency ratios, return ratios, and efficiency ratios.

8.2 Profit Margins

A profit margin is the ratio between a company's expenses and revenues. As there are several types of expenses, there are several margins allowing the investor to determine how much revenue gets converted to profit for different types of expenses. The formulas for the key margin measures are:

Gross Profit Margin = Gross Profit / Revenue

Operating Profit (EBIT) Margin = Operating Profit (EBIT) / Revenue

Net Income Margin = Net Income / Revenue

$$\text{EBITDA Margin} = \text{EBITDA} / \text{Revenue}$$

Margins can never be greater than 100%. Higher margins are better. As an industry becomes more competitive, profit margins usually converge towards 0%.

So what might investors use these formulas for? By looking at the various numbers overtime, an investor can determine, past a certain level of expenses, whether a company is converting more or less of its revenue into profit. This is very helpful information. Investors might look for trends, such as increasing or decreasing margins overtime. A rising trend is generally better for the prospects of the business.

Investors might also compare a company with its competitors. Suppose company A has an EBITDA margin of 25% and company B has an EBITDA margin of 15%. Going further, suppose the two companies are competitors selling a very similar product. What might cause the difference in EBITDA margin? Perhaps company A has a competitive advantage. Maybe company B allocates its resources poorly. Regardless, when a company has a superior margin relative to its peers, it is important to understand why that phenomenon exists and whether it is sustainable.

Margins vary significantly between industries. Very competitive industries have low margins. Less competitive industries or industries in which a few companies have significant competitive advantages have higher margins.

8.3   Liquidity Ratios

Liquidity ratios measure the ability of a company to meet its short term liabilities and short term debt obligations. They are calculated by dividing current assets (or a subset of them) by current liabilities. These ratios give an idea of the financial security and health of a company in the near term. The formulas for the key liquidity ratios are:

$$\text{Quick Ratio} = (\text{Cash} + \text{Marketable Securities} + \text{Accounts}$$
$$\text{Receivable}) / \text{Current Liabilities}$$

$$\text{Current Ratio} = \text{Current Assets} / \text{Current Liabilities}$$

By the above definitions, the quick ratio is guaranteed to

be less than or equal to the current ratio. Quick ratio measures the most liquid (easily converted to cash) current assets relative to current liabilities.

Generally, a current ratio of at least 1 is required since this indicates the company can meet its short term obligations. However, an investor generally likes to see at least a slightly greater cushion than this, such as a current ratio of 1.5 or greater.

8.4 Solvency Ratios

Whereas liquidity ratios help determine the company's ability to meet near-term obligations, solvency ratios help determine the ability to meet long-term debt obligations. Some of these ratios measure the ability of a company to meet interest payments and others measure how levered (the level of debt) a company is relative to its income and assets. The formulas for the solvency ratios are:

Interest Coverage (IC) Ratio = EBITDA / Interest Expense

Fixed Charge Coverage Ratio = (EBITDA - Capital Expenditures) / Interest Expense

Leverage Ratio = Long-term Debt / EBITDA

Levered Free Cash Flow (LFCF) / Debt Ratio = LFCF / Debt

Debt Ratio = Long-term Debt / Total Assets

Debt-to-Equity Ratio (D/E) = Long-term Debt / Book Value of Equity

Loan to Value (LTV) = Debt / Market Value of Equity

Equity Cushion = Enterprise Value / Debt

Interest coverage ratio and fixed charge coverage ratio give an idea of a company's ability to produce liquidity (cash) in order to meet its mandatory financial obligations. These ratios are very important, and generally an investor prefers that these ratios are at least 2x or greater. This provides a reasonable cushion in case the company's operations go south.

The leverage ratio and levered free cash flow ratio portray "how levered" a company is. Leverage is the investment strategy of using borrowed money; therefore, how "levered" a firm is refers to how much money it has borrowed, relative to the earnings of the business. Of these two ratios, the leverage ratio is more widely used. This ratio can vary widely between industries.

Debt often gets a bad rap. But it is important to realize that debt actually magnifies returns *if things go well for the company*. Some industries require significant amounts of debt. Others, such as technology, require barely any debt. This being said, investors should be wary of firms with excessively high leverage ratios, especially if the leverage ratio is high relative to peers. A highly levered company unable to meet interest payments or repay its debt can go into bankruptcy, which is a usually a very costly process for investors. A "high" leverage ratio (remember, this depends on industry context) could be around 5.0-6.0x or greater. A "medium" leverage ratio is around 3.0x. A "low" leverage ratio is around 1.5x or less.

The debt ratio, D/E ratio, LTV ratio, and equity cushion all give one an idea of how levered a firm is relative to its. These formulas are much more relevant for analyzing an investment in the debt than its because it gives an idea of *downside protection* for the creditors in case the company's operations go south. This concept will make more sense after Chapter 10. Of the four formulas discussed in this paragraph, the two most used are LTV and equity cushion. They both depend on the market value of equity, which is generally a more reliable measure of downside protection or underlying asset value.

8.5   Return Ratios

Return ratios are a class of financial metrics that assess a business's ability to generate profits from its assets and long-term investments. Having a higher value relative to a competitor or the company's own history is a positive sign. The three main return ratios are:

$$\text{Return on Invested Capital (ROIC)} = \text{EBIT} / (\text{Working Capital} + \text{PPE})$$

$$\text{Return on Assets (ROA)} = \text{Net Income} / \text{Total Assets}$$

Return on Equity (ROE) = Net Income / Shareholder's Equity

ROIC is a very helpful measure for gauging the return actually generated by the investments of a company. Since it utilizes EBIT, or operating income, as the denominator, it measures returns independent of the financing decisions (the use of debt versus equity) of the business. This allows the investor to hone in on the core return potential of the operations of the business. A high ROIC is one of the chief signposts that a company has a significant competitive advantage. This is a topic we will come back to several times. It is important to note that there are several variations of the ROIC formula. The author believes the formula presented here is the most effective. ROA and ROE are, in the author's opinion, less useful than ROIC. However, ROE is more important for certain types of companies, particularly financial companies. Again, profitability ratios must be compared relative to industry peers and the company's own history to have context and significance.

There is a special version of the ROE formula called the DuPont Formula:

ROE = (Net Income/Sales)*(Sales/Assets)*(Assets/Equity)

In the DuPont Formula, the "sales" component and "assets" component cancel out, resulting in Net Income / Sales or ROE. So what is the purpose of the DuPont Formula? The important insight from the DuPont Formula is that ROE is determined by three main components in conjunction: profitability (net income / sales), efficiency (sales / assets), and leverage (assets / equity).

8.6 Efficiency Ratios

Efficiency ratios measure how efficiently a company uses its assets to generate revenues and its ability to manage those assets. The efficiency ratios are:

Asset Turnover Ratio = Sales / Total Assets

Inventory Turnover Ratio = COGS / Inventory

Receivables Turnover Ratio = Sales / Accounts Receivable

Payables Turnover Ratio = COGS / Accounts Payable

Efficiency ratios can provide crucial insight into the cash conversion cycle of a company. This is the topic of the next chapter.

9

Cash Conversion Cycle

9.1 Introduction

At the end of the previous chapter, we introduced the concept of efficiency ratios. Let us consider this concept in conjunction with the cash conversion cycle, the standard flow of cash between various current assets and liabilities.

Cash Conversion Cycle

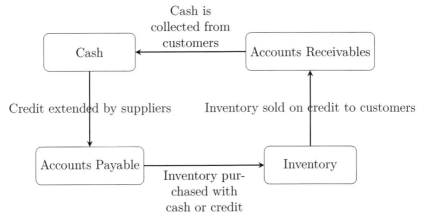

This diagram will provide a lot of the intuition for a formula we'll discuss later in this chapter.

9.2   Days Payables Outstanding

By combining the efficiency ratios from the last chapter with an annualizing days amount (such as 365), it is possible to calculate the average number of days that payables, inventory, or receivables stay as payables, inventory, or receivables. For example, to calculate days payables outstanding (DPO), the following formulas are used:

$$DPO = (1 \: / \: \text{Payables Turnover Ratio}) * 365$$
$$OR$$
$$DPO = (\text{Accounts Payable} \: / \: COGS) * 365$$

This measure reveals the average number of days a given accounts payable remains as an accounts payable. In other words, this metric indicates how long it takes the company to pay its suppliers back for supplies, on average. The lower the number, the quicker the business pays its liabilities. The higher the ratio, the better the credit terms a company gets from its suppliers. From a company's perspective, increasing DPO is an improvement.

9.3   Days Inventory Held

By the same logic, we can calculate the average number of days inventory stays as inventory before it is sold. This is called days inventory held (DIH). The formulas for this are:

$$DIH = (1 \: / \: \text{Inventory Turnover Ratio}) * 365$$
$$OR$$
$$DIH = (\text{Inventory} \: / \: COGS) * 365$$

This metric gives an idea of how long the company's cash is tied up in inventory. It is essentially a measure of the effectiveness of a company's inventory management. For this reason, it is valuable to compare a company's DIH to that of its competitors and own history to observe how inventory management is trending.

9.4   Days Sales Outstanding

Lastly, we can calculate the average number of days that inventory (when sold on credit) stays as accounts receivable. This metric, called days sales outstanding (DSO) indicates how long it takes customers to pay the company back. The formulas for this are:

$$DSO = (1 \text{ / Receivables Turnover Ratio}) * 365$$
$$OR$$
$$DPO = (\text{Accounts Receivable / Sales}) * 365$$

DSO provides helpful insight regarding the nature of a company's cash flow. A high DSO indicates that the company is selling a lot of its goods on credit. This also shows the company is taking longer to collect cash from credit customers.

9.5 Tying Everything Together

Now, consider the diagram from the beginning of the chapter in tandem with the concepts of DPO, DIH, and DSO. By combining these concepts, the cash conversion cycle (CCC) formula can be derived:

$$CCC = DSO + DIH - DPO$$

First, why is DPO subtracted? Well, DPO relates to the company's payment of its own bills. If this value can be maximized, then the company holds on to cash longer, which allows it to invest that cash in other areas during the time period. This maximizes the investment potential of that cash. Because of this, a longer DPO is better.

What is the significance of the CCC? The CCC measures the speed (in days) a company can convert cash on hand into more cash. The CCC captures this by considering the cash as it is first spent to purchase inventory (DIH) and pay down accounts payable (DPO), then through sales and the receipt of cash from customers (DSO), and finally back into cash. This metric helps to measure the effectiveness of the management team at handling working capital. Usually, a lower number is better. Consider the case of Amazon.com, which has a negative CCC. This negative CCC means that Amazon.com has so little cash tied up in handling inventory and getting paid back by customers, that the credit it receives from suppliers is actually great enough to finance the firm's long-term investments, such as new warehouses. Insights like this are valuable for the investor, and make the CCC essential to understand and utilize.

Part III

Debt and Capital Structure

10

Debt Basics

10.1 Introduction

Debt investing focuses on assessing whether both interest and the initial debt amount (principal) will be paid by the issuer. In contrast, equity investing depends on other people deciding to pay more for the equity than you initially paid. Assuming the issuer pays both interest and principal, the debt investor knows exactly what their return will be going into the investment. In general, when you purchase stock, the only way the investment generates a return (excluding the impact of dividends) is when more people come to believe that they should pay more for the stock than you previously did. There is no such dependency in credit, assuming both interest and principal are paid.

In credit investing, an investors right to an interest payment and principal repayment is contractually guaranteed. The only exception to this is the case of bankruptcy, which is rare, especially for investment grade debt. Because debt investment provides a return to investors only if the company manages to pay interest and repay principal, credit analysts focus on protecting downside risk in an investment by considering how things could go wrong. By contrast, equity investors often focus on what can go right, since the equity investors capture all the benefits of things going well in the form of share price appreciation. The potential return for credit investors is capped/fixed at the yield of the investment (with the exception of total return bond investment strategies which will be covered later). For this reason, credit or debt is often called fixed income.

As mentioned previously, credit analysts focus on protecting their downside and understanding risk very well. This requires a cynical approach to the company analysis process. If a bond (a publicly traded debt instrument) is purchased and held to maturity, then the price movement in the interim does not matter. Think back to the return formula in Chapter 1. The only determinants of the return of a debt instrument are: the price paid upfront, the cash payments (interest or coupon payments) to the investor over the course of the investment, and the amount of money received at the end (principal repayment).

When performing credit analysis, the investor must also remember the investment is heading towards a terminal date or a conclusion since the debt instrument will eventually mature. This is not the case with equity, which lasts indefinitely (as long as the company remains solvent), or until the equity is sold.

Credit analysis focuses on two main concepts: liquidity and asset coverage. Liquidity is the ability of the company to generate cash to make interest and principal payments over the life of the loan. Asset coverage is important when liquidity is not sufficient, since the debt holder then depends on the value of the company's assets to get repaid.

It is important to remember that debt is not necessarily bad. Some industries utilize a lot of debt. This is also called being "highly-levered" or "debt-intensive." Despite industry influences, individual management teams decide how to lever their company.

10.2   Common Terms

Debt is produced when a lender (investor) provides capital to an entity (issuer). Buying debt is the act of providing cash now (investing) with the expectation of having it returned at a later date. Investors, however, expect to be compensated for providing capital. This compensation comes in the form of interest or coupon payments paid by the issuers to the investor over the time the money is lent. Below is a list of common terms in debt parlance and their relevant definitions:

- Capital Structure: the combination of debt and equity that finances a firms operations. This is the focus of Chapter 11.

- Principal/Par/Face Value: the amount of capital provided by the investor to the issuer.

- Interest Payment/Coupon Payment: the payment the investor receives in compensation for taking on the risk of lending to the borrower/issuer. This payment amount is calculated by multiplying the interest rate or coupon rate by the *current* principal amount.

- Maturity: the date on which the principal is supposed to be paid back in full. Typically expressed in terms of years. For example, one might say "the debt has a maturity of 5 years" which means the debt principal must be paid back in 5 years. Generally, as maturities increase, the interest rate on the debt also increases. During a longer time span, there is a greater chance for negative things to happen to a company, and investors want to be compensated for taking on that additional risk.

- Amortization: the pay-down of principal. Includes early prepayment of principal (paying down some or all of the principal in advance of the maturity date). Often times, debt comes with a required amortization schedule for scheduled early prepayments. For example, a 1%, 2%, 3% structure is common, which means that 1% of debt principal must be paid back in year 1, 2% of debt principal must be paid back in year 2, and 3% of debt principal must be paid back in year 3. These amortization payments are paid in addition to interest payments.

- Call Date: a date on which a debt can be paid back before maturity. This is a date (or series of dates) at which the borrower/issuer has the option to repay some or all of their debt, for a specific debt. In some cases, the borrower/issuer might see advantages to the early prepayment of debt, such as if the issuer believes they can raise new debt at a lower interest rate, or if the issuer seeks to deleverage their capital structure.

- Call Protection: investors often do not want debt to be repaid early at the call dates. They want to collect their interest payments for longer periods of time without having to reinvest that capital. As such, there are provisions called call protection provisions that prevent or make it more expensive for the issuer to retire the debt early. For example, the issuer might not be able to retire debt early for several years. Or, if the issuer has the ability to retire debt, they might have to do so at a premium to par. For example, if the debt has a

103/102/101 call protection provision, this means the debt,
if retired early, must be retired at a 3% premium to par in
the first year, a 2% premium to par in the second year, and
a 1% premium to par in the third year. For example, a 3%
premium to par means it costs the issuer $1.03 to payback
$1 of principal early.

- LIBOR: the London Interbank Offering Rate. This is the
  interest rate that very high quality government securities are
  charging. A recent common range for LIBOR is 1.5%-3%.

- Spread: the difference between the quoted rates of return between two different debt instruments. For example, if LIBOR
  is 1.5% and a debt has a 9% interest rate, the spread is 7.5%.

- Spread to Worst: this is the worst possible spread that will
  be achieved, when making the most pessimistic assumptions
  regarding call dates and principal repayments.

- Yield: the income return on an investment. This is slightly
  different than interest rate. The yield is usually expressed as
  an annual percentage return rate based on the investment's
  cost or current market value. The current yield is the bond
  interest rate as a percentage of the current price of the bond.
  This nuance mainly matters for publicly traded debt.

- Yield to Maturity: an estimate of what an investor will receive in terms of interest rate if the bond is held to its maturity date.

- Yield to Worst: this is the worst possible yield that will be
  achieved, when making the most pessimistic assumptions regarding call dates and principal repayments.

- Covenants: provisions in a credit agreement that protect
  the creditor/investor from losing money on their investment.
  There are three types of covenants: maintenance/financial,
  affirmative, and negative covenants. These will be elaborated
  on later.

- Original Issuance Discount (OID): when the amount of debt
  provided at issuance is slightly lower than the principal amount.
  For example, in a 97 OID, the investor lends $97 for each $100
  they will be repaid at maturity.

- Seniority: refers to the order of repayment in the event of a sale or bankruptcy. Senior debt must be repaid before subordinated (or junior) debt is repaid.

- Refinancing: the act of raising new debt, with hope at a lower coupon rate (from the issuers perspective), and using that new debt to retire old debt.

- Bankruptcy: when a company "defaults" on its debt and fails to make an interest payment or principal repayment. Bankruptcy can also occur because of a "technical default" which is the violation of a covenant.

- Primed: when a new debt instrument is issued senior to an existing instrument.

- Lien: a lien is a legal right granted by a company to a creditor. A lien serves as insurance or collateral for the repayment of a loan. If the repayment of the loan is not satisfied, then the creditor may have the right to seize the asset or try and force its sale to get cash.

- Secured Debt: debt that has been granted a lien on some or all of the underlying assets of a company (such as the accounts receivable, inventory, and PPE).

- Unsecured Debt: debt that has not been granted a lien. Unsecured debt is riskier than secured debt, and therefore usually has a higher interest rate.

- Zero Coupon Bond: a bond that pays no interest payments over its life, meaning it is issued at a deep original issue discount (OID). It is important to note that zero coupon bonds do not affect the yearly cash flows of a company since all payments related to the zero coupon bond occur at maturity.

10.3 The Participants

10.3.1 The Issuers

The issuers of debt are the people raising/borrowing/taking on/issuing debt. The issuers of debt typically have some projects or objectives that require money now. However, often times they do not have that money in hand, so they raise debt to fund capital expenditures/government programs etc. The cost of raising

money through debt financing comes in the form of interest pay-
ments/coupon payments that the borrower must pay to the lender.
There are several different types of issuers: governments, corpo-
rates (companies), and cities (municipalities) are a few.

10.3.2   The Sell Side

The sell side consists of investment banks and other entities
that facilitate the connection between the buy side and issuers. The
sell side does not actually provide debt financing or lend money.
Instead, the sell side uses its network, expertise, and understanding of capital markets to help connect an issuer to investors and
structure the investment appropriately. For example, the capital
markets division at an investment bank might have Company A as
a client. Company A decides that they want to raise new debt to
fund the development of a new product. So, Company A, without direct connections to lender, goes to the investment bank and
requests help with raising debt. Then, the investment bank will
connect Company A with their extensive network of lender and
help intermediate the lending. Beyond this, the investment bank
will help advise the client and the lenders on key provisions of the
debt including: covenants, interest rate, maturity, the market's
reaction to the issuance, etc.

10.3.3   The Buy Side

The buy side consists of the investors. These are the actual
providers of capital or debt. These individuals or entities have
money now that they can lend. These lenders expect to receive a
return on their investment. With debt, that generally comes from
interest payments or coupon payments. The buy side can come
in the form of several entities, such as a hedge fund or a business
development company (BDC).

10.3.4   Private Equity

Private equity firms are a special type of issuer often called
financial sponsors. Private equity firms raise debt to finance the
acquisition of companies or to pay special dividends to themselves.
Private equity is the subject of Part VII.

10.4 Ratings Agencies

Ratings agencies are entities that rate the credit quality of a debt instrument. The three main rating agencies are Moody's, S&P, and Fitch. These agencies assign credit ratings evaluating a debtor's ability to make their interest and principal payments. The highest quality debt is usually considered AAA. Bonds rated BBB- or higher are called investment grade bonds. Bonds rated below this are called high yield bonds, speculative grade bonds, or junk bonds. Riskier debt is referred to as leveraged finance, or high yield debt investing.

If a corporate debt issuer was once an investment grade issuer and falls to a speculative or junk rating, this company is referred to as a "fallen angel."

10.5 Time Value of Money and Present Value

Would you rather have $100 now or $100 a year from now? Naturally, the investor would rather have $100 now. This is because the investor can generate a return on his investment over the next year, securing more than $100 a year from now. This introduces the concept of future value. The formula for future value (FV) is:

$$\text{Future Value} = (\text{Present Value})*(1 + r)$$

In the preceding formula, r is the rate of return generated by the investment operations of the investor over the year. It is also called the *discount rate* or *required rate of return* or *cost of capital*. Let us suppose that we have $100 now (present value or PV) and can generate a 10% return over the next year. Using the above formula, the future value (FV) of the investor's money is $110. What if the investor can generate a 10% return over the next *two* years? This requires an expansion of the previous formula to reflect the impact of compounding (discussed earlier):

$$\text{Future Value} = (\text{Present Value})*(1 + r)^2$$

Therefore, the FV of $100 invested at a 10% return rate for the next two years is $121. We can generalize the formula of the future value of an initial cash outlay with rate of return r and time periods of compounding t as:

$$FV = PV*(1 + r)^t$$

With hope, this discussion makes a lot of sense as it operates on core concepts of finance: compounding and the time value of money. Now, let us introduce a new scenario: what if we know the FV, r, and t, but not PV. Can we solve for PV? By simply moving the previous equation around, we sure can:

$$PV = FV/(1 + r)^t$$

This very powerful concept is called present value. Our formula suggests the present value or price (P_0) of an asset should equal the future value of the cash flow returned by the asset divided by a required rate of return, r, over t time periods. Since the quantity $(1 + r)$ is almost always greater than 1, this suggests that projected cash flows in more distant time periods are going to be less valuable (or more uncertain) than cash flows in earlier time periods. This intuitively makes sense, and is consistent with the notion that $100 now is better than $100 later. But, what if the asset produces multiple cash flows over several years? This is not a big issue. We just expand the formula to combine the impact of the multiple cash flows into the PV or P_0:

$$P_0 = \frac{C_1}{1+r_1} + \frac{C_2}{1+r_2} + ... + \frac{C_T}{1+r_T}$$

In the preceding formula, C_1 and C_2 refers to the cash flow of the asset in year one and year two, respectively, while r_1 and r_2 refer to the required rate of return in year one and year two, respectively. T is the final time period, or the number of years the asset produces cash flows. This formula can be expressed in simpler terms as a summation:

$$P_0 = \sum_{t=1}^{T} \frac{C_t}{(1+r_t)^t}$$

This formula is extremely important. The interpretation of this formula is: the value or price (P_0) of an asset is equal to the sum of the *discounted* cash flows of the asset. Discounted, in this context, refers to the reduced value we place on more distant (and inherently more uncertain) cash flows. This is one of the reasons that r_t is called the discount rate, since it captures the required rate of return of a given set of cash flows, and is the rate at which we discount future cash flows.

So what is the point of all this? Good question. Let us apply this formula to an actual asset, say, a bond. Imagine a bond pays a 5% interest rate, with a face value of $100, and a maturity of three years. Furthermore, suppose the interest rate demanded by investors or *required rate of return*, r, is also 5%. We could calculate the price of the bond as follows:

$$P_0 = \frac{\$5}{1.05} + \frac{\$5}{1.05^2} + \frac{\$105}{1.05^3}$$

By solving that equation, we determine that the price of the bond is exactly $100. When the price of the bond is exactly the same as the face value of the bond, the bond is priced at *par*. However, this is not always the case. Later in this chapter we will go into a deeper discussion of the alternative scenarios; first we must establish the key differences between loans and bonds.

10.6 Loans Versus Bonds

This is a critical section and aims to clarify several confusions the author had about debt for a long time. When companies need to raise money to continue or expand their operations, they generally have the option to choose between loans and bonds. Long-term loans and bonds work in a similar fashion. With each financing option, a company borrows money that it agrees to repay at a certain time and at a predetermined interest rate.

When a company takes out a loan, it is typically a private arrangement not open to the public or publicly tradable. Loans are often made by banks. Loans also have other components of their structure that are more restrictive than bonds. For example, the interest rate of loans is usually "floating" which means they are a spread off of LIBOR (e.g. LIBOR + 7.5%). This protects the lender from interest rate risk. Furthermore, loans typically have much more restrictive covenants. Lastly, the debt is often repaid over the life of the loan more (i.e. the debt has a fixed amortization schedule).

Bonds, on the other hand, have a fixed coupon rate, generally a longer maturity, less restrictive covenants, and a less restrictive amortization schedule. Bonds are publicly traded, making them a security. Unlike loans, bonds can be bought and sold in the public markets. A key corollary of this fact is that bonds have a *price* in the public markets that is disjoint from the *face value/principal* amount of the debt. This also means there is a difference between the yield/yield-to-maturity of the debt and the coupon rate. Beyond all that, prices of bonds are quoted as a percent of face value. For example, the price of a bond might be 80, which can be interpreted as 80% of principal. This means the bond is trading at a discount, which means the yield to maturity of buying this debt is *higher* than the coupon rate. If the price of the bond is 120, then the bond is trading at a premium, and the yield to maturity of buying this debt is lower than the coupon rate. See section 2: Key Terms if the language here is confusing.

The key takeaway from this section is that loans and bonds are very different. Only bonds have the unique characteristic of being a publicly traded security.

10.7   Bond Example

Having established that bonds have a price that is disjoint from the face value, let us consider a more involved example. Previously, we discussed an example in which the bond was trading (another term for priced) at par. Suppose that the interest rate investors demand or *required rate of return*, r, is also 5%. The calculation of the price of the bond is as follows:

$$P_0 = \frac{\$5}{1.05} + \frac{\$5}{1.05^2} + \frac{\$105}{1.05^3}$$

By solving that equation, we determine that the price of the bond is exactly $100. Notice that, in this case, the interest rate of the bond precisely equals the rate of return, r, demanded by investors.

Now suppose the company that issued this same debt announces that its cash flow from operations (CFO) will decrease significantly in the coming years. Therefore, the company will be producing less liquidity to meet interest payments. Due to this, the *credit quality* of the company has deteriorated and investors will perceive an investment in the company's debt as riskier. To be compensated for taking this higher risk, investors will demand a higher rate of return on their debt investment. Let's say 10%. How is this change reflected in the price of the bond? Let's write out the formula again:

$$\$87.57 = \frac{\$5}{1.10} + \frac{\$5}{1.10^2} + \frac{\$105}{1.10^3}$$

Notice, the price has dropped to about 87.6 (as % of face value). This makes sense. As the company becomes riskier (due to the deterioration in the liquidity of the underlying business), the price investors will pay to buy the company's bonds in the bond market will necessarily decrease. Put differently, the bonds are now *less sought after* than they were before, because they are riskier. Therefore, investors will pay less for the bonds by the rule of demand (as demand decreases, prices also decrease). Also notice, the *cash flows* of the bond (such as the interest payments and principal payment) are unchanging since they are inherent to the financial instrument. In contrast, the required rate of return is dynamic, reflecting market conditions and the level of investor demand. This is then reflected in the price of the bond.

In this scenario, imagine an investor purchases the bond at $87.6 and then holds the bond to maturity. The interest rate on the bond is still 5%, but the *yield* is different. To review what yield and yield-to-maturity are, refer to the "Common Terms" section of this chapter. Yield-to-maturity is basically the annualized return an investor would receive if the bond was purchased at its current price and held to maturity. The calculation for yield-to-maturity (YTM) is fairly involved. In this case, the YTM is 5.7%, slightly more than the interest rate of the bond. This makes sense, because we are paying less for the bond than we were at issuance, so the return for the same cash flows should be slightly greater. A bond that has a price below the face value of the bond is said to be trading at a *discount*.

Now imagine the inverse scenario. Suppose the credit quality of the company has improved since issuance, and the required return that investors demand decreases to 3%. What happens to the price?

$$\$105.66 = \frac{\$5}{1.03} + \frac{\$5}{1.03^2} + \frac{\$105}{1.03^3}$$

By the precisely opposite reasoning, the price of the bond has increased to 105.7. Investors are willing to pay more for a bond that is less risky. Since investors are paying more for the same cash flow profile, the YTM is less than the interest rate. The YTM is about 4.7% in this case. A bond that is trading at a price above par is said to be trading at a *premium*.

Having established the concept of bond prices, it is important to note the two main strategies in traditional debt investment: yield investing and total return investing. In yield investing, investors are focused on the interest payments they will receive and the yield-to-maturity of the bond. Investors hope to generate their returns by buying the bond, holding it to maturity, and collecting interest payments and principal repayments. The bond holder, remember, is contractually guaranteed to these cash flows, outside of bankruptcy. Yield investing is focused on the cash flows paid out by the company to the investor. A higher yield does not necessarily mean the debt is a better investment. Remember that the higher yield exists because the bond is perceived as riskier and more likely to default. Investing exclusively based on the yield of the investment is commonly referred to as "reaching for yield."

In contrast to yield investing, total return investing focuses on the price of the bond, similar to stock investing, though there are yield investors in stocks who focus on dividend payments. Therefore, a total return investor is hoping to buy (if he goes long) the bond at the market price, maybe collect some interest payments, and then sell the bond at a higher price at a later date. To do so successfully, the total return investor must correctly anticipate a change in the markets perception of the issuers credit quality, which is difficult to do. If the total return investor anticipates a deterioration in the credit quality of the issuer, then the investor might short the bond.

To wrap up this section, it is helpful to review the four key laws of bond prices we covered here:

- Bond prices vary *inversely* with yield; an increase in yield results in a decrease in bond prices; conversely, a decrease in yield results in an increase in bond prices

- When yield = interest rate, the bond is trading at par

- When yield > interest rate, the bond is trading at a discount

- When yield < interest rate, the bond is trading at a premium

10.8   Revolvers

Revolvers are a special type of debt generally provided by commercial banks. Revolvers, also called a "line of credit," basically function as a credit card for a company. The commercial bank and the issuer will agree on a "commitment amount," such

as \$100M, for a set period of time. This means the company can
"draw" up to \$100M at any time, in the same way a credit card
allows a consumer to "draw" up to their credit limit at any time.
Issuers then pay back the revolver when they need to or have the
funds to do so. During this time, the issuer pays interest on the
"drawn" amount. Usually, the interest rate on a revolver is spread
off of LIBOR (like a loan) and is relatively low. The issuer also
pays a small "commitment fee" as a percent of the commitment
amount.

Why do companies use revolvers? The main reason is that
it gives the company an additional source of liquidity, if they ever
need it. To give one concrete example, imagine a company that
has very seasonal sales and cash flow, such as a company that sells
Halloween costumes. This company, in anticipation of Halloween,
could draw their revolver to purchase inventory that they will sell
during Halloween. Then, once cash flow is produced from the sale
of Halloween costumes, the company can pay back the revolver and
collect the difference as profit. In this way, the company is able to
have a consistent and regular source of liquidity without having
to raise a new loan or bond everytime the new Halloween season
comes around.

Having established revolvers as a key source of liquidity,
what are other key sources of liquidity (cash) companies can use
to pay down debt and fund operations if needed? The first and
foremost is cash itself. The combination of excess revolver capac-
ity is often *available liquidity*. These are the most readily available
sources of cash for the company in a pinch. Beyond this, they can
raise cash in other ways such as: liquidation of assets (basically,
the selling of assets such as inventory and PPE for cash), equity
issuance, debt issuance, and actual cash generated by the business.
In extreme cases, companies can negotiate reduced interest rates
or file for bankruptcy to improve liquidity.

10.9 Covenants

Covenants are defined in the credit agreement that is created at the time the money is transferred from the investor to the
issuer. Covenants help preserve value for creditors. This is essential, since most management teams aim to maximize value for the
shareholders, which can encourage risky behavior, and creditors do
not like risky behavior. There are three types of covenants: financial, affirmative, and negative covenants.

Financial covenants are also called maintenance covenants because they refer to ratios that a firm must maintain. For example, a maintenance covenant might specify a specific EBITDA / interest expense ratio or current ratio the firm must maintain over the life of the loan.

Affirmative covenants are actions the firm must take. Examples of key affirmative covenants are: requirement to pay all business and employment related taxes, requirement to maintain current financial records and to deliver to the lender certain financial statements, requirement to maintain adequate insurance policies for the business, and a requirement to maintain the business entity in good standing with the state it was formed.

Negative covenants are actions the firm cannot take. Examples of key negative covenants are: limiting the total amount of indebtedness for the business, restricting or forbidding distributions and dividends paid to shareholders, preventing a merger or acquisition without the lender's permission, preventing of investment in certain capital equipment without the lender's permission, and preventing the sale of assets without the lender's permission.

A company that fails to comply with any covenant is said to be in technical default. A company can attempt to convince creditors to modify both covenants and the money terms (interest rate, maturity, face value) of a loan or bond. This is either called an amendment (an official change to the credit agreement) or a waiver/consent (a one-time forgiveness of the violation of a term or covenant).

10.10   Other Types of Debt

This discussion has focused on corporate debt. There are a wide variety of other types of fixed income products, such as government debt (called U.S. treasuries in the United States or sovereign debt in the case of international governments), municipality debt (the debt of cities), consumer debt (called consumer credit, such as credit card debt and auto loans), and derivative fixed income products (CLOs, CDOs, MBSs which are not discussed in this book).

For the average investor, the area of focus will be on U.S. treasuries, with perhaps some additional on municipality debt and corporate debt. U.S. treasuries are considered "riskless" since it is generally believed that the U.S. government cannot default on its debt. For this reason, the interest rates on U.S. debt are usually lower than that of corporate debt. The U.S. sells debt across a huge spectruym of maturities, ranging from 6 months to 30 years.

While investors can lock in a "riskless" interest rate from the government, it is important to realize that to be completely safe from permanent loss of capital, the investor must hold the U.S. treasuries until maturity. If the 10-year U.S. treasury bond yield is 2.35%, and the government increases interest rates to 5% over that time span, then the investor will lose money on the price depreciation of the 10-year bond *if he sells it prior to maturity.* Remember, bond prices vary inversely with interest rate changes. In this scenario, if the U.S. treasury (or any bond, assuming default does not occur) is held to maturity, then the intermediate price fluctuations do not matter.

11

Capital Structure

11.1 Debt versus Equity

Capital structure, put simply, is the mix of long-term debt and equity financing that a firm utilizes to fund its operations. The value of equity + long-term debt is called total capitalization. Equity, meanwhile, is an ownership claim on the business. Equity holders share in the rise in value of the overall firm. Maximizing shareholder value is also the focus of the board of directors and company management. Beyond share price appreciation, equity investors also make a return through discretionary dividends, which are decided by management. Since they capture all the benefits of successful or perceived growth, equity holders often focus. In contrast, long-term debt investors generally have fixed upside. Therefore, debt investors are focused on protecting downside risk (through asset coverage or asset protection) and on the ability of the company to meet interest payments (produce liquidity).

Some people believe that, for a given firm in a given industry, an *optimal* capital structure exists. This intuitively makes sense, because, in theory, a firm could balance out the pros and cons of debt with the pros and cons of equity. In practice, it is not this simple. In truth, determining optimal capital structure for a firm is very difficult.

Pecking order theory is an important concept to establish here in the search for optimal capital structure. Its premise: that firms prefer to finance their operations in a specific order. The preference goes: reinvested profits > debt > equity. Reinvested profits are obviously the preferred form of financing as if a firm can reinvest its own cash in the business, it does not have to pay out interest payments (via debt) or give up a portion of its upside (via equity). Debt is preferred over equity (with some *very important* caveats) since paying out interest is generally "cheaper" than giving away a portion of the company's upside in the form of equity. Put more succinctly, the cost of debt is generally considered lower than the cost of equity.

Why then do firms raise equity at all if the act gives away a portion of their upside? Mainly because a firm's debt level is balanced between two opposing forces: tax shields and costs of financial distress.

11.1.1   Tax Shields

Observe the following two income statements (note, these income statements start with EBIT to focus on the key point):

Income Statement Comparison		
Scenario	**Scenario A**	**Scenario B**
EBIT	$100	$100
Interest Expense	$0	$20
Profit Before Tax	$100	$80
Tax Expense	$40	$32
Net Income	$60	$48

In this analysis, assume a 40% tax rate. Notice EBIT is the same in scenario A and B. But, interest expense is $20 higher in scenario B. One might expect scenario B to have a net income that is also $20 lower in this case. However, notice the net income in scenario B is only $12 lower. The reason for this: the increased interest expense reduces profit before tax, and therefore the tax expense. The exact tax expense reduction = (Interest Expense) * (Tax Rate). In this case, we have a $20 interest expense a 40% tax rate, result in an $8 "tax shield". By subtracting the tax shield from the interest expense, we get the total impact on net income: $12 lower in scenario B than scenario A. We can check above to see this is exactly the case.

What we have observed here is called the tax deductibility of interest expense or the tax shield effect of interest expense. This effect causes the *cost of debt* to be lower than the interest rate paid on the debt. This makes debt financing attractive for firms, especially firms that pay a lot of taxes.

11.1.2 Costs of Financial Distress

Offsetting the benefits of tax shields and the relatively lower cost of debt (as compared to equity) is the possibility of financial distress. Financial distress is another word for bankruptcy, or defaulting on an interest payment/principal repayment. Naturally, as interest and debt levels increase, the probability of financial distress also increases. It is essential to understand that bankruptcy is a very expensive process, both directly and indirectly. Directly, bankruptcy has significant legal and consulting expenses. Indirectly, a company's competitive position, relationships with suppliers and customers, brand reputation, and other critical qualitative aspects can deteriorate significantly during the bankruptcy process.

Beyond that, companies have to be able to actually pay interest payments in order to raise debt successfully. This is why start-ups do not raise debt: there is no simply way they could meet the interest payments since they are almost always facing negative cash flow. No debt investor would lend to a startup, since he basically knows the company would end up in bankruptcy.

11.2 Weighted Average Cost of Capital (WACC)

Weighted average cost of capital (WACC) is the blended return demanded by all providers of capital to the company. WACC can be thought of as the required rate of return or cost of capital for an entire firm. The WACC is the discount rate (think back to the time value of money concept) that reflects the riskiness of an entire business. Previously, we have referenced the concepts of "cost of debt" and "cost of equity". For calculating WACC, we determine both the cost of debt and the cost of equity, then weight these costs by their respective proportion of the capital structure. Cost of debt is the return demanded by the debt investors of the business. Primarily, the cost of debt reflects the default risk of the company (the likelihood that the company cannot meet interest payments or principal repayments). As default risk increases, cost of debt also increases. Cost of equity is the return demanded by equity investors.

The formula for WACC is:

$$\text{WACC} = r_d * (1 - T) * \frac{D}{D+E} + r_e * \frac{E}{D+E}$$

In the preceding formula, r_d is the cost of debt, T is the tax rate, the quantity $1 - T$ captures the impact of the tax shield (discussed previously) on the cost of debt, $\frac{D}{D+E}$ is the proportion of debt in the capital structure, r_e is the cost of equity, and $\frac{E}{D+E}$ is the proportion of equity in the capital structure. Since the costs of each form of capital (debt versus equity) are weighted by their respective proportions in the capital structure, it makes sense that this metric is called the weighted average cost of capital. Also, D or debt usually refers to the book value (or par value) of debt, in practice, this can be found on the balance sheet or the footnote related to long-term debt in a 10-K. E usually refers to the market value (or market cap, calculated by multiplying shares outstanding by share price) of equity. T is 35% for most corporations, but to be more accurate, simply divide the tax provision by profit before tax on the income statement to arrive at the approximate tax rate.

To give an example, suppose r_d is 5%, T is 40%, book value of debt is \$100, market cap is \$300, and cost of equity is 12%. What would WACC be? Simply plug into the formula:

$$9.75\% = 5\% * (1 - 40\%) * \tfrac{100}{400} + 12\% * \tfrac{300}{400}$$

What this examples takes for granted is the cost of debt and cost of equity, which will be discussed now.

11.2.1   Cost of Debt

There are three main ways to calculate the cost of debt. In order of increasing effectiveness/accuracy: use comparable debt, use most recent interest expense, and use weighted average yield-to-maturity (YTM) method.

Previously, we established the role and function of the credit rating agencies. By observing the credit rating (and associated YTM) of the debt of similarly-rated companies, one can estimate the cost of a firm's debt. This comparable approach is quick and easy, but less effective. For example, imagine the company in question has a AA credit rating. We could go look on the ratings agencies' websites to determine the YTM of other AA rated debt and use this is as the cost of debt for the company in question.

Another approach to calculate the cost of debt is to simply take the most recent annual interest expense and divide it by the average debt outstanding during the year. This is usually accurate, but still inferior to the weighted average YTM method.

The most effective way to calculate the cost of debt is the weighted average yield-to-maturity (YTM) method. The formula for this method is as follows:

$$\text{Weighted Average YTM} =$$
$$\frac{YTM_1 * DebtAmount_1}{TotalDebt} + ... + \frac{YTM_n * DebtAmount_n}{TotalDebt}$$

In the preceding formula, n is the total number of interest bearing debts in the company's capital structure (remember, a company can have some loans, some bonds, and several of each). The following chart shows an example of the weighted average YTM method:

Weighted Average YTM Example				
	Amount	YTM	% of Debt	Weighted YTM
Debt 1	$100	3%	22.2%	0.67%
Debt 2	$200	5%	44.4%	2.22%
Debt 3	$150	8%	33.3%	2.67%
Total	$450	NA	NA	5.56%

In the preceding chart, the weighted average YTM is 5.56%. This would then serve as the cost of debt, r_d, in the WACC formula.

11.2.2 Cost of Equity

Cost of equity is the return demanded by the equity holders or owners of the business. As discussed earlier, we will find that the cost of equity is generally the most expensive type of capital.

Capital Asset Pricing Model (CAPM) is a model designed by academic communities. It is the main way that academics, investment banks, and some hedge funds calculate cost of equity. However, many hedge funds and investors use their own proprietary calculating methods. Some firms also simply utilize a fixed % without any calculation at all, such as 10%. So we see there are several ways to possibly calculate cost of equity. In this book, we will focus on the essential concept of CAPM.

CAPM theory states there are two types of risk: asset-specific risk and systematic risk. Asset-specific risk is the associated with a specific company or asset. Systematic risk, which is called beta or β, is the sensitivity of a given asset's returns to changes in the market's rate of return. In theory, if given what the market will return and β, we can calculate what the specific asset will return. Note: β is, to the author, one of the most unintuitive concepts in all of finance. It is completely normal for this to not make sense at first.

Technically, β is the covariance of an asset with the market divided by the variance of the market. To give a concrete example of β, a β of 1.1 means the following: if the market as a whole goes up by 10%, the asset will go up by 11%. A β of -1 means that if the market as a whole goes up by 10%, then the asset will go down by -10%.

The underlying assumption here is that we know what the market as a whole will return. Sadly, we do not know this quantity, since we do not know the future. However, we can use the historical average returns of the market, in excess of some normalizing benchmark, like the risk-free rate (the yield on U.S. treasuries) as an estimate for what the market will return. This quantity, the average return of the stock market, in excess of the risk free rate, is called the market risk premium. This is considered the premium investors demand for taking on the additional risk of investing in equity. By multiplying β by the market risk premium, we get an estimate of the cost of equity. There is one item to add: at a minimum, investors will demand at least the risk-free rate since it is basically a guaranteed return they can get without risk. Therefore, the risk-free rate is added to the β multiplied by the market risk premium. In accordance, the formula for cost of equity under the CAPM looks like this:

$$\text{Cost of Equity} = r_f + \beta * (r_m - r_f)$$

In this formula, r_f is the risk-free rate. Usually, the yield on the 5-year or 10-year U.S. treasury is used for this. At the time of this writing, the 5-year U.S. treasury yield is about 2.2%. The market risk premium in the U.S., or the quantity $(r_m - r_f)$, is about 6%. As a reminder, this is the average return the stock market has achieved throughout history in excess of the risk-free rate. One question remains - how do we calculate /beta?

To calculate β in Excel, take the covariance between the market's returns and the asset's returns and divide that by the variance of the market's returns. Other resources, such as Yahoo Finance and Google Finance, disclose the βs of companies, but the effectiveness of the calculation is often questioned.

The β calculated using the procedure discussed in the preceding paragraph or found on Yahoo Finance/Google Finance is called a raw beta, levered beta, or β_L. This means that the calculated β_L or raw beta is affected by the leverage or capital structure of the business.

As companies take on more debt, their β_L tends to increase, since the more leverage a company has the riskier their returns become. This generally results in greater equity value volatility. Therefore, we have to normalize β_L to get a measure that is normalized for the company's capital structure. This process is called *unlevering* β and results in β_U or beta unlevered. There are dozens of formulas for unlevering beta. The formula used by the author is: $\beta_U = \beta_L * (\frac{E}{D+E})$.

Finally, we can describe the full process for calculating the β_L of a specific company (company Z) using the following steps:

1. Collect a set of comparable companies from the industry of company Z

2. Calculate the raw βs or β_Ls of the comparable companies

3. Unlever the comparable companies' β_Ls using the respective capital structure of each company and the formula $\beta_U = \beta_L * (\frac{E}{D+E})$

4. Average the β_Us of the comparable companies

5. Relever the averaged β_Us with the capital structure of company Z using the formula $\beta_L = \beta_U * (\frac{D+E}{E})$

The table below provides an example of this process:

Beta Calculation Example					
Company	β_L	**Market Cap**	**Debt**	**E/(D+E)**	β_U
Comparable A	1.10	$1000	$200	83.33%	0.92
Comparable B	0.90	$500	$300	62.50%	0.56
Comparable C	1.30	$1500	$1000	60.00%	0.78
Company Z	1.18	$800	$450	64%	0.75

The β_U of company Z in the preceding table equals the average of the β_Us of the comparable companies. By relevering this average β_U with the capital structure of company Z, we then arrive at the β_L of company Z, which is 1.18. Finally, we have calculated all the necessary components to determine the cost of equity. The risk-free rate, or r_f, is about 2.2%. The market risk premium, or $(r_m - r_f)$, is about 6%. The β_L of the target company is 1.18. Plugging into the formula, we get:

$$9.28\% = 2.2\% + 1.18 * 6\%$$

11.2.3   Tying Everything Together

As a reminder, the formula for WACC is:

$$\text{WACC} = r_d * (1 - T) * \tfrac{D}{D+E} + r_e * \tfrac{E}{D+E}$$

The calculated cost of debt is 5.56%. The calculated cost of equity is 9.28%. The book value of debt is \$450. The market value of equity is \$800. Therefore, $\frac{D}{D+E}$ is 36% and $\frac{E}{D+E}$ is 64%. For T, the standard corporate tax rate of 35% will be used. Tying this all together, we calculate the WACC as:

$$7.24\% = 5.56\% * (1 - 35\%) * 36\% + 9.28\% * 64\%$$

11.2.4   ROIC versus WACC

The combination of ROIC and cost of capital is powerful. A company has some cost associated with its funds. This is the cost of capital, which was calculated previously. ROIC is the approximate return generated on that capital. Incremental ROIC is the approximate return on *new* capital invested. Incremental ROIC is difficult to calculate, but it is an important concept to understand. A company that generates an incremental ROIC > WACC is creating value for the company by investing in its business. A company that generates an incremental ROIC < WACC is actually destroying value by reinvesting in its business, since the cost of that capital is more expensive than the return generated by it. If incremental ROIC < WACC, the company is best off returning some or all of the cash it produces to shareholders (in the form of dividends or share buybacks), since the company destroys value by investing that cash in the business.

11.3   Seniority and Security

In a company's capital structure, there are two important concepts: seniority and security. Seniority refers to the hierarchy or order of repayment in the event of a company sale or bankruptcy. Senior debt must be repaid before subordinated debt is repaid. Equity is the most junior or least senior part of the capital structure. As seniority increases, the prospective return of the security decreases. As investors take additional risk by investing in a more junior portion of the capital stack, they demand to be compensated for their added risk in the form of higher expected returns. The graphic below exhibits a standard version of the "capital stack":

Highest seniority, lowest risk, lowest return

> **Senior Secured Debt**
> 0-25% of capital stack
> 2-6% targeted returns

> **Senior Unsecured Debt**
> 0-25% of capital stack
> 6-12% targeted returns

> **Mezzanine Debt**
> 0-15% of capital stack
> 12-15% targeted returns

> **Preferred Equity**
> 0-10% of capital stack
> 15-20% targeted returns

> **Common Equity**
> 25-100% of capital stack
> 20%+ targeted returns

Lowest seniority, highest risk, highest return

There are a few key takeaways from this diagram. First, as described, senior securities are less risky, so they have a lower expected return. In contrast, junior securities are more risky, so they have a higher expected return. The reason senior securities are less risky is because they get paid back first in the event of a company failure or default. Beyond this, the diagram also indicates a company must always have equity in its capital structure. This makes sense since a company must have owners. By contrast, debt is optional, and is decided on by the owners of the company or the management team. We have already discussed the reasons a management team would decide to add debt to the capital structure.

Another key attribute of the capital stack is security. Security refers to whether the debt investor has a lien on the collateral of the business. As mentioned previously, potential collateral might include: accounts receivable, inventory, or PP&E. Secured debt instruments are generally the most senior part of the capital structure. In the event of the bankruptcy or liquidation of a firm, the value of the secured creditors claim is supported by the specific assets they have a lien on. For example, if a company has to liquidate (sell all its assets and return cash to investors), then secured creditors get all the cash associated with the selling of the collateral associated with their debt instrument, up until their claim (face value) is repaid.

We can see that most portions of the capital stack are not secured. Naturally, these portions demand higher returns than the secured portions.

What specific securities make up each portion of the capital stack?

Senior Secured Debt

The senior secured part of the capital stack generally consists of a revolver and secured loans/secured term loans provided by commercial banks and hedge funds/institutional investors. Revolvers are usually provided by commercial banks. The term loans provided by commercial banks are usually called Term loan A(s) or TLA(s). The characteristics of loans were described previously in Chapter 10. TLAs typically have significant amortization requirements over the life of the loan.

Beyond TLAs, there are term loans provided by hedge funds and other institutional investors in the senior secured portion of the capital stack. These are called Term Loan B(s) or TLB(s) and have less stringent amortization requirements (a greater proportion of principal is repaid at maturity) and a longer dated maturity.

Beyond TLAs and TLBs, the last common possible portion of the senior secured section of the capital stack is second lien term loans. These have a second priority claim on the assets of the borrower. Institutional investors such as hedge funds often invest in second lien term loans, when they exist in the capital stack.

Senior Unsecured Debt

Senior unsecured debt mainly consists of high yield bonds. As a reminder, the attributes of bonds were discussed in Chapter 10. Generally, the principal of high yield bonds are repaid entirely at maturity (this is called a bullet payment structure). This also means that high yield bonds do not have a required amortization schedule. Also, high yield bonds usually pay interest at a fixed rate, rather than a floating rate.

Mezzanine Debt

Mezzanine debt is the portion of the capital structure that lies between traditional debt and equity. Mezzanine debt instruments are usually tailor-made for the needs and desires of the investor and company. Mezzanine debt has a high targeted return of 12-15% (sometimes higher). Hedge funds and specialized mezzanine funds invest in the mezzanine debt portion of the capital stack. Because of the tailor-made nature of the mezzanine debt portion of the capital structure, there are a variety of common mezzanine debt structures. These various structures are the subject of Chapter 12.

Preferred Equity

Preferred equity is a senior type of equity, but also sometimes considered a special type of mezzanine debt. Private equity investors, such as buyout funds, growth equity funds, and venture capital funds, often invest in the preferred equity of a company. Preferred equity is also elaborated on in Chapter 12.

Common Equity

Finally, at the bottom of the capital stack, with the greatest risk and the greatest potential reward, is common equity. Common equity is the portion of the capital stack traded in the stock market. When an individual buys shares of a company, they are buying common equity. Equity provides a cushion for lenders and bondholders. For example, if equity represents 40% of the capital stack, then the value of the entire enterprise (the capital stack as a whole) must deteriorate by 40% for the principal of the debt holders to be in jeopardy.

11.4   Structural Subordination

Generally, a publicly traded company actually consists of several companies in a hierarchy. The company at the top of the hierarchy is called the parent company or the holding company (HoldCo). A HoldCo is basically a company that owns other companies. Companies existing directly under the HoldCo are the *subsidiaries* of the HoldCo. Usually, the operating assets or actual cash producing assets (such as trucks, factories, etc.) of the firm are owned by the subsidiaries of the company, or the lower rungs of the corporate hierarchy. For this reason, the subsidiaries are often called operating companies (OpCos).

Consider a business with three main business lines: a trucking business, a retail business, and an advertising business. All of these separate businesses, or OpCos, are owned by the HoldCo that represents the combined entity. The corporate structure diagram below exhibits this relationship.

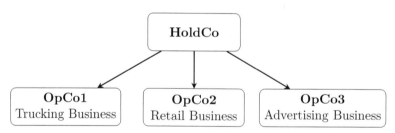

When investing in the debt or equity of a company, it is important to realize where the debt or equity lies in the corporate structure. For example, using the preceding diagram, is the equity that is publicly traded on the stock market the equity of the HoldCo or one of the OpCos? This is an important question to answer. It is possible for a company to have a fraction of its equity publicly traded on the stock market. OpCo1 could, for instance, have 50% of its equity on the stock market with the other 50% owned by the HoldCo.

Debt, however, can be raised by any of the companies in the corporate structure, such as HoldCo, OpCo1, OpCo2, or OpCo3.

This raises a dilemma. Is debt raised by OpCo2 senior or junior to debt raised by the HoldCo? For our answer we must turn to the concept of structural subordination. In a nutshell, structural subordination means debt that is *closer* to the operating assets of the company is structurally senior to debt further away from the operating assets of the company. The debt of OpCo2 is structurally senior to the debt of HoldCo because OpCo2 owns operating assets. This is true even if the debt at the OpCo2 level is labeled "subordinated debt" and the debt at the HoldCo level is labeled "senior debt".

But why is this the case? Remember that *each* of the companies in the preceding diagram has its own capital structure. Furthermore, remember that every capital structure has equity. Finally, remember that HoldCo owns OpCo2. Therefore, HoldCo is actually an equity owner (or 100% shareholder) of the equity of OpCo2. Now, both OpCo2 and HoldCo have debt. Since debt is senior to equity in the capital structure, the debt of OpCo2 is actually senior to the equity claim that HoldCo has on OpCo2. So we see then that, OpCo2's debt actually gets paid back first (from the cash produced by the operating assets) and is structurally senior to the debt of HoldCo. Think of it this way: since HoldCo is an equity holder of OpCo2, when cash trickles up from OpCo2 to HoldCo, it is basically an internal dividend payment. Interest and principal payments are higher priority than dividend payments, so the debt of OpCo2 is paid back before the debt of HoldCo, which can only be paid back via dividend payments from the OpCos. For this reason, it is essential to understand where debt lies in the corporate structure.

The only exception to structural subordination is a *subsidiary guaranty*. This is simply a contractual guaranty by the OpCos to pay back the debt of HoldCo first. In a contract, basically anything that both parties agree to is fair game. So, if both parties agree to a subsidiary guaranty, then HoldCo debt can "overcome" its structural subordination to the debt of the OpCos.

Obviously, the structural subordination of a debt, or lack thereof, affects the risk of an investment. Therefore, investors will with hope price this in to the returns they require for their investment.

11.5   Signaling

Information asymmetry exists between a management team (which decides the capital structure of a company) and investors. Put differently, the management team knows more about the company and its prospects than investors. Therefore, investors closely watch the actions of management for clues regarding their future expectations. This is the concept of signaling through capital structure and financing decisions.

In a nutshell, it is often considered a positive signal whenever the company increases the cash it is paying out. This includes: raising debt (since the company will increase its interest expense), raising or starting a dividend, or repurchasing shares. The logic: if management is increasing cash paid out to investors, then they must be optimistic about future cash generation. Repurchasing its own shares also suggests the company believes its stock is undervalued. However, in the case of dividends and share repurchases, the company might just be paying out cash to shareholders because it does not have any identifiable projects with a ROIC > WACC.

It is often considered a negative signal when the company reduces the cash it is paying out or raises equity financing. A company cutting its dividend is a bad sign. A company raising equity financing through the stock market, saying essentially "we think the amount of cash we can raise per share right now is good" is often interpreted negatively as well. However, rules of thumb like this are rarely completely effective in investing and every scenario should be considered on a case-by-case basis. For example, a company might just be raising equity funding to help finance a very high ROIC project.

12

Mezzanine Securities

12.1   Introduction

In Chapter 11, the mezzanine portion of the capital stack was introduced. This portion of the capital structure that lies between traditional debt and equity. It makes up a small slice of the capital stack and has a targeted return rate of about 12-20%. Here we will discuss varying structures of securities that lie specifically in the mezzanine portion of the capital structure. These securities will often attach some form of equity upside in order to increase the potential for return. We will discuss a few examples of this.

12.2   High-Yield Loans (Leveraged Loans) or High-Yield Bonds

The classic high yield loan or bond can still be placed in the mezzanine portion of the capital structure. No further detail need be provided here since the mechanics of high-yield loans and bonds were discussed extensively in Chapters 10 and 11.

12.3   Debt with Warrants

Often times, mezzanine investors will invest in a high yield loan or bond and also receive warrants from the company they invest in. A warrant is a complex security that gives investors a small portion of equity upside potential. In a nutshell, a warrant confers the owner the right, but not the obligation, to buy a security – normally an equity – at a certain price before expiration. The price at which the underlying security can be bought or sold is referred to as the exercise price or strike price.

Warrants given to mezzanine investors by the company issuing debt, give the mezzanine investors the *right* to purchase equity in the company at a specific price before a certain time. Through warrants, a mezzanine investor has the right to purchase a very small portion of the equity before a certain time period elapses. Warrants are a form of "sweetener" or "equity kicker" that juice the potential returns of the investment by allowing the loan or bond holder to share in a small portion of the equity upside. A warrant is almost identical to a *call option* which is discussed extensively in Chapter 46.

12.4   Convertible Debt

With a convertible debt obligation an investor has the option to have their principal repayment through a fixed number of shares of equity rather than in cash.

For example, suppose a mezzanine investor invests in a convertible debt with a face value of $1000. Furthermore, the convertible debt gives the investor the *option* to have his principal repaid either in cash at $1000 (like a normal debt) or in the form of 50 shares of the company. In this scenario, the share price of the company would have to be worth more than $20 (which is $1000/50 shares) for the investor to choose the share option. Otherwise, the convertible debt investor would just choose the $1000 in cash.

So why would an investor want to invest in convertible debt? Convertible debt gives the investor the ability to take part in equity upside (through the option to be repaid in equity) while also protecting the investor from downside risk, since, if the company does poorly and the share price decreases, the investor can elect to receive his principal repayment in the form of cash. Because of this powerful optionality for the investor, convertible debt generally has an interest rate that is relatively lower than a standard loan or bond of comparable seniority and maturity.

12.5   Paid-in-Kind (PIK) Debt

A PIK is a type of high yield debt obligation in which the interest payments are made by increasing the outstanding principal rather than through cash interest payments. Therefore, the outstanding debt increases over the life of the PIK instrument. A similar structure to this is a toggle, in which the company has the choice to pay interest expense either by increasing debt or through cash payment.

However, a PIK produces a "non-cash interest expense" that flows through the income statement. Therefore, PIK instruments still produce tax shields. Because the PIK instrument saves the firm cash in the form of tax shields, while not costing the firm cash in the form of interest expense, PIK instruments actually increase the cash flow of a firm up until the maturity (at which point the face value and accumulated interest expense is due).

12.6 Preferred Equity

Preferred equity is sometimes considered a mezzanine security and sometimes consider a senior version of equity. Preferred equity is a class of ownership (or special type of debt) with a higher claim on a company's assets and earnings than common stock. Preferred shares generally have a required dividend (often in the form of a PIK). Preferred stock has features of debt, since it has a fixed dividend payment and a face value. Preferred equity also has features of equity, particularly if it is a special type of preferred equity with the ability to convert into common stock (like a convertible debt). This is a common structure for preferred equity. Preferred equity has a wide variety of structures and nuances. It is also the main portion of the capital structure that growth equity and venture capital investors invest in.

Part IV

Valuation and
Financial Modeling

13

Valuation Basics

13.1 The Core Concepts of Valuation and Financial Modeling

Valuation is the art of determining what a security is *worth*. The value of a security is different than its price. If someone asked you what price would you pay for an apple tree, what would you say? Two main approaches come to mind. The first is to consider the future cash flows of the apple tree produced by selling apples and paying out associated expenses. The second is to look at what other people are paying for comparable apple trees. The cash flow focused technique, in the case of a company, is called discounted cash flow analysis. The relative valuation technique actually has two forms: comparable companies analysis and precedent transactions analysis. These three methods: discounted cash flow analysis, comparable companies analysis, and precedent transactions analysis are the main ways of valuing a company. They form the focus of Part IV where we will also cover three statement modeling – a useful financial modeling technique for areas such as credit analysis.

13.2 Art Versus Science

Is investing an art or a science? Art is a more qualitative practice in which the "correct" answer is less clear. Science, by contrast, is generally quantitative and has an objectively accurate answer. In approaching valuation, it is easy to be lulled into the belief that investing is more of a science, since the models and methods discussed in Part IV will produce a precise measure of company value.

However, models are just that – models. A model is only a

strong as its forecasts and inputs; even then, forecasts of the future are generally wrong. An investor must strive to be incredibly rational and honest regarding the inputs to a model, since an investor can manipulate the inputs to produce any result desired. Due to this, it is essential, in the author's opinion, to take all valuation approaches with a grain-of-salt. Valuation techniques can easily give an investor a false sense of security.

Valuation techniques are mandatory for areas where a specific transaction price is required for a deal to go through, such as the M&A group of an investment bank and buyout private equity. This helps explain why buyout private equity and the M&A operations of an investment bank are generally very heavy on financial modeling. Furthermore, financial modeling (especially three statement modeling) is useful for credit analysis, since the investor can analyze the ability of the company to produce enough liquidity to meet interest expenses under varying conditions. A three statement model, in tandem with an equity valuation model, enables an investor to analyze the two core aspects of a credit analysis: 1) liquidity and 2) asset protection (where the equity value is a proxy for asset protection).

This being said, the author believes investing is more of an art than a science. The qualitative aspects of a business, such as the competitive position, the industry dynamics, the value proposition, and much more, ultimately determine the long-term success of a business and the quality of an investment. As mentioned in Chapter 1, this focus on the microeconomic characteristics (whether qualitative or quantitative) of a business is called fundamental analysis. In fundamental analysis, the correct answer is often unclear, because of the importance of qualitative factors. If an investor chooses to utilize valuation techniques at all, they must be employed judiciously, with rational and honest expectations grounded in the economic reality and qualitative fundamentals of the business.

Regardless of the investor's personal opinion on financial modeling and valuation, it is essential to understand valuation techniques, as they are a core part of the industry. If the investor decides to employ valuation techniques, a deep understanding of the techniques discussed here in Part IV will prove very useful. If the investor chooses not to employ valuation techniques, the core intuitions and mental framework that a business is worth the sum of its future discounted cash flow is essential to understand. Beyond this, it is also helpful to understand valuation just to know how a significant portion of the finance and investing community thinks about companies and investing decisions.

13.3 Where We Stand

Parts I-III of this book covered essential technical concepts that help an investor find information, speak the language of investing, and understand what is going on with a company. Deeply internalizing the concepts in Parts I-III (whether by reading these parts multiple times or referring to the additional resources discussed in the Further Exploration section at the end of this book) will prove extremely valuable to an aspiring investor.

In Part IV, all the technical concepts covered thus far culminate in the art of security valuation and financial modeling. Part V covers *many* key qualitative and fundamental attributes of a business that are the ultimate determinants of a company's long term cash flow, worth, and liquidity production. Part VI covers a philosophical framework, called value investing, through which to approach the markets and the concepts introduced in the rest of the book. Parts IV-VI, when internalized, considered in tandem with Parts I-III, and effectively employed, equip the investor with enough knowledge to be dangerous in the investing world.

Part VII covers the various forms of private equity, which is reasonably different from public investing. In Part VII, we will also explore leveraged buyout models, a special financial modeling technique for evaluating the acquisition of a company. Lastly, Part VIII will cover advanced and selected topics.

14

Discounted Cash Flow Analysis

14.1 Introduction

Previously, when discussing bond pricing, we established that any asset is worth the sum of its discounted cash flows. This concept is reflected by the following formula:

$$P_0 = \sum_{t=1}^{T} \frac{C_t}{(1+r_t)^t}$$

When looking at the preceding formula, the pricing of a debt instrument comes very naturally, since the cash flows (the numerator in the equation) are inherent to the instrument itself. Furthermore, the discount rate or yield is readily determined. But, in the case of valuing equity, applying this formula is more complex. Discounted cash flow (DCF) analysis is the process of using this formula to value a company's equity or the entire firm. The price produced by a DCF is called *intrinsic value*. This is the most common valuation technique.

In Part III we already covered the cost of capital or required rate of return for a firm: weighted average cost of capital or WACC. This will serve as r_t in the preceding formula. Apart from this, most of the work involved in creating a DCF is associated with calculating the cash flows, or C_t, for each time period. We discussed several cash flow formulas in Chapter 6. However, a DCF uses a slightly different cash flow formula than those previously discussed.

14.2 A Slightly Different Cash Flow Formula

Let us think back to the discussion on tax shields from Chapter 11. Remember the WACC formula we derived serves as the discount rate, or r_t, for the purpose of valuing a firm. The formula for WACC is repeated here for convenience:

$$\text{WACC} = r_d * (1 - T) * \frac{D}{D+E} + r_e * \frac{E}{D+E}$$

Notice how here the WACC formula captures the effect of the tax shield by multiplying the cost of debt by $(1-T)$. However, many of the cash flow metrics covered in Chapter 6 also capture the effect of the tax shield by reducing the tax provision. Therefore, we must utilize a slightly different cash flow formula to avoid "double-counting" the impact of the tax shield. The modified cash formula simply calculates the tax expense from EBIT, like so:

FCF = EBIT$*(1 - T)$ - Capital Expenditures - (Δ in WC) + Depreciation + Amortization

In the preceding formula, T is the tax rate. Furthermore, this is a *cash flows to firm* formula, rather than a *cash flows to equity* formula since it includes interest expense. This, in combination with the WACC, which represents the firm-wide cost of capital, means the value produced by the summing the discounted cash flows will be an enterprise value rather than an equity value. We will revisit the importance of this at the end of the chapter. The quantity EBIT$*(1-T)$ is also called net operating profit after-tax (NOPAT).

We now have a framework for solving the sum of the discounted future cash flows. We also have the cash flow formula and the discount rate formula. From here, most of the work is related to actually forecasting and calculating the various components of the previous cash flow formula and WACC formula in order to calculate future discounted free cash flows.

An important note: we need not build full financial statements (income statement, balance sheet, cash flow statement) with a balance sheet that balances into the future (which is core to a three statement model). We need only to calculate the various components of the cash flow formula and WACC formula.

14.3   Capitalization Table

In our example DCF analysis, we'll be valuing Company Z. Before calculating the free cash flows and the discount rate, it is essential to layout the basics of the company's capital structure and recent operating results to provide context and a base level understanding of Company Z's capitalization.

14.4 Revenue Projection Model

First, the focus is on calculating NOPAT or EBIT*$(1 - T)$. To do this, we must build a forecasted income statement. All income statements start with revenue. The two different approaches to forecasting revenue or the top-line of the income statement are covered in this section: the top-down approach and the bottom-up approach. The part of a DCF model that forecasts revenue is called a revenue projection model (RPM). As we will see, most of the other components of a DCF depend on the sales projections. For this reason, we must be pragmatic in our sales predictions. Sales growth rates beyond 10-20% are very hard to sustain for mid-stage to late-stage businesses. Most companies well suited for a DCF analysis will have sales growth rates <10%.

Throughout a model, forecasts up until a specific year are utilized. Equity lasts forever, but we cannot forecast cash flows to infinity. Instead, we forecast the cash flows five years out (5-20 years out is standard) and then use one of two methods to value the cash flows from year five to infinity (called the "terminal value"). The forecasted years encompass the "projection period." To provide context and help shape our forecasts, a few years of historical data are also included in a DCF model. This data encompasses the "historical period".

One last note: the components of the model that dictate the values of key numbers in the projection period are called "assumptions" or "drivers."

14.4.1 Top-down Approach

The top-down approach focuses on the macro or industry environment of the company to forecast sales. For example, to arrive at the specific sales of Company Z, one might start with the total market size (this is the total annual sales produced by a given industry). Then, one can calculate the historical market share (the % of the market size Company Z makes up). From this, the investor can forecast the future market share and market size based on industry dynamics and business fundamentals.

In the case of the top-down example, the drivers are the *% Change* in market size and the *% Abs. Change* in market share.

This means that *we decide* the numbers/assumptions made in these line items. These assumptions *drive* the rest of the model. In this case, we have forecasted the market size will grow at 5% a year and that market share will initially increase and then decline. This results in overall sales that grow initially and then decline in the later years of the projection period.

14.4.2   Bottom-up Approach

The bottom-up approach focuses on the *Operating metrics* of the company. Operating metrics are a company's core operating units. Think of a store for a retail business, or a website visitor for an online news business. To forecast sales in the bottom-up approach, first forecast the Operating metrics. Then bridge the Operating metrics to sales by forecasting sales/operating metric. Finally, multiply the forecasted operating metric by the sales/operating metric amount to arrive at the total sales. In the case of the bottom-up example, the drivers are the *% Change* in the number of stores and the *% Change* in revenue/store. In the authors opinion, the bottom-up approach to forecasting sales is superior.

14.5   Forecasting the Income Statement to EBIT

The sales forecast produced by the RPM serves as the top-line of the forecasted income statement. From here, the main missing items on the income statement are: COGS (which will allow us to calculate gross profit), SG&A (which will allow us to calculate EBIT), and a tax rate (which will allow us to calculate EBIT*$(1 - T)$.

COGS and SG&A are almost always forecasted as a "% of sales". First, look at the historical level of COGS and SG&A as a percent of sales to get an idea of historical levels. Next, combine the historical results with your personal view on the company's prospects (do you expect COGS and SG&A, as a percent of sales, to increase or decrease, and why?). By doing so, one can build a "% of sales" forecast figure for both COGS and SG&A during the projection period. By multiplying the "% of sales" by the projected sales derived from the RPM,we realize the projected COGS and SG&A figures. For the tax rate, the historical effective tax rate usually works well.

With EBIT*$(1-T)$ calculated, we have determined the first component of the free cash flow formula. The next component of the free cash flow formula that we must calculate is the change in working capital from the balance sheet.

14.6 Forecasting Working Capital Items

As a reminder, working capital = current assets - current liabilities. Company Z only has accounts receivable, inventory, and accounts payable as current assets and current liabilities. For these specific items, we can utilize the "days sales outstanding (DSO)", "days inventory held (DIH)", and "days payables outstanding (DPO)" formulas from Chapter 9 to determine historical levels and forecast future assets and liabilities levels. However, for current assets or current liabilities beyond those that are apart of the cash conversion cycle, such as prepaid expenses or deferred revenue, are usually forecasted as a % of sales like COGS and SG&A.

Once future levels of DSO, DIH, and DPO (and any other current assets and current liabilities) are forecasted (based on our expectations or knowledge regarding changes, if any, in the company's cash conversion cycle and working capital needs), we can convert these metrics into specific values of accounts receivable, inventory, and accounts payable in the projection periods by reversing the formulas from Chapter 9. In the case of current assets or current liabilities forecasted as a % of sales, we simply multiply the % of sales forecast by the sales metric from the income statement for a given year.

Once the current assets and liabilities in the projection period are calculated, we can calculate working capital and Δ in working capital. Remember, Δ in working capital is subtracted to arrive at the cash flow impact of working capital changes.

14.7 Forecasting Cash Flow Statement Items

The only components of the free cash flow formula left to calculate are: capital expenditures, depreciation, and amortization. All of these items come from the cash flow statement. Similar to COGS and SG&A, capital expenditures, depreciation, and amortization are usually forecasted as a % of sales.

Table 14.10 shows the projected cash flow statement items, including capital expenditures, depreciation, and amortization. Table 14.11 contains the drivers influencing the figures seen in 14.10.

14.8   Calculating Free Cash Flow

All the components of the free cash flow formula have now been calculated, allowing us to determine the cash flows over the projection period. To do this, simply plug the calculated numbers into the following formula for each year in the projection period:

$$\text{FCF} = \text{EBIT}*(1 - T) \text{ - Capital Expenditures - } (\Delta \text{ in WC) +}$$
$$\text{Depreciation + Amortization}$$

Table 14.12 contains the free cash flow calculations.

14.9   Calculating WACC

It is important to remember the ultimate goal of a DCF: to calculate all the future cash flows of a firm and discount them at an appropriate discount rate. At this point, cash flows from year $t = 1$ to year $t = 5$ have been calculated. Now, the discount rate or WACC must be determined. Fortunately, we have already covered the process of calculating WACC based on a company's capital structure in Chapter 11. As a reminder, the formula for WACC is:

$$\text{WACC} = r_d * (1 - T) * \tfrac{D}{D+E} + r_e * \tfrac{E}{D+E}$$

To solve for the WACC, we must calculate r_d, r_e, the weights of debt and equity in the capital structure, and the tax rate, T.

14.9.1   Cost of Debt

As discussed in Chapter 11, r_d can be calculated in three different ways. In this example, the weighted average YTM method is utilized. Table 14.13 contains the r_d calculation. From the capitalization table in Table 14.1, $\tfrac{D}{D+E}$ is easily calculated. Finally, using the effective tax rate from the income statement assumptions allows us to determine T. By combining all these components, the debt portion of the WACC calculation is easy to determine, as exhibited in Table 14.14.

14.9.2   Cost of Equity

For r_e, the formula $r_e = r_f + \beta * (r_m - r_f)$ is used. An example β calculation is contained in Table 14.15. From there, the risk-free rate or r_f is determined using a long-dated U.S. treasury yield. In this case, the 10-year U.S. treasury yield is used. This is easily found on the internet. The market risk premium, $(r_m - r_f)$, is usually between 5-8%. In this case, 6.5% is used. Finally, $\frac{E}{D+E}$ is easily determined using the capitalization table in Table 14.1. From this, we arrive at the equity portion of the WACC calculation. Table 14.16 shows an example.

14.9.3   Tying it Together

By combining the debt portion and the equity portion of the WACC, we can calculate the WACC/discount rate/required rate of return for the firm. Table 14.17 contains an example.

14.10   Discounting the Cash Flows

Having calculated the discount rate and cash flows in the projection period, the discounted free cash flows are easily obtainable. The formula for the discount factor is:

$$\text{Discount Factor} = \frac{1}{(1+WACC)^t}$$

By multiplying the free cash flows over the projection period by the discount factor, the discounted free cash flows over the projection period are calculated. Table 14.18 contains an example.

14.11   Calculating Terminal Value

Thus far, we have focused on the cash flows associated with the projection period, $t = 1$ to $t = 5$. However, we have not considered the cash flows associated with the remaining time periods, $t = 6$ to $t = \infty$. That being said, it is irrational to explicitly project and calculate discounted cash flows for every year from $t = 6$ to $t = \infty$. Therefore, we must calculate a *terminal value* that serves as an approximation of the cash flow produced over the time period $t = 6$ to $t = \infty$. There are two main methods for determining terminal value: the exit multiple method and the perpetuity growth method.

The exit multiple method assumes that the company is *bought* at the end of the projection period at a multiple of some earnings metric. Usually, EBITDA is used as the earnings metric. By multiplying the assumed exit multiple, (enterprise value)/EBITDA (6-

10x is usually safe), by the EBITDA at the end of the projection period, a single cash flow that represents the worth of the company from $t = 6$ to $t = \infty$ is calculated. However, this cash flow must be discounted by the discount factor at the end of the projection period, since we assume the company is sold at the end of the projection period.

The perpetuity growth method assumes that the company produces cash into infinity, at some growth rate, g, and some discount rate, r. The simplified formula for an infinite cash flow with growth rate g and discount rate r is:

$$\text{Perpetuity Value} = \frac{FCF_{t+1}}{(r-g)}.$$

Note: this formula only works if $r > g$, which should always be the case. For our purposes, the WACC is used as r. g is determined by the modeler. Usually, g is 1-3%. FCF_{t+1} is the free cash flow in the final year of the projection period multiplied by $(1+g)$. Therefore, plugging into the preceding formula, the formula for the perpetuity value is:

$$\text{Perpetuity Value} = \frac{FCF_{t=5}*(1+g)}{(WACC-g)}$$

Finally, similar to the exit multiple method, this lump-sum cash flow is realized at the end of the projection period. Therefore, the perpetuity value must be discounted by the discount factor from the end of the projection period. An example of both terminal value methods is contained in Table 14.19.

14.12   Determining Enterprise Value

By summing the discounted cash flows over the projection period and adding the terminal value, we can finally calculate the value of the *firm*. It is important to note that the value we have calculated is the *enterprise value* since the cash flow formula we utilized includes interest expense and is a free cash flow to firm formula.

At this point, we can also calculate the terminal value as a % of the calculated enterprise value. This is important because it gives us an idea of how much of the calculated value of the company depended on cash flows from $t = 1$ to $t = 5$ versus $t = 6$ to $t = \infty$. Generally, this number is fairly high, in the 50-70% range, though, this largely depends on how many years the modeler forecasts the cash flows into the future and the terminal value assumptions, such as the exit multiple or long-term growth rate. Table 14.20 contains an example.

14.13 Determining Equity Value and Implied Return

Finally, we can determine the implied stock price calculated by our model. To do this, we must first convert the calculated enterprise value into equity value. As a reminder, the shorthand formula for enterprise value is:

Enterprise Value = Market Cap + Debt - Cash

By moving this formula around, we can determine the formula for converting enterprise value to equity value:

Market Cap = Enterprise Value - Debt + Cash

Fortunately, we have already calculated enterprise value and the debt and cash levels are easily found on the capitalization table in Table 14.1. From this, it is very easy to calculate the market cap or equity value of the company. Divide the implied market cap by the number of shares outstanding (also found in Table 14.1), to determine an implied share price. By comparing this value with the current share price (also found in Table 14.1), we can calculate the implied return on investment (ROI). This is the implied discrepancy between the current share price and the share price predicted by the assumptions in the model.

14.14 Sensitivity Analysis

It's hard to know whether a lot of our key assumptions, such as WACC, the exit multiple, or long-term growth rate are precise. For this reason, it is essential to perform a *sensitivity analysis* on these key metrics. This analysis, which calculates the implied ROI or implied share price for a wide variety of key inputs, such as various WACCs, long-term growth rates, and exit multiples, helps give an idea of how sensitive the model is to key inputs. For example, how much does a 1% WACC increase reduce implied ROI? This is very important to know, as high sensitivity to key inputs means the model is less reliable.

14.15   Different Scenarios

It is still hard to know whether our operating assumptions, which determine the free cash flows in the model, are a correct prediction of the future. A lot can happen in the span of a few years. For this reason, it is important to prepare a range of *scenarios* or operating assumptions that capture different levels of operating success for the company. Typically, a model will have a bull, bear, and base case. The bull case is the most optimistic set of plausible operating assumptions, such as sales growth, COGS levels, and SG&A levels. The bear case is the most pessimistic set of plausible operating assumptions. The base case is somewhere in between. By combining varying scenarios with a sensitivity analysis, an investor can acquire a much deeper understanding of a model and its reliability as a basis for investment.

14.16   Reference Model

In the following pages, a reference model is included to help readers understand the core concepts. Note: all figures (except per share data and operating metrics) are in thousands.

Table 14.1: Capitalization Table

Company Z Capitalization Table	
Shares Outstanding	100
Share Price	$8
Market Cap	$800
Debt	$500
Cash	$300
Enterprise Value (EV)	$1000
P / (LTM E)	20.0x
EV / (LTM EBIT)	10.0x
EV / (LTM EBITDA)	7.5x

Table 14.2: Top-down Revenue Projection Model

	Company Z Top-down Revenue Projection Model								
	Historical Period			Projection Period					
Year	2015A	2016A	2017A	2018E	2019E	2020E	2021E	2022E
Market Size	$1000	$1100	$1200	$1260	$1323	$1389	$1459	$1532
% Change	NA	10.0%	9.1%	5.0%	5.0%	5.0%	5.0%	5.0%
Market Share	50.0%	55.0%	60.0%	63.0%	63.0%	59.8%	53.9%	45.9%
% Abs. Change	NA	5.0%	5.0%	3.0%	0.0%	(3.1%)	(5.9%)	(8.0%)
Sales	$500	$605	$720	$794	$833	$831	$786	$703

| % Change | NA | 21.0% | 19.0% | 10.2% | 5.0% | (0.2)% | (5.4)% | (10.5)% |

Table 14.3: Bottom-up Revenue Projection Model

| Company Z Bottom-up Revenue Projection Model | | | | | | | | |
| | Historical Period | | | Projection Period | | | | |
Year	2015A	2016A	2017A	2018E	2019E	2020E	2021E	2022E
Number of Stores	1000	1100	1200	1297	1389	1474	1549	1612
% Change	NA	10.0%	9.1%	8.1%	7.1%	6.1%	5.1%	4.1%
Revenue/Store	$500	$550	$600	$612	$600	$564	$507	$436
% Change	NA	10.0%	9.1%	2.0%	(2.0%)	(6.0%)	(10.0%)	(14.0%)
Sales	$500	$605	$720	$794	$833	$831	$786	$703
% Change	NA	21.0%	19.0%	10.2%	5.0%	(0.2)%	(5.4)%	(10.5)%

Table 14.4: Forecasted Income Statement

| Company Z Forecasted Income Statement | | | | | | | | |
| | Historical Period | | | Projection Period | | | | |
Year	2015A	2016A	2017A	2018E	2019E	2020E	2021E	2022E
Sales	$500	$605	$720	$794	$833	$831	$786	$703
COGS	$300	$350	$400	$441	$463	$462	$437	$391
Gross Profit	$200	$255	$320	$353	$370	$369	$349	$313

	2015A	2016A	2017A	2018E	2019E	2020E	2021E	2022E
SG&A	$180	$200	$220	$243	$255	$254	$240	$215
EBIT	$20	$55	$100	$110	$116	$115	$109	$98
EBIT*(1 − T)	$13	$36	$65	$72	$75	$75	$71	$64

Table 14.5: Income Statement Assumptions

	Company Z Income Statement Assumptions							
	Historical Period			Projection Period				
Year	2015A	2016A	2017A	2018E	2019E	2020E	2021E	2022E
COGS (% of sales)	60%	58%	56%	56%	56%	56%	56%	56%
SG&A (% of sales)	36%	33%	31%	31%	31%	31%	31%	31%
Tax Rate	35%	35%	35%	35%	35%	35%	35%	35%

Table 14.6: Income Statement Margins

	Company Z Income Statement Margins							
	Historical Period			Projection Period				
Year	2015A	2016A	2017A	2018E	2019E	2020E	2021E	2022E
Gross Profit Margin	40%	42%	44%	44%	44%	44%	44%	44%
EBIT Margin	4%	9%	14%	14%	14%	14%	14%	14%

Table 14.7: Forecasted Balance Sheet Items

| | Company Z Forecasted Balance Sheet Items | | | | | | | |
| | Historical Period | | | Projection Period | | | | |
Year	2015A	2016A	2017A	2018E	2019E	2020E	2021E	2022E
Current Assets								
Accounts Receivable	$100	$110	$140	$152	$160	$159	$151	$135
Inventory	$60	$65	$70	$72	$76	$76	$72	$64
Total Current Assets	$160	$175	$210	$225	$236	$235	$223	$199
Current Liabilities								
Accounts Payable	$90	$95	$100	$109	$114	$114	$108	$96
Total Current Liab.	$90	$95	$100	$109	$114	$114	$108	$96

Table 14.8: Working Capital Calculation

| | Company Z Working Capital Calculation | | | | | | | |
| | Historical Period | | | Projection Period | | | | |
Year	2015A	2016A	2017A	2018E	2019E	2020E	2021E	2022E
Working Capital (WC)	$70	$80	$110	$116	$122	$121	$115	$103
Δ in WC	NA	$10	$30	$6	$6	($1)	($7)	($12)

Table 14.9: Balance Sheet Assumptions

Company Z Balance Sheet Assumptions								
	Historical Period			Projection Period				
Year	2015A	2016A	2017A	2018E	2019E	2020E	2021E	2022E
Days Sales Outstanding	73.0	66.4	71.0	70.0	70.0	70.0	70.0	70.0
Days Inventory Held	73.0	67.8	63.9	60.0	60.0	60.0	60.0	60.0
Days Payables Outst.	109.5	99.1	91.3	90.0	90.0	90.0	90.0	90.0

Table 14.10: Forecasted Cash Flow Statement Items

Company Z Forecasted Cash Flow Statement Items								
	Historical Period			Projection Period				
Year	2015A	2016A	2017A	2018E	2019E	2020E	2021E	2022E
Capital Expenditures	$40	$50	$60	$48	$50	$50	$47	$42
Depreciation	$15	$16	$17	$32	$33	$33	$31	$28
Amortization	$15	$16	$17	$32	$33	$33	$31	$28

Table 14.11: Cash Flow Statement Items Assumptions

Company Z cash flow statement Items Assumptions								
	Historical Period			Projection Period				
Year	2015A	2016A	2017A	2018E	2019E	2020E	2021E	2022E
CapEx (% of sales)	6%	6%	6%	6%	6%	6%	6%	6%
Deprec. (% of sales)	3%	3%	2%	4%	4%	4%	4%	4%
Amortiz. (% of sales)	3%	3%	2%	4%	4%	4%	4%	4%

Table 14.12: Free Cash Flow Calculation

Company Z Free Cash Flow Calculation					
	Projection Period				
Year	2018E	2019E	2020E	2021E	2022E
EBIT*$(1 - T)$	$72	$75	$75	$71	$64
− Capital Expenditures	$48	$50	$50	$47	$42
+ Depreciation	$32	$33	$33	$31	$28
+ Amortization	$32	$33	$33	$31	$28
− Δ in WC	($6)	($6)	$0	$7	$12
Free Cash Flow	$82	$86	$92	$93	$90

Table 14.13: Cost of Debt Calculation

Company Z Cost of Debt Calculation			
	Amount	YTM	% of Debt	Weighted YTM
TLA	$100	3%	20%	0.6%
TLB	$200	5%	40%	2.0%
Bonds	$200	8%	40%	3.2%
Total	**$500**	NA	NA	5.8%

Table 14.14: Debt Portion of WACC Calculation

Company Z Debt Portion of WACC Calculation	
Cost of Debt	5.8%
Debt (% of capital structure)	38%
Tax Rate	35%
Debt Portion of WACC	1.5%

Table 14.15: Cost of Equity Calculation

Company Z Beta Calculation					
Company	β_L	Market Cap	Debt	E/(D+E)	β_U
Comparable A	1.10	$1000	$100	90.9%	1.00
Comparable B	0.90	$500	$200	71.4%	0.64

| Comparable C | 1.20 | $800 | $100 | 88.9% | 1.07 |
| Company Z | 1.47 | $800 | $500 | 61.5% | 0.90 |

Table 14.16: Equity Portion of WACC Calculation

Company Z Equity Portion of WACC Calculation	
Beta	1.47
Risk-free Rate	2.35%
Market Risk Premium	6.5%
Cost of Equity	11.9%
Equity (% of capital structure)	62%
Equity Portion of WACC	7.3%

Table 14.17: WACC Calculation

Company Z WACC Calculation	
Debt Portion of WACC	1.5%
Equity Portion of WACC	7.3%
WACC	8.8%

Table 14.18: Discounting the Cash Flows

Company Z Discounted Free Cash Flow Calculation					
		Projection Period			
Year	2018E	2019E	2020E	2021E	2022E
Free Cash Flow	$82	$86	$92	$93	$90
Discount Factor	0.92	0.85	0.78	0.71	0.66
Discounted Free Cash Flow	$75	$73	$71	$67	$59

Table 14.19: Calculating Terminal Value

Company Z Terminal Value Calculation			
Method 1: exit multiple		*Method 2: Perpetuity*	
EBITDA (2022E)	$154	FCF (2023E)	$92
Exit Multiple	7.5x	Growth Rate	3%
Enterprise Value	$1155	Discount Rate	8.8%
Discount Factor	0.66	Perpetuity Value	$1466
Discounted CF	$759	Discount Factor	0.66
		Discounted CF	$963

Table 14.20: Enterprise Value Calculation

Company Z Enterprise Value Calculation	
Sum of DFCFs (2018E to 2022E)	$345
Terminal Value (from exit multiple)	$759
Enterprise Value	$1103
TV as % of EV	68.8%

Table 14.21: Equity Value Calculation

Company Z Equity Value Calculation	
Enterprise Value	$1103
− Debt	$500
+ Cash	$300
Equity Value	$903
Shares Outstanding	100
Implied Share Price	$9.03
Current Share Price	$8.00
Implied ROI	12.9%

15

Comparable Companies Analysis

15.1 Introduction

The basis of the comparable companies approach to valuation is: a company should be valued similarly, as a multiple of earnings, EBITDA, FCF, etc., to comparable companies. Previously, we explored the DCF methodology, which focuses exclusively on the ability of the firm to produce long-term cash flows. The DCF methodology calculates the *intrinsic value* of a firm, since it aims to determine the value of the discounted cash flows specific to that firm. In contrast, the comparable companies analysis looks at current market trading multiples (such as EV / EBITDA or P/E) for similar firms to determine an average trading multiple for those companies. The value of a specific company can be extrapolated from the value of the average trading multiple. This will make more sense over the course of this chapter. A solid understanding of the concepts in Chapter 7 will prove helpful for grasping this valuation method.

The DCF is a cash flow based, intrinsic valuation method. The comparable companies analysis, by contrast, does not consider the cash flow of the firm extensively. It instead depends primarily on the current market valuations of comparable companies. For this reason, comparable companies analysis is a *relative* and *market-based* valuation method. A comparable companies analysis (and other relative valuation methods) is generally much quicker to perform. The most time consuming component is gathering information on the comparable companies for the benchmarking exercise. This is covered later in this chapter.

15.2   Selecting Comparable Companies

The entire premise of a comparable companies analysis is that a company should be valued similarly to its peers. Therefore, an investor must think critically about whether the similarities between the company in question and a potential peer are significant enough to warrant them being valued similarly by the market.

Beyond this, the investor must also realize that there is often a reason (or many reasons) that a given company is valued differently than its peers. Therefore, when performing a comparable companies analysis, the investor must try and determine why (and if) the market is valuing the company in question differently than its peers. Then, based on the investors own perception of the rationality of the reason for the valuation discrepancy, the investor might decide that the valuation discrepancy is warranted or unwarranted and invest based on this view. One method for helping the investor understand pricing discrepancies between peer companies is a benchmarking exercise, discussed in the next section.

The most important component of a comparable companies analysis is selecting companies that are actually similar to the company you are trying to value. When performing a comparable companies analysis, quality of comparison is more important than the quantity of comparisons. There are many factors to consider when determining the similarity of two companies, such as: industry, target customers, size, products, and suppliers. Most free financial information resources, such as Google Finance, contain extensive lists of comparable companies for a given ticker. This is often a good place to start for trying to identify and select companies to include in a comparable companies analysis.

15.3   Benchmarking

When performing a comparable companies analysis, the investor must try and understand why pricing differences exist (if at all) between peer companies. When analyzing a group of similar companies, it is very helpful to *benchmark* the companies relative to each other to better understand the financial and qualitative characteristics of the a firm and its peers. A benchmarking exercise provides valuable context for understanding a group of peer companies and consists of the following: 1) list the comparable companies and the companies in question, 2) identify key metrics of interest to compare between each similar company (such as sales, EBITDA, net income, return, capital structure, solvency, etc. metrics), 3) calculate/determine all the relevant metrics for each company, and 4) determine the minimum, maximum, median, and mean of each metric across the comparable company set. Step 4 from the preceding list of steps is especially valuable. By calculating the min, max, median, and mean of each metric, the investor can analyze which companies in the set of peers are out-performers or laggards relative to the peer average levels. This is valuable information. If a company is a significant out-performer in a benchmarking analysis and is also valued higher relative to peers (covered in the next section), the investor might believe this relatively higher valuation is justified. However, if a company is a significant out-performer in a benchmarking analysis and is valued *lower* relative to peers, the investor might become suspicious and perform a deeper analysis on the company in question to understand better why this possible mispricing (or lack thereof) exists.

15.4 Performing the Valuation

Once the benchmarking exercise is complete, the last step is performing the valuation. To perform the valuation, the investor must: 1) calculate the *peer* mean for a variety of trading multiples (such as P/E, EV/Sales, EV/EBITDA, EV/EBIT, etc.), 2) multiply the peer mean by the respective metric or denominator (net income in the case of a P/E ratio), 3) depending on whether the original trading multiple is a firmwide or equity multiple, either an implied market cap or implied enterprise value will be calculated at this point. In the case that an implied market cap is produced (such as with a P/E ratio), the implied market cap is simply compared with the current market cap to determine the implied ROI. In the case that an implied enterprise value is produced (such as with an EV / EBITDA ratio), the enterprise value must be converted to an equity value (by subtracting debt and adding cash) to arrive at an implied market cap that is then compared with the current market value to determine an implied ROI.

15.5 Reference Model

In the following pages, a reference model is included to help readers understand the core concepts.

Table 15.1: Comparable Companies Analysis - Benchmarking

| Company | | Company Z Benchmarking | | | | |
| | Sales Metrics | | | EBITDA Metrics | | |
	Sales	3-year Sales Growth	EBITDA	3-year EBITDA Growth	EBITDA Margin
Comparable A	$1000	6%	$275	8%	27.5%
Comparable B	$800	8%	$200	9%	25.0%
Comparable C	$1300	5%	$375	7%	28.8%
Company Z	$900	7%	$250	10%	27.8%
Min.	$800	5%	$200	7%	25.0%
Max.	$1300	8%	$375	10%	28.8%
Median	$950	6.5%	$262.5	8.5%	27.6%
Mean	$1000	6.5%	$275	8.5%	27.3%

Table 15.2: Comparable Companies Analysis - Benchmarking

	Company Z Benchmarking								
	Net Income Metrics			Return Metrics			Solvency Metrics		
Company	Net Income	3-year NI Growth	NI Margin	ROIC	ROA	ROE	Debt / EBITDA	EBITDA / Int. Exp.
Comparable A	$150	7%	15%	25.3%	16.3%	9.0%	2.2x	2.1x
Comparable B	$130	10%	16.3%	23.5%	14.5%	9.6%	1.5x	2.3x
Comparable C	$210	9%	16.2%	26.4%	17.0%	10.2%	2.7x	3.4x
Company Z	$160	11%	17.8%	27.3%	15.2%	10.1%	2.4x	2.7x
Min.	$130	7.0%	15.0%	23.5%	14.5%	9.0%	1.5x	2.1x
Max.	$210	11.0%	17.8%	27.3%	17.0%	10.2%	2.7x	3.4x
Median	$155	9.5%	16.2%	25.9%	15.8%	9.9%	2.3x	2.5x
Average	$162.5	9.3%	16.3%	25.6%	15.8%	9.7%	2.2x	2.63x

Table 15.3: Comparable Companies Analysis - Benchmarking

| Company | Shares | Share Price | Capital Structure | | | | Market Multiples | | |
			Market Cap	Debt	Cash	EV	P / E	EV / Sales	EV / EBITDA
Comparable A	100	$9	$900	$605	$150	$1355	6.0x	1.4x	4.9x
Comparable B	90	$10.5	$945	$300	$100	$1145	7.3x	1.4x	5.7x
Comparable C	110	$11	$1210	$1013	$200	$2023	5.8x	1.6x	5.4x
Company Z	105	$8.5	$892.5	$600	$175	$1318	5.6x	1.5x	5.3x
Min.			$893	$300	$100	$1145	5.6x	1.4x	4.9x
Max.			$1210	$1013	$200	$2023	7.3x	1.6x	5.7x
Median			$923	$603	$163	$1336	5.9x	1.4x	5.3x
Average			$987	$629	$156	$1460	6.2x	1.5x	5.3x

Company Z Benchmarking

Table 15.4: Comparable Companies Analysis - Valuation

Company Z Valuation - Comparable Companies Analysis			
P / E Multiples Valuation			
Peer Mean P / E	Company Z Net Income	Implied Market Cap	Implied ROI
6.3x	$160	$1015	13.7%
EV / Sales Multiples Valuation			
Peer Mean EV / Sales	Company Z Sales	Implied EV	Implied Equity Value	Implied ROI
1.4x	$900	$1303	$878	(1.7%)
EV / EBITDA Multiples Valuation			
Peer Mean EV / EBITDA	Company Z EBITDA	Implied EV	Implied Equity Value	Implied ROI
5.3x	$250	$1337	$912	2.2%

16

Precedent Transactions

16.1 Introduction

The precedent transactions approach to valuation is very similar to comparable companies analysis. Both methods utilize a relative valuation technique (in which the valuation is based on similar companies) and a multiple based approach (in which the valuation is based on a firmwide or equity multiple of earnings, EBITDA, cash flow, etc.). The main difference between precedent transactions and comparable companies analysis is that precedent transactions focuses on multiples actually *paid* for similar companies in historical (usually 3-7 years back) mergers and acquisitions. In contrast, comparable companies analysis focuses on current trading multiples based on the market value of the firms' equity. Apart from this slight nuance, the process of performing a precedent transactions analysis is almost identical to a comparable companies analysis.

16.2 Comparable Companies Analysis Versus Precedent Transactions

There are several reasons for this implied ROI differs so much between a precedent transactions approach and a comparable companies analysis.

First, acquirers of companies will generally pay extra (above and beyond the current company market price) to actually control and own the company's operations. This extra payment is called a *control premium*. There is value to actually dictating and controlling a company's operations (and, in some cases, capitalizing on synergies between two merging companies). For these reasons, the control premium exists.

Second, as time passes, the market valuations of companies can significantly change. For example, at the time of this writing, the average P/E ratio of the constituents of the S&P was about 24x. In 2012, the average P/E ratio was 15x. Therefore, acquisitions in 2012 might have occurred at a 15-22x P/E multiple, meaning the companies might have been acquired for a price equal to 15-22x net income. In 2012's market context, this acquisition multiple included a healthy control premium above market levels. However, in the market context of 2017, a significant discrepancy exists between the acquisition multiples paid five years ago and the current market trading levels. In rising market conditions valuations as a multiple of earnings are increasing. Even with a control premium factored in, under such conditions, a comparable companies analysis might yield a greater implied ROI than a precedent transactions analysis. The reason: a precedent transactions approach includes transactions from several years prior, when valuations were lower. By the opposite reasoning, in falling market conditions, a comparable companies analysis might yield a lower implied ROI than a precedent transactions analysis.

If there are several *comparable* and *recent* M&A transactions, then the market conditions becomes less of a factor. In such a case the precedent transactions approach will generally produce a higher implied ROI due to the inflating effect of the control premium. A comparable companies analysis focuses exclusively on market conditions and is classified as a *current* valuation approach. A precedent transactions analysis is less current, factoring in historical M&A transactions several years back.

Precedent transactions also help investors gain an understanding of what other companies or investors might pay for the *entire firm* with a control premium factored in. If the investor expects that the company in question will be acquired, this can be a very valuable analysis. However, whereas the universe of legitimately comparable companies (on the basis of key characteristics such as industry, target customers, size, products, and suppliers) is already small, the universe of comparable companies that were recently acquired is even smaller. For this reason, it can be very difficult to perform a precedent transactions analysis for companies without many similar (and acquired) competitors.

16.3 Performing the Valuation

The actual process of performing a precedent transactions analysis is almost identical to that of a comparable companies analysis. First, an appropriate and reasonable set of comparable and acquired companies must be selected. This can be difficult to do in practice, since finding extensive information on M&A deals is not easy. Access to Bloomberg greatly facilitates this process. If Bloomberg is not available, then a good way find historical transaction information is to develop a list of public and private competitors of the company in question (using competitor lists on Google Finance and contained in the company's 10-K). The investor can then search the internet specifically for the acquisition history (if any exists) of the competitors/comparable companies.

A benchmarking exercise, almost identical to that performed in a comparable companies analysis, is then necessary. However, the benchmarking exercise will generally be more difficult to perform in a precedent transactions analysis since many of the companies under inspection will no longer have recent and publicly available financial information (because they were acquired).

Finally, we come to actually valuing the company. Instead of using current market multiples, the investor utilizes the multiples paid in precedent transactions. Once these multiples are determined, the investor aggregates them (either using the mean or median) and then multiplies the average multiple by the metric or denominator specific to the multiple (net income in the case of an average P/E ratio). An implied equity value or implied enterprise value is produced. In the case of an equity multiple, simply calculate the implied ROI by comparing the implied equity value with the current market cap. In the case of a financial statements, first convert the enterprise value to an equity value by subtracting debt and adding cash. Then, calculate the implied ROI by comparing the implied equity value with the current market cap.

Therefore, the only real differences between a comparable companies analysis and precedent transactions analysis is the type of multiple used (trading multiple versus transaction multiple) and the size of the universe of comparable companies. Beyond this, actually finding information for a precedent transactions analysis is much more difficult relative to a comparable companies analysis.

Because of the significant similarities between the precedent transactions and comparable companies valuation methods, no reference model, beyond that provided in Chapter 15, is necessary.

The only difference between the comparable companies example model in Chapter 15 and a precedent transactions model is the type of valuation multiple utilized. Therefore, to consider an example of a precedent transactions analysis, simply substitute transaction multiples in place of market multiples.

17

Sum-of-the-Parts

17.1 Introduction

All the valuation models covered so far work under the assumption a company has one main business line. But, what if the company is a conglomerate with multiple business lines, such as a retail clothing business, an advertising business, and a grocery business? Ideally, if the company "breaks out" the information regarding each business line in their financial statements, each business line could be valued separately. The value of each individual business line can then be combined to arrive at a more accurate enterprise value for the entire business. From there, the enterprise value is easily converted into an equity value that can be compared with the current market cap to determine an implied ROI. This is the basis of the sum-of-the-parts valuation approach.

17.2 Performing the Valuation

To actually perform a sum-of-the-parts analysis, the investor first values each business line individually using one of the three methods we have covered: discounted cash flow, comparable companies analysis, and precedent transactions. The simplest approach to a sum-of-the-parts analysis is to perform a comparable companies analysis for each business line. For example, the average clothing store business likely trades at a very different EV/EBITDA multiple than the average advertising business, making it simple to perform a comparable companies analysis for each business line. After that, the enterprise values of each individual business line are easily summed to arrive at a total enterprise value. From there, the enterprise value is converted into an equity value and the implied

ROI calculated.

This produces a much more robust and accurate valuation of the conglomerate company than simply trying to perform a single comparable companies analysis for the entire enterprise (especially since there are likely few comparable conglomerates). By focusing on comparable businesses of the individual business lines, the number of quality comparisons increases significantly and the accuracy of the average trading multiple, for each specific business line, improves significantly.

17.3   Reference Model

On the remainder of the page, a reference model is included to help readers understand the core concepts.

Table 17.1: Sum-of-the-Parts Analysis

Company Z Sum-of-the-Parts		
Business Line	**Valuation Method**	**Enterprise Value**
Clothing Store	Discounted Cash Flow	$800
Advertising	Precedent Transactions	$1000
Grocery	Comparable Companies Analysis	$600

Company Z Sum-of-the-Parts	
Total Enterprise Value	$2400
- Debt	$400
+ Cash	$200
Implied Equity Value	$2200
Current Equity Value	$2000
Implied ROI	10%

18

Three Statement Modeling

18.1 Introduction

At this point, we have covered the core valuation methods utilized by investors: discounted cash flow, comparable companies analysis, and precedent transactions. We also introduced sum-of-the-parts, the main way to combine various valuation methods to value a conglomerate company. However, these valuation methods focus on determining the value of a company's equity and provide little insight into the interest coverage and deeper financial statistics. This is the role of a three statement model. A three statement model aims to entirely recreate and forecast all three financial statements (the income statement, balance sheet, and cash flow statement) for a company. As such, a three statement model is likely the most difficult technique covered so far.

What makes a three statement model technically difficult to implement? Well, two reasons in particular. First, over the projection period, the balance sheet must balance (A = L + E) for the model to be correct. This seems easy in theory, but in practice, it can be tricky to develop a model that balances. This also leaves zero room for any error. Second, interest expense is very tricky to calculate. This is because the calculation of interest expense produces a *circular reference*. A circular reference occurs when a model loops back into itself in the calculation. How does this happen? Consider the following chain: net interest expense (including interest income) affects net income → net income is the top line of the cash flow statement → the cash flow statement determines the cash balance and revolver balance → the cash balance and revolver balance influences the net interest expense. As one can see, a circular reference is created since net interest expense eventually influences net interest expense due to the way the three statements connect. Since a three statement model has zero room for error and the added complexity of calculating interest expense, it is quite involved.

This being said, three statement models are one of the best ways to cement and understand core accounting principles covered in Chapter 5. Before attempting to build your own three statement model, a solid grasp of Chapter 5 is essential. Furthermore, since three statement models include debt pay-down assumptions and interest expense, they are essential for analyzing the credit quality of a business. In Part VII we will discuss leveraged buyout models. An understanding of three statement modeling will be a must.

18.2   Three Statement Model Steps

18.2.1   Assumptions

Before building the model, the investor must make several assumptions for the three statements and debt schedule over the projection period. Similar to discounted cash flow analysis, a three statement model consists of a historical period and a projection period. The historical period helps serve as a basis for future projections or drivers.

Income Statement Assumptions

The key items to forecast on the income statement are: the sales growth rate (for a more involved analysis, a revenue projection model is necessary), COGS (usually forecasted as a % of sales), SG&A (usually forecasted a a % of sales), the tax rate (usually forecasted as a % of profit before tax), and the payout ratio (forecasted as a % of net income). The payout ratio is the % of net income paid out as dividends.

Balance Sheet Assumptions

The key items to forecast on the balance sheet are: accounts receivable (usually forecasted as DSO or as a % of sales), inventory (usually forecasted as DIH or as a % of sales), other current assets (usually forecasted as a % of sales), accounts payable (usually forecasted as DPO or as a % of sales), and other current liabilities (usually forecasted as a % of sales).

Cash Flow Statement Assumptions

The key items to forecast on the cash flow statement are: depreciation (usually forecasted as a % of sales), amortization (usually forecasted as a % of sales), capital expenditures (usually forecasted as a % of sales), debt repayment (usually forecasted as a $ amount), and debt issuance (usually forecasted as a $ amount). Other possible items to forecast on the cash flow statement are: changes in other long term assets or liabilities and share repurchases.

Debt Schedule Assumptions

The key items to forecast on the debt schedule are: interest income/expense as a % of the average cash/revolver balance and interest expense as a % of the average debt balance.

18.2.2 Building the Income Statement

Once the assumptions are all in place, the modeler can begin building the three statements. As with the DCF method, the values of the various line items in the historic period must be manually filled in. For the income statement projection period, sales are easily forecasted using the sales growth rate assumption. From there, all the other line items on the income statement are easily calculated based on the assumptions. The income statement should include dividends paid (calculated as a % of net income) and reinvested earnings (equal to net income minus dividends). Both of these line items appear below net income on the income statement. However, it is *essential* to leave the interest income and interest expense line items blank at this point in the modeling process. The step of adding interest income and interest expense is saved for last because of the circular reference.

18.2.3 Building Minimal Cash Flow Statement

Before proceeding to the balance sheet, the modeler must first forecast a few select cash flow statement items. Specifically, the line items depreciation, amortization, capital expenditures, debt issuance, and debt pay-down must be filled in. All of these items are forecasted as a % of sales, except for debt issuance and debt pay-down, which are easily forecasted as an absolute dollar amount.

18.2.4   Building Most of the Balance Sheet

From here, the modeler can forecast all of the balance sheet *except for* the cash and revolver line items, which are left blank for now. The current assets and current liabilities on the balance sheet are easily forecasted using the assumptions and the relevant items from the income statement.

For PPE, the formula $\text{PPE}_{t+1} = \text{PPE}_t + \text{Capital Expenditures} - \text{Depreciation}$ is used. From the historic period, PPE_t is easy to obtain. Furthermore, at this point, capital expenditures and depreciation are already forecasted on the cash flow statement. Therefore, PPE can be calculated for all years in the projection period.

For goodwill (and other intangible assets, when they exist), the formula $\text{Goodwill}_{t+1} = \text{Goodwill}_t - \text{Amortization}$ is used. Again, the initial Goodwill_t is found from the historic period. Since amortization is forecasted on the cash flow statement, goodwill can be determined for all projected time periods.

The modeler can easily determine the amount of long-term debt for each year in the projection period using the debt repayment assumption (reflected on the cash flow statement) and the historic level of long-term debt.

For retained earnings, the formula $\text{Retained Earnings}_{t+1} = \text{Retained Earnings}_t + \text{Reinvested Earnings}$ OR $\text{Retained Earnings}_{t+1} = \text{Retained Earnings}_t + \text{Net Income} - \text{Dividends}$ are used. Again, using the reinvested earnings figure from the income statement and the historical level of retained earnings, the modeler can project the value of retained earnings for all periods in the projection period.

For all other balance sheet line items, assuming the modeler has not made other assumptions regarding changes in these other line items, simply "flat-line" these line items into the future. "Flat-lining" is the practice of simply forecasting a line item into the future, unchanged.

At this point, the balance sheet should be completely built except for cash in the current assets section and the revolver in the current liabilities section. The modeler should calculate the value of current assets, total assets, current liabilities, total liabilities, shareholder's equity (SHE), and total liabilities plus SHE. Finally, the modeler should put in a "balance check" line item below "total liabilities + SHE". The value of the balance check line item should equal "total assets − (total liabilities + SHE)". The balance check line item is an easy way to see whether the balance sheet is balanced (and the model correctly built). When the balance sheet is balanced, the balance check line item will be "0.000" for all time periods. At this stage of the model, the balance sheet should *not* be balanced. That comes later.

18.2.5 Building the Remainder of the Cash Flow Statement

The rest of the cash flow statement can be filled in from the balance sheet and income statement. Notably, the modeler can fill in changes in the working capital accounts (current assets and current liabilities) and dividends, linked from the income statement. At this point, CFO, CFI, and CFF are easily calculated. By summing CFO, CFI, and CFF, the modeler determines the change in cash over the year. Using the formula $\text{Cash}_{t+1} = \text{Cash}_t + \Delta$ in Cash, the modeler can calculate the next periods cash balance using the previous periods cash balance and the change in cash. A negative cash balance indicates the revolver has been drawn. The notation to indicate this in the model is: C/-R for Cash/-Revolver.

18.2.6 Linking Cash and Revolver

The cash or revolver balance is now calculated, so the modeler can complete the balance sheet. The modeler must link the cash line item on the balance sheet, for a given year t, to the maximum of the C/-R end-of-period (EOP) balance and 0, for the same year t. The maximum between the C/-R balance and 0 must be used as any C/-R value below \$0 indicates a revolver draw, in which case the cash balance is assumed to be \$0. After this the modeler must link the revolver line item on the balance sheet, for a given year t, to the *negative* minimum of the C/-R EOP balance and 0, for the same year t. The *negative* minimum between the C/-R balance and 0 must be used, because any negative C/-R value indicates a revolver draw (and will also be below 0). The negative sign in the front flips the sign of the revolver draw to a positive on the balance sheet. These two rules can be summarized as follows:

$$\text{Cash}_t = max(\text{R/-C Balance}_t \text{ EOP}, 0)$$
$$\text{Revolver}_t = -min(\text{R/-C Balance}_t \text{ EOP}, 0)$$

At this point, the cash or revolver balance should reconcile all remaining differences between the asset and liability sides of the balance sheet. Furthermore, the balance sheet equation, $A = L + E$, should be satisfied. Therefore, the "balance check" line item should have "0.000" for its value in all time periods.

18.2.7 Building the Debt Schedule

At this point, the modeler can finally complete the debt schedule, which will allow the modeler to calculate interest expense. Using the balance and cash flow statement, the modeler can simply link the debt schedule to existing line items to determine the C/-R BOP and EOP balances for all time periods. Then, to determine interest income/(expense) due to the C/-R balance, the modeler simply multiplies the assumed interest rate for the C/-R balance by the average C/-R balance for a given year. The average C/-R balance for a given year is simply the average of the C/-R BOP and EOP values for a given year. By following an identical process for long-term debt, the modeler can determine the interest expense associated with long-term debt.

18.2.8 Linking Interest Expense

Finally, the modeler links the interest expense associated with C/-R on the income statement to the associated line item from the debt schedule. The modeler performs the same action for the interest expense associated with long-term debt. As a result, the circular reference will be created. It is possible that the modeling software (such as Microsoft Excel) will produce a warning at this point. This is normal. Simply turn on circular references in the settings (File $\rightarrow$ Options $\rightarrow$ Formulas $\rightarrow$ Check Enable Iterative Calculation). If the rest of the model is made correctly, the balance sheet should still balance completely in all time periods. At this point, apartment from actually analyzing the model, the model is essentially complete.

Sometimes if something is wrong, when a circular reference is created, the model can "blow-up." "In Microsoft Excel, a "blow-up" manifests via the appearance of "#REF" all over the model. To remove the "#REFs" and try to debug the model, simply delete the entries for the interest income and interest expense line items on the income statement. This should remove the circular reference. If the "#REFs" still appear after removing the interest expense line items, hit the "calculate" button on the bottom left of the Microsoft Excel sheet to refresh the calculations in the model. From there, the modeler can try and debug the linkages and formulas in the model to determine why a "#REF" appears when a circular reference is introduced.

18.2.9 Analyzing the Model

One of the main burdens of a three statement model is handling interest expense. However, when done correctly, this is also one of the main benefits. With a completely balanced and functional three statement model, the investor can analyze all of the ratios covered in Chapter 8, for a given set of assumptions, including solvency ratios, which are essential for credit analysis.

18.3 Reference Model

In the following pages, a reference model is included to help readers understand the core concepts.

Table 18.1: Forecasted Income Statement

Company Z Forecasted Income Statement	Historic	Projection Period				
Year	2017A	2018E	2019E	2020E	2021E	2022E
Sales	$1000	$1050	$1103	$1158	$1216	$1276
COGS	$200	$210	$221	$232	$243	$255
Gross Profit	$800	$840	$882	$926	$972	$1021
SG&A	$700	$735	$772	$810	$851	$893
EBIT	$100	$105	$110	$116	$122	$128
Interest Expense/(Income):						
C/-R Expense/(Income)	($2)	($2)	($1)	($1)	$0	$0
Interest Expense	$30	$28	$23	$18	$13	$8
Profit Before Tax	$72	$79	$89	$99	$109	$120
Tax Provision	$25	$28	$31	$35	$38	$42
Net Income	$47	$51	$58	$64	$71	$78
Dividends	$14	$15	$17	$19	$21	$23
Reinvested Earnings	$33	$36	$40	$45	$50	$55

Table 18.2: Forecasted Income Statement Assumptions

Company Z Forecasted Income Statement Assumptions						
	Historic	Projection Period				
Year	2017A	2018E	2019E	2020E	2021E	2022E
Sales Growth Rate	NA	5%	5%	5%	5%	5%
COGS (% of sales)	20%	20%	20%	20%	20%	20%
SG&A (% of sales)	70%	70%	70%	70%	70%	70%
Tax Rate (% of PBT)	35%	35%	35%	35%	35%	35%
Payout Ratio (% of NI)	30%	30%	30%	30%	30%	30%

Table 18.3: Forecasted Balance Sheet

Company Z Forecasted Balance Sheet						
	Historic	Projection Period				
Year	2017A	2018E	2019E	2020E	2021E	2022E
Current Assets:						
Cash	$100	$71	$45	$23	$4	$0
Accounts Receivable	$100	$105	$110	$116	$122	$128
Inventory	$50	$53	$55	$58	$61	$64
Prepaid Expenses	$50	$53	$55	$58	$61	$64
Total Current Assets	$300	$281	$265	$254	$248	$255
Long-term Assets:						
PPE	$500	$532	$565	$599	$636	$674
Goodwill	$200	$179	$157	$134	$109	$84
Other LTA	$50	$50	$50	$50	$50	$50
Total Assets	$1050	$1041	$1037	$1037	$1043	$1063
Current Liabilities:						
Revolver	$0	$0	$0	$0	$0	$10
Accounts Payable	$50	$53	$55	$58	$61	$64
Deferred Revenue	$50	$53	$55	$58	$61	$64
Total Current Liabilities	$100	$105	$110	$116	$122	$137

Long-term Liabilities:						
Long-term Debt	$300	$250	$200	$150	$100	$50
Other Long-term Liabilities	$50	$50	$50	$50	$50	$50
Total Liabilities	**$450**	**$405**	**$360**	**$316**	**$272**	**$237**
Equity Accounts:						
Common Stock	$200	$200	$200	$200	$200	$200
Retained Earnings	$400	$436	$476	$522	$571	$626
Shareholder's Equity	**$600**	**$636**	**$676**	**$722**	**$771**	**$826**
Total Liabilities + SHE	**$1050**	**$1041**	**$1037**	**$1037**	**$1043**	**$1063**
Balance Check	*0.000*	*0.000*	*0.000*	*0.000*	*0.000*	*0.000*

Table 18.4: Forecasted Balance Sheet Assumptions

Company Z Forecasted Balance Sheet Assumptions						
	Historic	Projection Period				
Year	2017A	2018E	2019E	2020E	2021E	2022E
AR (% of sales)	10%	10%	10%	10%	10%	10%
Inventory (% of sales)	5%	5%	5%	5%	5%	5%
Prepaid Expenses (% of sales)	5%	5%	5%	5%	5%	5%
Accounts Payable (% of sales)	5%	5%	5%	5%	5%	5%
Deferred Revenue (% of sales)	5%	5%	5%	5%	5%	5%

Table 18.5: Forecasted Cash Flow Statement

Company Z Forecasted Cash Flow Statement					
			Projection Period		
Year	2018E	2019E	2020E	2021E	2022E
CFO:					
Net Income	$51	$58	$64	$71	$78
+ Depreciation	$21	$22	$23	$24	$26
+ Amortization	$21	$22	$23	$24	$26
Changes in Current Assets (Inc.)/Dec.:					
Accounts Receivable	($5)	($5)	($6)	($6)	($6)
Inventory	($3)	($3)	($3)	($3)	($3)
Prepaid Expenses	($3)	($3)	($3)	($3)	($3)
Changes in Current Liabilities Inc./(Dec.):					
Accounts Payable	$3	$3	$3	$3	$3
Deferred Revenue	$3	$3	$3	$3	$3
Changes in LTA or LTL:					
OLTA	$0	$0	$0	$0	$0
OLTL	$0	$0	$0	$0	$0
CFO	$88	$97	$105	$114	$123

CFI:					
Capital Expenditures	($53)	($55)	($58)	($61)	($64)
Acquisitions	$0	$0	$0	$0	$0
CFI	($53)	($55)	($58)	($61)	($64)
CFF:					
Dividends	($15)	($17)	($19)	($21)	($23)
Share Repurchases	$0	$0	$0	$0	$0
Debt Issuance	$0	$0	$0	$0	$0
Debt Repayment	($50)	($50)	($50)	($50)	($50)
CFF	($66)	($68)	($70)	($72)	($74)
C/-R BOP	$100	$71	$45	$23	$4
Net Change in Cash	($29)	($26)	($22)	($18)	($14)
C/-R EOP	$71	$45	$23	$4	($10)

Table 18.6: Forecasted Cash Flow Statement Assumptions

Company Z Forecasted Cash Flow Statement Assumptions					
		Projection Period			
Year	2018E	2019E	2020E	2021E	2022E
Depreciation (% of sales)	2%	2%	2%	2%	2%
Amortization (% of sales)	2%	2%	2%	2%	2%
CapEx (% of sales)	5%	5%	5%	5%	5%
Debt Repayment (dollar amount)	($50)	($50)	($50)	($50)	($50)

Table 18.7: Forecasted Debt Schedule

Company Z Forecasted Debt Schedule						
	Historic	Projection Period				
Year	2017A	2018E	2019E	2020E	2021E	2022E
Cash/-Revolver BOP	NA	$100	$71	$45	$23	$4
Cash/-Revolver EOP	$100	$71	$45	$23	$4	($10)
Interest Income/(Expense)	$2	$2	$1	$1	$0	$0
Long-term Debt BOP	NA	$300	$250	$200	$150	$100
Long-term Debt EOP	$300	$250	$200	$150	$100	$50
Long-term Debt Interest Expense	$30	$28	$23	$18	$13	$8

Table 18.8: Forecasted Debt Schedule Assumptions

Company Z Forecasted Debt Schedule Assumptions						
	Historic	Projection Period				
Year	2017A	2018E	2019E	2020E	2021E	2022E
Interest Income (% of average C/-R)	2%	2%	2%	2%	2%	2%
Long-term Debt Interest Expense (% of average debt)	10%	10%	10%	10%	10%	10%

Table 18.9: Credit Analysis

Company Z Forecasted Credit Analysis					
	Projection Period				
Year	2018E	2019E	2020E	2021E	2022E
Debt / EBITDA (x)	1.9x	1.5x	1.1x	0.7x	0.4x
Net Debt / EBITDA (x)	1.3x	1.1x	0.9x	0.7x	0.4x
EBITDA/Interest Expense (x)	5.7x	7.2x	9.6x	13.9x	23.7x
(EBITDA - CapEx)/Interest Expense (x)	3.7x	4.6x	6.2x	8.9x	15.2x

Part V

Fundamental Analysis

19

Good Businesses

19.1 The Importance of Good Businesses

At this point, Parts I-IV have covered the quantitative essentials of investing, including accounting, ratio analysis, valuation, and the core techniques of financial modeling. The quantitative aspects of investing are important. They help the investor read and interpret the financial health of a company and determine its value under a given set of assumptions. However, as described previously, a financial model is only as good as the quality of its assumptions. To really become an effective investor, it takes more than a knowledge and understanding of the previously discussed technical concepts. Once the technical concepts are internalized, an investor should focus on understanding and identifying the characteristics of *good businesses*.

At its core, the fundamental analysis of companies hinges on the belief that owning a stock is the same as owning a share of an underlying business. In the same vein, owning a debt is the same as being a creditor to an underlying business. Traders, momentum investors, and other tribes consistently forget this concept. As a fundamentals-based investor in underlying businesses, one should naturally gravitate towards investing in high-quality business with positive qualitative and quantitative characteristics. In this part of the book, the goal is to develop a much deeper understanding of the characteristics consistent with good businesses. Beyond this, we will also touch on other tools, concepts, and quantitative methods that might help the investor identify a great business (or lack thereof).

19.2   What Makes a Good Business?

In a nutshell, what makes a good business? To consider this question, think back to the discounted cash flow methodology of valuing a business. The determinant of the long-term value of a business is its ability to produce cash flow into perpetuity. Therefore, a good business is one that can produce a *sustainable* stream of cash flow, ideally with some growth prospects in that cash flow stream. Some famous investors, such as Warren Buffett, put the same concept differently – a good business is one that has a *wide economic moat*, or a competitive position that is easily defensible. A good business has characteristics intrinsic to its operations and business model that give it a defensible, long-term competitive advantage relative to its peers. Furthermore, businesses do not exist in isolation. The industry context and competitive dynamics of an industry influence the sustainability of a company's economic moat, if one exists.

Now, we will give the *wide economic moat* analogy, coined by Warren Buffett, more attention. Consider an actual castle that has a moat around its walls. For simplicity, assume the castle only produces beef that it sells to other kingdoms. Therefore, the castle will have several key components to its operations: herders (who raise the cattle), butchers (who prepare the cattle for distribution), and traders (who actually distribute the cattle to other kingdoms in exchange for money). A castle also has a governing body, a royal family, the goal of which is to maximize the longevity and value of the castle and its denizens.

However, there are other kingdoms that also produce beef. These kingdoms are in vicious competition, constantly trying to destroy the other beef producing kingdoms and improve their own longevity and worth. In this dynamic, a wide moat around a given castle's walls would prove invaluable to ensuring the security of the castles operations. Beyond this, a strong army or offensive operation would also enhance the ability of a kingdom to erode the competitive position of other castles.

This analogy, using a castle in place of a company, introduces several essential concepts of fundamental analysis: industry analysis (the competitive dynamics between the various beef producing castles), corporate strategy (how a given castle aims to erode the competitive position of other castles and improve its own competitive position), competitive advantage (the presence of a moat around the castles walls that helps defend its operations from attackers), and risk (the various factors that could cause the downfall of a given castle). These topics are the subjects of the next several chapters.

20

Industry Analysis

20.1 Industry Classification

To understand the relationships between the various constituents of an industry, the investor must first classify the key characteristics of the industry itself. This might include: where the industry is in its life cycle, the industry's relationship with the business cycle, other external factors.

Industry Life Cycle

There are four main phases of an industry's life cycle: the pioneer, growth, mature, and decline phases. The pioneer phase is the riskiest in industry context. Companies in pioneering industries are generally cash flow negative and have significant capital requirements. These pioneering firms acquire capital from firms that focus on high-growth startups, such as venture capital firms and sometimes growth equity firms. These early stage companies might not even have many customers yet. Because the potential risk of early stage, unproven companies is greatest, so is the potential return. However, the failure rate of companies in the pioneer stage is also very high. A modern example of a pioneering industry is the crypto-currency space and the associated companies that offer crypto-related products.

Companies in a growth industry are generally closer to cash flow positive or are actually cash flow positive. These companies still require heavy capital investment, via growth equity firms, debt, and internal reinvestment, to fund their significant growth opportunities. These companies often have established and recurring customer relationships and are beginning to become an entrenched part of the micro-economies they serve. A specific example of a growth industry is the space of algorithmic-based consumer lending, a subset of financial technology.

Companies in mature industries are cash flow positive. Mature industry companies do not require much external capital, since their growth opportunities are limited. When growth opportunities do arise, a mature company can reinvest its cash from operations into the business. Companies in mature industries have low to moderate sales growth (such as 0-12%). Often times, mature companies start returning some of the cash they produce to shareholders in the form of share buybacks or dividend payments. Mature companies have less return potential than pioneer or growth companies since they are less risky and much more established. The automotive industry is an example of a mature industry. Furthermore, mature companies have very stable customer relationships and significant recurring revenue.

Companies in declining industries have begun to lose sales and customers. Another pioneer or growth industry has usually come along to steal away the customers of declining companies. Industries in decline generally have no (or very limited) growth opportunities, and can become cash flow negative. Warren Buffet refers to investing in declining industries, or declining companies, as *cigar butt* investing. It is generally pretty risky to invest in declining industries, since the risk is high, and the prospective returns are fairly low. A modern example of a declining industry is retail.

Almost any industry falls into one of the preceding four phases. Because the phases progress linearly from one phase to the next (i.e. pioneer to growth) and the final phases is the eventual extinction of a company, these phases are referred to as an industry's life cycle. However, it is possible to identify specific companies within an industry classification that have differentiated or unique characteristics. For example, an investor might identify a specific company with growth-like characteristics in a pioneer industry, or a company with mature-like characteristics in a declining industry. Identifying opportunities like this can make great investments.

Business Cycle Dynamics

The business cycle is the ebb and flow of the economy. The U.S. economy has consistently experienced periods of expansion, followed by temporary contractions. This process, called the business cycle, repeats itself over several time periods.. There are three main relationships that an industry can have with the business cycle: growth, defensive, and cyclical:

- **Growth** - in relation to the business cycle, a growth industry continues to experience significant expansion, irrespective of the macroeconomic context

- **Defensive** - a defensive industry maintains stable sales and profitability throughout the business cycle; an example of a defensive industry is consumer staples, which includes businesses like grocery stores

- **Cyclical** - a cyclical industry has significant variability in its sales and profitability depending on the current status of the business cycle; an example of a cyclical industry is the automotive sector, since, during periods of macroeconomic compression, fewer consumers spend money on expensive, discretionary products such as cars

Other External Factors

There are several other external factors that can influence an industry's dynamic and the financial results of a company in a given industry. These include:

- **Government Regulations** - government regulations can greatly impact the financial results of certain industries. For example, biotechnology is an industry that is very sensitive to changes in government regulation and modifications of old laws.

- **Demographic Conditions** - a changing demographic environment is important to investors. For example, the United States, Japan, and other very developed countries have an aging population, which changes the long-term trajectory of some industries.

- **Social Changes** - social shifts can greatly influence the success or failure of certain industries and companies. For example, Amazon did well to capitalize on the social trend towards instant gratification by adding "one-click order" functionality to its website.

- **Technological Innovation** - innovation can disrupt mature industries and force them into a declining phase. An example of technological innovation in an industry is the algorithmic-based lending industry.

20.2   Financial Analysis

Understanding the relative financial performance of the companies in an industry is essential. In practice, this is very similar to the benchmarking exercise performed in a comparable companies analysis or precedent transactions analysis. Key questions to answer in the financial analysis of an industry are:

- What is the market share of the leading companies in the industry?

- Which companies are taking market share in the industry?

- Is the overall industry growing or shrinking?

- What is the relative profitability of the companies in the industry?

- Is the industry a monopoly (one firm dominates), an oligopoly (a handful of firms dominate), or highly competitive (no single firm or group of firms dominates)?

- What are the key inputs to the industry?

- Do companies in the industry have pricing power (the ability to enforce higher prices on customers)?

- What are the cost barriers to entering into the industry?

- Is access to capital the only barrier to a new entrant entering the industry, or are there deeper competitive advantages (more on competitive advantage in Chapter 22)?

20.3   Supply and Demand

As the supply of a product increases, the price of the product decreases. In economics, this is the law of supply. The law of demand states: as the demand of a product increases, the price of the product increases. The effects of the law of supply and the law of demand balance each other out to produce an equilibrium price for the industry. As price, along with volume, is one of the chief determinants of revenue, it is essential to understand the supply and demand dynamics of an industry.

The three main factors to analyze regarding the level of customer demand for industry products are: the stage of the industry in its life cycle; macroeconomic factors that influence the industry (such as GDP growth); and other headwinds (impeding factors) or tailwinds (supporting factors) arising from external factors, such as demographic shifts or government changes.

Supply is more difficult to analyze. The investor must acquire an understanding of how difficult it is for new, competitive firms to enter the industry. Several factors could influence this, such as the time it takes to actually enter the industry, or the costs associated with launching a company and training a new staff. From there, the investor should seek to understand how many nascent companies are actually on the way.

For example, in analyzing companies that produce commodities such as coal, investors will often prepare an analysis that details all the incoming coal plants and the expected annual production. This gives investors a precise understanding of the supply dynamics of the coal industry. By combining this supply analysis with a demand analysis, the investor can get an idea of where the industry could be headed. However, it is difficult to analyze supply with this level of granularity outside of the commodities industry. With that said, models aiming to precisely predict the price of commodities are often wrong. It is the author's opinion that predicting macroeconomic factors such as supply and demand for an entire industry is very difficult and often inaccurate. For this reason, while a supply/demand analysis is necessary, an investor should approach the results with a grain-of-salt.

20.4 Porter's Five Forces

In economic theory, returns on invested capital should be equivalent across all firms and industries. However, empirical evidence suggests that this is not the case. Why might this be? One explanation is the structure of the industry, or the characteristics that define an industry. A famous economist named Michael Porter produced a framework for thinking about industry structure. He distills industry structure into five forces exhibited by the diagram below. The investor can rank each of these five forces as low, medium, or high to get a comprehensive understanding of the competitive dynamics within an industry.

Porter's Five Forces

Threat of Substitutes

Substitute products are competing products produced by other industries. If an industry's products have several substitutes, then customers have more options. This constrains the ability of companies in the industry to raise prices. For example, the competition created by the advent of the airline industry greatly reduced the ability of railroad companies to exert significant pricing pressure on customers. Customers now had two choices for transportation and shipping needs. Airlines and railroads are substitutes (for non-transoceanic transportation), but are not rivals in the respective industry of each.

Threat of New Entrants

Existing firms are not the only threat to firms in an industry. The possibility of new firms entering an industry is called the threat of new entrants. An industry that is difficult to enter has high *barriers to entry* and low threat of new entrants. Some significant barriers to entry are:

- **Economies of Scale** - economies of scale refers to the concept that larger enterprises achieve a reduction in costs relative to smaller firms. This serves as a barrier to entry since it allows the incumbent firm(s) to charge prices that are uneconomical for new entrants.

- **Government Regulations and Patents** - some industries have government sanctioned monopolies, such as utilities and biotechnology (through extensive patent protection). This is a great barrier to entry.

- **Asset Specificity** - certain industries require assets that are very specific to the industry. This serves a barrier to entry since new firms with capital are less likely to spend money on "do-or-die" assets. Instead, these firms would likely prefer to purchase non-specialized assets that can be converted into other uses in the event of a failure.

- **Brand Loyalty** - other industries develop significant customer relationships and brand loyalty with their customers. For example, Coca-Cola customers are famously loyal to the brand and spend much less money, if any, on competing soda products. This brand/customer loyalty inhibits new firms from entering the industry.

- **Supplier and Distribution Relationships** - most industries require extensive supplier and distribution networks. Industries where the incumbent firms have entrenched and high-quality relationships with their suppliers and distributors can be difficult to enter.

Supplier Power

Most industries have inputs, such as raw materials, employees, and other core operating expenses. Therefore, the relationship that a supplier-dependent industry has with its suppliers is critical. When suppliers have more power in the relationship, they have a higher degree of supplier power and negotiation leverage. Suppliers are generally more powerful when: 1) suppliers are concentrated (there are not many suppliers) or 2) it is expensive for firms in the industry to switch suppliers. Suppliers are weak when: 1) there are many suppliers, 2) the suppliers sell a commoditized good, and 3) there are few firms in the industry to purchase products from the suppliers.

Buyer Power

When the customers of an industry have a lot of power in the relationship with that industry, buyer power is high. When there are many suppliers and few buyers, buyer power is high.

When there are few suppliers and many buyers, buyer power is low. When buyer power is high, the buyer is able to negotiate and set the price they pay for the good. To break the concept down even further: buyers are strong when: they are concentrated or they purchase a significant amount of the goods produced by the industry. Consequently, buyers are weak when: 1) they are not concentrated, 2) they have high switching costs (costs associated with changing suppliers), and 3) they purchase a small portion of the goods produced by the industry.

Rivalry

Rivalry refers to the intensity of the competition between firms in an industry. Some industries have low rivalry and the participants do little to gain a competitive advantage. However, in most industries, the incumbent firms seek to displace their competitors. Examples of aggressive actions that increase industry rivalry are: modifying or improving product differentiation, changing prices, capitalizing on supplier relationships, and utilizing distribution channels in unique ways. Some characteristics of industries with high rivalry are: numerous firms, minimal product differentiation, and low market growth.

21

Corporate Strategy

21.1   Generic Strategies

At this point, we have discussed frameworks and methods for analyzing the attractiveness of an industry. Equally important is a firms position within a given industry. To this end, we will review several frameworks for identifying strategically sound companies; for considering future strategic options for a company; and, in later chapters, for evaluating competitive advantage.

The same economist from the preceding chapter, Michael Porter, argues that a firm's strengths fall into one of two categories: product differentiation or cost advantage. To strategically outperform competitors, firms must leverage their strengths. Furthermore, firms can either employ a cost leadership or differentiation strategy in a broad or narrow scope, resulting in three generic strategies: "cost leadership strategy," "product differentiation strategy," and "focus strategy." The diagram below exhibits the generic strategies.

| | | **Strategy** | |
		Cost	Differentiation
Scope	Broad	Cost Leadership	Differentiation
	Narrow	Focus	Focus

Cost Leadership Strategy

Here the objective is to be the low cost producer in an industry at a particular quality level. The firm can price its products in two ways: 1) above market prices (to increase profitability) or 2) below market prices (to increase market share). Aggressive pricing actions like this can result in a "price war" – an aggressive lowering of prices by the participants in an industry. If a firm has a low cost advantage, than it can outlast the other competing firms in the industry during the price war. Eventually it becomes uneconomical for these firms without a cost advantage to sell at the price levels sustained by the company with a cost advantage.

There are several ways that companies can develop a cost advantage: maintaining relatively stronger supplier relationships, access to low cost materials, and improving operational efficiencies. A cost leadership strategy has risks, since, eventually, competing firms are likely to innovate and make up for their prior cost disadvantage, at which point a price war ensue. If several firms in an industry utilize a focused cost leadership strategy, then it is possible for each individual company to develop pricing power or a low cost advantage within its market niche.

Product Differentiation Strategy

A product differentiation strategy entails the production of a good or service that has unique, differentiating attributes. As a result, the goods or services are valued higher by customers, who then begin to prefer the unique goods or services over a competing firm's product. Generally, this higher quality or unique product allows firms to charge a premium price. The objective is that the higher price will exceed the additional costs resulting from producing the differentiated product. Firms that successfully develop a product differentiation strategy often have "pricing power" and can enforce price increases on their customers due to the unique characteristics of their products. This is because there are limited substitute goods or services for the customers.

The strengths associated with a differentiation strategy are: an effective product development team, a solid corporate brand, and a successful sales operation. The biggest risk are changes in consumer preferences and competitor imitation of the unique products/services.

Focus Strategy

In a focus strategy, the company focuses on a small subset of a market. Within that market, the company aims to achieve either a differentiation advantage or cost advantage. There are many benefits to a focus strategy, such as customer loyalty. Simply put: the needs and desires of a group are generally better satisfied by focusing entirely on that single group. The biggest risk to a focus strategy is the possibility that a larger, broad-market leader alters its product to compete with the focus company.

By considering the generic strategies in tandem with the industry analysis framework discussed in the previous chapter, the investor is armed with a powerful set of tools for analyzing the prospects, strategy, and economic viability of a given company.

21.2 SWOT Analysis

Assessing the environment and internal factors is an essential component of strategic planning. Factors internal to the firm are called strengths or weaknesses. Factors external to the firm are called opportunities or threats. Analyzing a company's strategic prospects under this framework is called SWOT analysis. The combination of internal and external factors results in several, specific strategies, as exhibited by the SWOT matrix pictured below.

	Strengths	**Weaknesses**
Opportunities	S-O strategies	W-O strategies
Threats	S-T strategies	W-T strategies

S-O strategies try to leverage the strengths of the company to capitalize on opportunities in the industry or marketplace. S-T strategies utilize a firm's strength to help deter potential threats. W-O strategies attempt to overcome weaknesses to profit from specific opportunities. W-T strategies are defensive in nature. The objective of a W-T strategy is to reduce the susceptibility of the firm to its threats by focusing on addressing its weaknesses.

22

Competitive Advantage

22.1 Introduction

A competitive advantage is a characteristic, or set of characteristics, that enables a business to generate above-average profits and cash flow. A sustainable competitive advantage is one that will last for a long time. In an earlier chapter, this concept was referred to as a "wide economic moat." Good businesses are able to generate high returns on invested capital (ROIC) because they have competitive advantages. Bad businesses are the opposite. However, it is very difficult to identify businesses with a sustainable competitive advantage, because they are rare. In this chapter, we will discuss several key sources of competitive advantage and explore the various signposts that can reveal evidence of a competitive advantage.

22.2 Switching Costs

Switching costs are one of the best sources of competitive advantage. A "sticky" customer is a great customer. A sticky customer is one that starts spending money with a business and then stays spending money with that business for a while. A "sticky solution" is a product or service offered by companies that naturally develops sticky customers. A sticky solution that creates sticky customers is a sign of high switching costs, which is great for a business.

Sticky solutions that make it difficult to switch products or services are very valuable. High switching costs greatly increase the *stability* of a cash flow or revenue stream, since fewer customers will change to a competing product or service. If it is difficult for customers to switch to a competing product or service, a company can

also charge the customer more money, which influences the growth
of the company's cash flow or revenue stream and maintain a high
ROIC.

High switching costs arise from a few main sources: product
integration into the customers operations, actual monetary switching costs, psychological switching costs, and onerous switching procedures. Each of these is covered below:

- **Product Integration** - for many companies, the solution
  that they provide becomes a critical part of the day-to-day
  operations of their customers. For example, consider accounting software companies. This type of product has an initial
  learning curve, but once all the accounting information is entered into the software, a firm is much less likely to switch
  to new accounting software. This is for two reasons: 1) it
  takes a lot of time to transfer all the data to new accounting software and 2) the users of the accounting software are
  accustomed to the current product they are using.

- **Monetary Switching Costs** - some firms charge an actual
  fee when customers switch to a competitor. Consider an en-
  ergy company that charges customers a fee if they switch to
  a competitor.

- **Psychological Switching Costs** - another source of switching costs is psychological in nature. There is a well known
  behavioral bias, called the endowment effect, in which people
  ascribe more value to things simply because they own them.
  Another concept, called anchoring, makes it difficult for people to make subsequent judgments after an initial judgment.
  The combination of these two behavioral biases (and frankly,
  many more) make it difficult for people to switch companies
  in certain scenarios.

  A good example is the financial wealth adviser industry. Individuals hire financial wealth advisers. Then, even
  if the adviser performs terribly, they have great psychological difficulty 1) admitting they made a mistake, 2) believing
  the adviser has done poorly, and 3) actually switching financial advisers. If you are intrigued by the topic of behavioral
  biases, which fall in the realm of social science, which is discussed more fully in Chapter 35.

- **Onerous Switching Procedures** - for other businesses,
  it is just difficult and annoying to switch to a competing

product. A great example is a brokerage firm (through which people deposit money to trade financial securities, such as stocks). Once people deposit their money with a brokerage firm and begin purchasing stocks or bonds, it is very tedious and frustrating to move it to another firm. The same concept applies to banks. Notice that very few people change banks or brokerage firms.

22.3 Network Effects

A powerful source of competitive advantage, a network effect is when the value and usefulness of the product or service a company sells actually increases with the number of people that use it. This means, as a company grows its customer base, its existing customers are deriving more value from the product. At the same time, new customers are extracting more value from the product, while the attractiveness of the product to potential customers is also increasing. It is easy to see how a network effect can have a profound impact on both the stability and potential growth of a company's cash flow stream. Once established, a network effect is a difficult competitive advantage to erode, making it durable.

However, network effects are rare. For a company to have a network effect, the value of the product *to the customer* has to actually increase with the network. For almost every businesses, the customers of the business do not consider what other customers are doing.

Two notable examples of businesses/industries with network effects: credit card and social network companies. The size of the network of people and businesses that accept a particular credit card effects the value of the service to new customers. In the case of a social network business, the website's value to the customer increases as more of their friends and acquaintances sign up. Network effects are fairly rare in businesses that deal with physical goods.

22.4 Cost Advantages

Cost advantages are a competitive advantage that arise from a business having the capability to produce the same goods as its competitors for a cheaper price. Whereas the competitive advantages discussed thus far allow a firm to charge a premium, a cost advantage allows a firm to undercut competitors and win customers

based on price. Cost advantages, however, are often easy to repli-
cate, making them a short term edge really. That being said, there
are three main ways to create a *durable* cost advantage: proprietary
knowledge, high-quality supplier relationships, and unique access.

- **Proprietary Knowledge** - a proprietary production process, such as a unique manufacturing concept or internal software that optimizes some aspect of a company's operations,
  can be a source of a cost advantage. However, all cost advantages rooted in proprietary knowledge are somewhat easily
  replicated by other firms by simpling hiring people from the
  competing firm to acquire the proprietary process/

- **High-Quality Supplier Relationships** - some companies
  are able to establish very positive relationships with their
  key suppliers, enabling them to purchase goods at a cheaper
  rate than competitors. If this cheaper rate is contractually
  guaranteed for some number of years, then this competitive
  advantage has more durability.

- **Unique Access** - some firms have unique access to high
  quality resources. For example, a firm in the mining industry
  that owns a mine with softer rock than the competitor average will have an easier time extracting ore from that rock,
  and thus a cost advantage based on this unique access.

22.5   Size Advantages

Firms that are relatively bigger than competitors often have
a competitive advantage due to their size and scale. A larger firm
has more negotiating leverage with industry suppliers (since they
make-up a larger portion of the suppliers income) and has some
cost advantages through *economies of scale*, the concept that a
firms marginal costs gradually reduce as the firm grows larger.

The advantages of size are mostly cost-centered. However,
a firm with a larger size also has an easier time experimenting
with, and releasing new and differentiated products and services.
If these products/services are successful in developing a customer
base, then the firm can develop a market niche and grow the revenue component of the business.

22.6 Product Quality

Though not discussed in academic or investing books much, product quality is a fantastic source of competitive advantage. Simply offering a higher quality product, relative to competitors, for a given price point, is one of the best competitive advantages a firm can have. Product quality is often ignored as a source of competitive advantage because it is difficult to quantify or assess.

Product quality is similar to brand, though. Brand focuses more on the reputation a company has, where product quality focuses exclusively on the customer experience. It is possible for a company with a good or reputable brand to reduce its product quality (which will eventually deteriorate the brand). In a sense, product quality is the precursor to a good brand, for a given price point. A brand arises from the level of product quality, service, and other factors associated with a company.

22.7 Intangible Assets

Intangible assets includes brands, regulatory licenses, patents, and other similar, non-physical assets. A strong brand is a great source of a competitive advantage. Consider the Coca-Cola company, which Warren Buffet famously invested in largely on the basis of the company's brand. A strong, reputable brand creates customer loyalty. Customer loyalty results in recurring revenue and stable cash flow. A stable cash flow stream is much easier to grow than a cash flow stream that is regularly losing customers and revenue.

Customer loyalty also makes it difficult for competitors to steal market share. However, popular brands are not necessarily profitable brands, so there is some nuance to assessing a brand's value. Furthermore, it is difficult to precisely value the worth of a brand. The big question: is the brand strong enough to influence customer behavior? Will customers pay a premium for the product or regularly purchase the product? If the answers are yes, then the brand likely confers a strong competitive advantage.

While patents prevent other companies from selling an identical product, there are many risks still associated with patent-based competitive advantages. Notably, any threats to the patent, such as legal challenges or expiration (all patents have a finite life), will severely jeopardize the worth of the company.

Regulatory barriers and licenses also make it difficult for new

companies to enter an industry. Consider the slot machine industry, which is heavily regulated and requires government licensing.
As evidence of the barrier that regulation produces, there are only
four companies in the slot machine industry. Beyond that, few, if
any, new competitors have entered the industry in recent history.

22.8   Evidence of a Competitive Advantage

We have discussed several notable sources of competitive advantage. So what signposts can the investor look for in industries
and businesses pointing towards the presence of a competitive advantage? Consider the following:

- Has the company produced a ROIC in excess of the WACC
  over a long period of time?

- Have other firms been able to enter the industry successfully?

- Have many firms been forced to leave the industry?

- Has the company increased or decreased prices overtime?

- How has the company's market share changed overtime?

- Has the market become more or less consolidated?

Based on the answers to the preceding questions,if there is
strong evidence of a competitive advantage, the investor must work
to identify the source of the competitive advantage and evaluate
whether its strength is increasing or decreasing overtime. Furthermore, the investor must also try to determine the duration of the
competitive advantage to assess its durability.

Remember, the sole determinant of the long-term value of
a business is its ability to produce a sustainable (and with hope
growing) cash flow stream through some durable competitive ad-
vantage(s). Therefore, understanding this chapter and its intrica-
cies is critical.

23

Risk

23.1 What is risk?

Risk must be understood, recognized, and controlled. Investing deals with the future, which is inherently uncertain. This uncertainty introduces a range of possible outcomes.

At this point, several topics have been discussed to help the investor analyze whether an investment generate returns. However, little attention has been given to the things that can go wrong with a business and impair returns. The catch-all for this is risk.

Think back to Chapter 1: The goal of investing is to *maximize after-tax return* while *minimizing risk*. Most investors spend all their time thinking about maximizing return, without deeply considering risk. As such, a risk-focused investing process can differentiate an investor. To many great investors, risk is the most important aspect of an investment decision. Since risk is also defined as "the permanent loss of capital" and the goal of investing is to grow and preserve capital, it makes sense that anything that could result in such a loss would be the focus of a sound investing approach. Regardless of whether risk is the first, second, or third item considered by the investor, it is essential for the investor to at least address and understand.

The importance of minimizing risk, while also maximizing return, is captured by the following formula, called the Sharpe ratio, which is an industry standard concept for portfolio management:

$$\text{Sharpe Ratio} = \frac{E[r_p] - r_f}{\sigma_p}$$

The goal is to optimize an investment portfolio by maximizing the Sharpe Ratio. In the Sharpe ratio, $E[r_p]$ is the expected return of the portfolio. r_f is the risk-free interest rate. σ_p is the standard deviation of the portfolio's returns (this is what academic and quantitative financial professionals often utilize to capture risk). The precise formula is less important than the intuition introduced by the formula, which is to maximize the following:

$$\max\left(\frac{Return}{Risk}\right)$$

What are the important takeaways from this formula? First, *every* investment comes with risk. Second, risk *detracts* from the attractiveness of the return. Third, investing must consider return and risk *in tandem*. *Risk-adjusted returns* is the industry term that captures these insights. Great investors seek high risk-adjusted returns.

While it is generally true that return correlates positively with risk. The goal of a fundamentals and value-oriented investment process is to find *asymmetric* risk-reward opportunities – places where the potential reward significantly outweighs the potential risk or chance for permanent capital loss. Many academics and professionals believe these opportunities do not exist. The dozens of investors who have amassed fortunes actually employing this concept would beg to differ.

Risky investments are investments where the range of possible outcomes is wider. Put differently, riskier investments are ones where the rosy, return generating scenario is less likely, because alternate scenarios are relatively more likely.

For those tempted to distill risk into the concept of volatility (think back to β from the CAPM), it is enticing and convenient to believe that a concept as complex as risk can be aggregated into a single, beautiful, catch-all number. Volatility, in a nut-shell, is the variability in a securities price. Is an investment that is virtually certain to return money in the future inherently risky because the price movement between now and the future is bumpy? Not at all. In investing, the destination is more important than the journey.

Furthermore, in general, volatility decreases as a securities price increases. Therefore, to an academic, risk actually decreases as a securities price appreciates! This is exactly contrary to the old investing adage "buy low, sell high!"

Risk is incredibly complex. There is a lot that we do not know. It is tempting to believe that life and its events will proceed as normal. However, history has proven, time and again, that this is not the case. Life is defined by unexpected, often unpredictable phenomena. These events are called *unknown unknowns*.

Black swans are another common name for these events. These are events or other things we do not know that we do not know. Furthermore, there are *known unknowns*. These are events or other things we know that we do not know, such as inflation. We know that inflation will exist and have a number next year, but we do not know what that number will be. Where concepts like competitive advantage are somewhat tangible and observable in a business model, risk is mysterious, un-concrete, and elusive.

Beyond this, risk is subjective! An investment may be risky to one individual and safe to another. This relates to an incredibly important concept – correctness. To be a great investor, you have to be right or lucky, both of which are very difficult to obtain. An investor can be convinced he has accurately assessed the risk of a situation and still be proven wrong. Market and business realities proceed independently of one over-confident individuals expectations.

With hope, these few pages have helped the reader understand risk and its importance. However, this small introduction only touches the surface of one of the most complex, misunderstood, and, to the author, interesting concepts in investing and finance. From here, we will explore some common types of risk. Then we will explore ways to combat risk.

23.2 Types of Risk

According to Benjamin Graham, the father of value investing, there are three main types of risk: valuation risk, business risk, and balance sheet risk. In this discussion, the most attention will be given to these three types of risk.

Valuation Risk

Valuation risk refers to buying an asset for more than it is worth. When the investor buys an overpriced asset, he or she is reliant on all the good things that are factored into the price of the asset actually occurring. An asset that does not have a price well below its intrinsic value has a lot of valuation risk, since the investor is dependent on a rosy future to avoid a permanent loss of capital. One of the most consistent mistakes investors make is overpaying for the hope of growth. We will discuss the best way to combat valuation risk, and other risks, later in this chapter.

Business Risk

Business risk refers to all the fundamental risks that could affect a businesses' ability to sustain and grow cash flow. Business risk is a huge, catch-all term, but incredibly important. Business risk is the possibility of a deterioration in the sustainability or growth of a business' cash flow stream due to one or more economic changes. Notice, "economic changes" captures a wide variety of potential risks: new competitors, substitute products, a competitor developing a proprietary process, exchange rates changing, the list goes on. However, the business risk concept condenses all the risks that could potentially affect the cash flow of a firm. In some communities, this is called "basic business risk" or BBR.

Balance Sheet Risk

Balance sheet risk is associated with the possibility or occurrence of financial distress. Balance sheet risk is best controlled through a sound, reasonable, and fundamental analysis of a company's balance sheet strength and cash flow producing prospects, in excess of associated interest expense.

Other Risks

There are dozens of other risks, such as reinvestment risk, interest rate risk, and more. However, for a fundamentals based investor, grappling with and understanding valuation risk, business risk, and balance sheet risk is a fantastic place to start and focus.

23.3   Combating Risk

Unfortunately, the best ways to combat risk are often very subjective and elusive, much like risk itself. Some effective risk management approaches are:

- Paying less than an asset is worth and demanding a healthy *margin of safety* between purchase price and intrinsic value

- Focusing on controllable factors of the investing decision, such as process and investor behavior

- Performing deep due diligence on a potential investment while constantly asking (and trying to answer) "what are the core determinants of the long term cash flow of this business" or, put simply, "what is the question"?

- Working hard

- Utilizing a long-term perspective and ignoring day-to-day market fluctuations

24

Company Analysis in Detail

24.1　Classifying the Company

In the same way that industries are classified into a set of buckets, companies fall into a set of buckets as well. The main buckets a company can fall into are: pioneer, growth, mature, cyclical, declining, and turnaround.

Pioneer

A pioneer company is focusing on creating a new market or entering into an established market in a differentiated way. A pioneer company is generally experiencing rapid growth. It is difficult to perform financial analysis on a pioneer company since they are generally newer and have little operating history or cash flow. A pioneer company is usually cash flow negative, and, in the event the company is cash flow positive, heavily reinvesting the cash flow into the business.

Valuation of pioneer companies is very difficult, since the future growth rate of the firms revenue and cash flow is very difficult to assess. When considering investing in a pioneer company, the investor must think hard about the qualitative attributes of the business since the quantitative aspects are either 1) not available or 2) mostly guess-work. A pioneer company is heavily dependent on investor capital to fuel its survival and growth until it becomes cash flow positive.

Growth

A growth company is experiencing high growth in cash flow and sales. A growth company has more established customer relationships than a pioneer company and is further along in establishing a market or intruding into an existing market. A growth company is still very dependent on investor capital to fuel its growth, even if it is cash flow positive.

Mature

A mature company has a well-established product with recurring customer relationships. A mature company is generally cash flow positive and returning a portion of that cash to shareholders in the form of dividends or stock buybacks. Since investable opportunities are likely limited or have a low prospective ROIC, mature companies do not regularly raise capital from investors. A company with stable revenues and stable cash flow is most likely a mature company.

Cyclical

A cyclical company has revenue and cash flow that varies greatly with the business cycle. At the peak of the business cycle (when things are going best in the economy), a cyclical business will have its maximum cash flow. At the trough of the business cycle (when things are going worst in the economy), a cyclical business will have its minimum cash flow. Cyclical companies are often commodity exposed, or dependent on the level of mass consumer spending, such as consumer automobile businesses.

Declining

A declining company has declining revenue and cash flow. Many factors can cause a decline in revenue or cash flow such as: a reduction in demand for the company's products, increasing competitive pressures, and increasing supplier pressure. A declining business is not an inherently bad investment, but, to really make significant returns investing in a declining business, it is optimal if the declining business is a realistic turnaround story. Declining businesses usually have been mature companies at some point in history.

Turnaround

A turnaround business is a declining business that has the potential (or has successfully managed) to stop the decline in revenue and cash flow and restore mature company status. In some rare cases, a company can turnaround into becoming a growth company again. Correctly identifying a successful turnaround story *early* can result in big profits for investors. However, successful turnarounds are rare birds.

24.2 Revenue Considerations

In this section, some pragmatic points related to revenue are discussed. Namely, the key components of revenue, volume and price, and the most attractive form of revenue, recurring revenue.

24.2.1 Volume and Price

The fact that revenue has two components, volume and price, is a simple, but often forgotten, concept:

$$\text{Revenue} = \text{Volume} * \text{Price}$$

In the preceding formula, volume is the number of goods sold and price is the price per good. Consequently, firms can grow revenue in one of three ways: 1) increase volume, 2) increase price, or 3) increase volume and price at the same time. Growing revenue through item 3) is somewhat rare, and potential evidence of a competitive advantage. But why is this rare?

The reason that it is rare to grow volume and price at the same time is because price has an inverse relationship with volume. As price increases, naturally, less people will be attracted to buying the product, reducing volume. In contrast, as price decreases, more people will be attracted to buying the product, increasing volume.

Let us consider an example. Suppose the price of a good is $1.20 and the volume of units sold is 50. Therefore, revenue is $60. Now, the company decreases the price per unit to $1.00 to grow volume. As expected, volume grows, in this case, to 60 units. However, the total revenue is still $60. This makes sense, because there is no free lunch – right? Not necessarily.

The concept introduced here is called *price elasticity of demand*. Price elasticity of demand describes the change in quantity demanded (volume) associated with a price change. The formal formula for price elasticity of demand is:

$$\text{Price Elasticity of Demand} = \frac{(\%\Delta Quantity)}{(\%\Delta Price)}$$

In the earlier example, the price elasticity of demand was -1.2. The % increase in quantity demanded (20%) precisely offset the reduction (-16.7%) in price, resulting in no impact on revenue. But what if the price elasticity of demand was less than this, let's say -1.5. Using the numbers from the preceding example, this would result in a % increase in quantity demanded of 25%, relative to a percent reduction in price of 16.7%. Therefore, the price per good is still \$1 after the price change, but the quantity demanded has increased by 25%, resulting in about 63 sold units. Therefore, because of the price elasticity of demand, revenue has actually increased by \$3 or 5% simply by changing the price!

What are the key takeaways from this economic insight? First, a business lowering prices is not necessarily bad. It depends on *why* the company is lowering prices. If the price elasticity of demand for the business and industry is very negative, then the price change might actually result in revenue growth for the company. Second, a business raising prices is not necessarily good, since it might have a negative impact on volume and destroy revenue. The big question is, does the business have a great enough competitive advantage to retain customers (maintain volume) while also increasing prices? This is called pricing power and is a powerful source of revenue growth, but rare. If a company does have pricing power, though, this is strong evidence of a competitive advantage. Third, a business, in theory, has an optimal price level that maximizes revenue by balancing out the effects of volume and price. Therefore, a management team that naively sets prices without much deliberation or analysis exhibits weakness, since they could be sitting on free revenue growth simply by charging more or less for the same product that they already offer!

24.2.2   Recurring Revenue

Is a dollar of revenue always worth the same? No, a revenue stream that is recurring is more valuable than one-time revenue. Remember, there are two main factors that contribute to the value of a business: the sustainability of the existing cash flow stream and the growth of the existing cash flow stream. Having significant recurring revenue positively contributes to the *sustainability* of a company's cash flow stream and makes a business more valuable.

Recurring revenue is also evidence of *customer retention,* a concept which will be elaborated on later in this chapter. Recurring revenue is important because it evidences the company has a strong *value proposition.* A value proposition is the actual reason that a customer purchases a company's products. A strong value proposition, supported by customer behavior, is evidence of product quality, one of the significant competitive advantages discussed previously.

What businesses have a high degree of recurring revenue? Software-as-a-service (SAAS) businesses immediately come to mind. These are basically businesses that sell subscriptions to software. The revenue stream associated with their service is inherently recurring, since the company is paid a monthly or yearly subscription fee, rather than a one-time fee upfront. From the businesses perspective, a smaller amount of recurring revenue is more valuable than a relatively larger amount of one-time revenue since recurring revenue increases the stability of the business and its cash flow.

24.2.3 The Five Sources of Revenue Growth

The discussion on volume and price is essential to understanding revenue. But, what are the tangible ways a company can actually grow volume or price, and thus revenue? There are five main ways:

- **New Customer Wins -** the classic way to grow revenue – just get more customers to buy the product! This is much easier said than done.

- **Cross-Sells -** this is the act of selling an existing customer other products or services offered by the company. For example, a company might offer both website hosting and analytics services with separate costs and subscriptions. An individual customer might purchase only the website hosting services. A successful cross-sell is when the sales team convinces that customer to purchase an additional service, such as the analytics service. This is not a new customer win, since this customer was already buying a product or service from the company.

- **Upsells -** this is the act of selling an existing customer a more expensive version of the product they are currently purchasing. For example, a company might offer a basic and premium subscription to its website. Assume that the basic and premium subscriptions are mutually exclusive. A customer might be currently subscribed to the basic plan. A successful up-sell is when the sales team convinces that customer to upgrade to the premium plan. This is not a new customer win, since this customer was already buying a product or service from the company. This is not a cross-sell, because the customer switched to a service that is mutually exclusive with the service previously purchased.

- **Price Increases** - this refers to revenue growth achieved by simply increasing the price of the same good or service for existing customers.

- **Acquisitions** - this refers to revenue growth resulting from acquiring other companies. This is basically the same as acquiring new customer wins. This type of growth is called *inorganic* growth, considered less attractive than organic growth (the name for growth coming from the other four sources of sales growth).

24.3   Products and Markets

When analyzing a business, it is important to understand all the products that they offer and the respective markets of each. Consider a company with two differing business lines: Line A that makes up 90% of revenue and Line B that makes up 10% of revenue. Line A is also a declining business. Most analysts probably focus on Line A and value the business based mainly off of Line A. Therefore, the focus on Line A likely impairs the market valuation of the business. However, Line B is a new business line, in a high growth industry, that is uncompetitive. Since Line B offers promise (the investor must assess how *real* this promise is) but is not the focus of analysts, a scenario could arise where there is *hidden* value in the company due to Line B. This hidden value might be significant enough (adjusted for risk) to justify investment. Because of situations like this, an investor must strive to understand all the products and markets of a business, since an ignored area could be where the value is hidden.

24.4 Sales

It is tempting to focus exclusively on a company's product and its quality to assess the ability of the company to sell its product. However, this ignores a huge component of selling a product – the actual sales team! To many investors, the sales team and its culture is the chief determinant of a company's ability to sell its product. As if assessing product quality was not already subjective enough, assessing sales culture is now thrown into the mix.

A company with a great product, but a sales team incapable of communicating the benefits of that product to potential customers will never sell a thing. A company with a lackluster product, but an incredibly capable sales team will likely experience great success.

For this reason, especially for earlier stage businesses, an investor must make an assessment of the sales culture and the people who make-up the sales team. If a business is dependent on new customer wins to survive, such as a start-up or consulting business, it is essential to understand *how* and *who* will secure these new customer wins!

Tying back to recurring revenue, the more recurring revenue a business has, the less important sales becomes. The importance of subsequent new customer wins decreases as the longevity of the revenue stream associated with previously won customers increases.

But how can the investor decide what makes a great sales team and culture? The answer is simple, but difficult and time consuming – study great sales teams from history. Study the attributes of influence and learn to analyze the possession of these attributes in other people. Learn to recognize the characteristics of a great salesman and positive culture by studying precedent examples.

24.5 Total Addressable Market

Total addressable market (TAM) is the prospective total annual sales amount of a market at maturity. Every word in the preceding definition is critical to understanding TAM, particularly, *prospective* and *market at maturity*. There is a big difference between market size (the current total annual sales of a market) and TAM. Market size generally refers to the size of the current market for a given type products. TAM refers to the size of the market at maturity. Therefore, market size is strictly smaller than or equal to TAM. However, in a consulting context, market size and TAM are sometimes used interchangeably.

Most start-ups and early stage companies depend on selling to investors the idea that TAM for their products and services is much greater than the current market size. Analyzing TAM is particularly important for un-saturated markets, where the TAM is much greater than the current market. In a mature market, the TAM is approximately the same as the market size, so there is little additional analysis required beyond aggregating the sales of the markets constituents.

In a TAM analysis for an early stage market, the process is more involved. As an example, consider the market for a particular type of drug therapy in the United States. Let us make some assumptions: the current market size is $100M, the United States population is 300M, the incidence rate of the disease that the drug treats is 2%, the expected long-term price per month of the drug is $25, and the disease is severe enough that the percent of people seeking treatment is 90%. What is the TAM in this scenario? Simply multiply all the assumptions together, adjusted into annual terms. Therefore, TAM = (300M people) * (2% of population with disease) * (90% of people with disease seeking treatment) * ($25 per month for treatment) * (12 months in a year) = $1.62B annual sales. Therefore, the TAM of this drug in the United States, based on the assumptions, is much greater than the current market size.

For drug therapies and healthcare in general, a TAM analysis is much easier, since several of the key assumptions are known with a reasonable degree of confidence: 1) the population, 2) the incidence rate of the drug, and 3) the percent of people seeking treatment. For most other industries and companies, the key assumptions are much harder to determine and require a deep level of analysis.

What is the missing ingredient of this discussion? The actual market share of a specific company! A company does not necessarily "own" the entire current market or prospective TAM, in fact, a "winner-take-all" scenario like this is very rare. Market share is the portion of a market that a company controls. Therefore, prospective market share, in combination with a TAM analysis, enables the investor to try and predict the eventual annual sales a company could achieve. Current market share is the proportion of a company's sales relative to the current market. However, predicting market share is difficult, and requires a consideration of several factors discussed thus far, such as product quality and sales.

Perhaps the best way to predict market share is to first understand the dynamics of the market: is it likely to end up as a monopoly, oligopoly, or a highly competitive market? Using precedent examples and comparable industries will help give the investor an idea of how to answer this question. If the market is likely to be a monopoly, who will control the market and why? If the market is likely to be an oligopoly, which companies will survive and why? If the market is likely to be highly competitive, are you sure you want to invest? This is why assessing relative product quality, relative value proposition, and relative sales culture is critical, since these factors can provide a plausible rationale for why a company will grow or maintain market share over time.

24.6 Operating Leverage

At this point, a lot of attention has been given to factors and points of analysis regarding sales and its growth. But what about profits? Specifically, what about the bridge between sales growth and operating income (EBIT) growth? This is called operating leverage. But, why does operating leverage exist? Wouldn't a 5% change in sales result in a 5% change in operating income (EBIT)? Not necessarily. At a high level, a business has two types of costs: fixed costs (one time costs for long-term assets) and variable costs (the costs associated specifically with selling the product). For the sake of understanding operating leverage, assume that EBIT = (Price - Variable Costs)*Volume - Fixed Costs (in accounting, fixed costs are normally counted as a capital expenditure and do not impact EBIT except through depreciation). The formal formulas for degree of operating leverage (DOL) are:

$$DOL = \frac{\%\Delta EBIT}{\%\Delta Sales}$$

OR

$$DOL = \frac{(\text{Price-Variable Costs})*\text{Volume}}{(\text{Price - Variable Costs}) * \text{Volume - Fixed Costs}}$$

For an example, consider a coffee shop. A coffee shop has the fixed costs of purchasing/establishing a location and purchasing coffee brewing equipment. For variable costs, a coffee shop has to purchase coffee cups and supplies, coffee beans, and pay for labor associated with producing the coffee. Let us say the upfront costs (fixed costs) total $50. Furthermore, the variable costs associated with selling a cup of coffee total $1 per coffee cup. Suppose the company can sell coffee for $2 and sells 100 cups of coffee. Plugging into the second formula above, we get:

$$2.0 = \frac{(\$2-\$1)*100}{(\$2-\$1) * 100 - \$50}$$

We see that, based on the economics of this business, a 10% increase in sales results in a 20% increase in EBIT. But what if the fixed costs of the business are increased to $75?

$$4.0 = \frac{(\$2-\$1)*100}{(\$2-\$1) * 100 - \$75}$$

In this scenario, we see that a 10% increase in sales results in an increase in EBIT of 40%. So, the operating leverage actually increased with the fixed costs. What if the fixed costs of the business are $25? The DOL will decrease to 1.33.

What economic forces are at play here? The important takeaway is that operating leverage, the bridge between sales growth and EBIT growth, depends on the *ratio* of fixed costs to variable costs. As a firm has more fixed costs as a portion of its cost structure, it has more operating leverage. As a firm has less fixed costs as a portion of its cost structure, it has less operating leverage.

Is operating leverage good? As with all leverage, it is not inherently bad. It just increases volatility – it increases the magnitude of positive developments and negative developments. A company with high operating leverage and high sales growth will experience rapid profit increases. However, if sales start to decline, profits will also decline rapidly.

As an example of a business with high operating leverage, consider a software business that produces a software platform upfront and then sells access to that software platform. Producing the software platform initially is very expensive and requires a lot of software development labor. However, once the platform is up and running, most of the software developers are no longer needed (except for a few to maintain the platform). In this scenario, fixed costs are high relative to variable costs. Therefore, as the business grows sales, its operating profits will rapidly increase. Put differently, a *lot* of the sales growth will fall to the bottom line.

24.7   Operating Metrics

Operating metrics are the core *operating* units of a business. For example, in a retail business, the core operating metric is often the number of stores. In a software business, the core operating metric is often the number of recurring customers or website visitors. Operating metrics drive the financial results of a firm. A financial model that analyzes the historical and prospective values of the operating metrics of a business is called an operating model.

24.8 Unit Economics

Unit economics refer to the profitability or economics associated with a single operating metric. For example, the "unit economics" of a retail business refers to the unit level of profitability associated with a single store. The formula for unit level ROIC (the best way to analyze unit economics, in the authors opinion) is:

$$\text{Unit Level ROIC} = (1 - T) * \frac{\text{(Unit Revenue - Unit Variable Costs)}}{\text{Unit Invested Capital}}$$

Unit economics are incredibly important. A business with terrible unit economics should not spend money on growth, since the growth will destroy value. If a business cannot make money at a unit level, how can it hope to generate profits at scale? As an example, consider a business that provides a short-term loan to help consumers finance the acquisition of a reasonably expensive item, like a tractor. To understand this business, it is very helpful to understand the unit economics of a single loan. Let us suppose that the business receives 1.7x their initial loan amount by the end of the year. On the variable costs side, the business has costs associated with paying staff, insurance, and other basic business costs that total $300 a year at the unit level. Further, let us suppose that the standard tractor costs $1000 and that the business finances the entire purchase of the tractor. Lastly, assume the tax rate is the standard business tax rate of 35%.

Therefore, the initial invested capital in this business, at a unit level, is $1000. The revenue at the end of the year associated with this initial investment is $1700. The unit variable costs are $300. The tax rate is 35%. Plugging into the formula above, the unit level ROIC is calculated as:

$$91\% = (1 - 35\%) * \frac{(\$1700 - \$300)}{\$1000}$$

Based on the characteristics of this business, the unit level ROIC is an astounding 91%! However, actually calculating unit level ROIC is difficult and often requires a transparent management team, which is rare. Understanding unit economics, though, often gives more insight into a business than any other area of analysis. The takeaway: any difficulty associated with procuring insights into unit economics is well worth it.

24.9   Scalability

Just because a company has great unit economics does not mean it is a great investment. A key question is – are the unit economics of the business scalable? Can the business grow its unit or operating metric count and sustain a high-level of great unit economics?

For example, consider an extremely profitable store that generates a unit level ROIC of 100% per year. However, the store has a fantastic, unparalleled location that is the main contributor to the great unit level economics. Therefore, if the company tried to scale the business and grow the number of units, the unit economics at the new stores would not be nearly as good as those at the original store. Therefore, this business has poor scalability.

To analyze scalability, consider whether there are any aspects of the current units of the business that cannot be replicated in future units. Then consider whether competitors can easily enter the market, which would erode the unit level economics. This is one of the many reasons why understanding competitive advantage is important!

Considering scalability in tandem with an operating model, an understanding of unit economics, and an assessment of competitive advantage is a *powerful* analysis toolkit for any fundamentals investor.

24.10   Customer Concentration

Customer concentration refers to the amount of revenue concentrated in a subset of customers. For example, a company with high customer concentration has a high percent of revenue concentrated in a small portion of customers. Concretely, suppose the three largest customers of a company make-up 50% of the revenue of the company. This is a fairly high level of customer concentration. If each of the three largest customers make-up an even split of that 50%, then each customer makes-up about 17% of the company's revenue. That is a huge portion of revenue for a single customer!

High customer concentration is considered a risk. In the preceding example, if a single one of the top three customers is lost, then the company loses 17% of revenue, a massive portion. For this reason, be wary of investing in companies with a high level of customer concentration, particularly if the customers do not have contracts with the company requiring that they maintain a relationship for an extended period of time.

24.11 Customer Retention

To survive and generate cash flow, a business must have customers who actually buy the company's products. Customer retention refers to the ability of a company to maintain existing customers. A high level of customer retention is great for a business. Remember, the determinant of the long-term value of a business is the sustainability of its cash flow stream and the growth of that cash flow stream. Therefore, customer retention is critical for understanding the sustainability of a business' cash flow stream.

Customer retention also provides deep insight into the company's product quality and value proposition. A high level of customer retention exhibits that a company's product actually adds value to its customers lives or businesses. Why else would they continue to purchase or use it? Customer retention is easier to assess for some businesses. For SAAS businesses, customer retention is an industry standard assessment metric. For something like a retail business, it is much harder to assess customer retention, since it is difficult to know whether a customer who previously went to a retail store will continue to go back to the same retail store.

Formally, customer retention rate (CRR) can be thought of as:

$$CRR = \frac{\text{Year End Customers From Set of Beginning of Year Customers}}{\text{Beginning of Year Customers}}$$

Churn rate is just the opposite of retention rate. Churn rate is the number of lost customers since the beginning of the year, over the number of customers at the beginning of the year. This being said, there are many different ways to calculate customer retention rate and churn rate. The formulas discussed here are just some of the most common.

Just because a new customer stays with a business for a long time does not mean it is profitable for the business. For this reason, it is important to consider some customer retention or churn based metric in tandem with the *cost* associated with acquiring that customer.

A common industry technique is to track the lifetime value (LTV) of a customer relative to customer acquisition cost (CAC) associated with winning that customer. The LTV of a customer combines the churn rate, annual revenue, and gross profit margin to estimate the profits that a single customer will contribute to a business over the life of that customers engagement with the business. This analysis is called LTV to CAC. Usually, the annual marketing spend per customer is used as the CAC measure.

24.12 Seasonality

Seasonality refers to the variability of a company's revenues and cash flows over the course of a year. For some businesses, this does not matter at all. But, for certain businesses, this is critical to understand. For example, a business that helps people set up holiday decorations during November and December will experience an influx of cash flow during that time of year. However, apart from those months, the business will have little to no revenue or cash flow.

24.13 Company Culture

Company culture refers to the dynamic, environment, and personal/professional attributes cherished by an organization. For a service based company, or any business heavily dependent on the performance of its *people*, company culture is incredibly important. Company culture is a hard-to-assess intangible asset, though. A poor company culture can actually destroy value. However, a great company culture can increase worker productivity, improve hiring capability, and encourage innovation. To assess company culture, conversations with former or existing employees are helpful. Conversations with management can give some insight, but management teams often try to make things sound better than they are.

24.14 Capital Allocation

Capital allocations refers to how management decides to allocate the cash it generates. There are five things a company can do with cash flow:

- Reinvest in the business in the form of capital expenditures

- Acquire other businesses (a special kind of capital expenditure)

- Pay dividends

- Repurchase shares

- Pay-down debt

Since cash is king, it is important the investor understands the capital allocation policy of a business and management. Where is cash going, and why? If the cash is being reinvested in the business, is it going towards high ROIC projects? If the cash is funding acquisitions, are these acquisitions likely to increase or help sustain long term cash flow? If there are limited high ROIC projects and poor acquisition opportunities, is cash being used to deleverage (pay-down debt) if there is any debt or is it being returned to shareholders?

24.15 Management

Management is one of the most controversial topics in investing. Despite the controversy, there are a few, important, pragmatic points about management: 1) a business with poor economics and great management will still be a business with poor economics and 2) a business with great economics and poor management will still be a business with great economics. It is the authors belief that, in general, the economics of a business are much more important than management.

This being said, what are some of the characteristics that a long-term, fundamentals, and cash flow focused investor would like to see? The list below provides some insight:

- A long-term focus

- A focus on cash flow and not earnings

- A focus on establishing durable competitive advantages

- A willingness to return cash to shareholders when investable opportunities are limited

- Honesty

- Integrity

- Character

- A sensible capital allocation policy

- An interest in establishing and maintaining a great company culture

- An excitement about potential long-term, cash flow, durable competitive advantage focused investors

Even if management possesses all the preceding characteristics, the statements of management must be taken with a grain-of-salt. This is because the investors perception of honesty, integrity, and character could be wrong, and management is still incentivized and emotionally invested in seeing the company succeed and have a strong investor base.

24.16   Maintenance Versus Growth

All capital expenditures are not created equal. In fact, apart from acquisitions, there are two main types of capital expenditures: maintenance and growth. Maintenance capital expenditures replace, replenish, and rebuild depreciating long-term assets. Growth capital expenditures go towards purchasing new long-term assets.

For example, suppose a company buys a machine. This initial purchase is a growth capital expenditure. However, the machine begins to break down over time and some parts must be replaced. The costs associated with replacing these parts are maintenance capital expenditures. Suppose the company buys another machine. This is a growth capital expenditure.

Maintenance capital expenditures are considered "more mandatory" than growth capital expenditures since maintaining an existing cash flow stream is often more important than growing cash flow (remember, a bird in the hand is worth two in the bush).

A company should only spend money on growth capital expenditures if the potential ROIC on the assets being purchased is high.

24.17   Dilution

Dilution is when an investors proportional ownership of a business is reduced through the issuance of new shares. For example, if an investor owns 10% of a business, and that business issues new equity, the number of shares outstanding overall increases, reducing the original investor's ownership percent of the business. With market cap held constant, and a great number of shares outstanding, presumably this would negatively impact the share price for the original investor. In reality, this is not always the case. Dilution still reduces the size of dividends per share and earnings per share to which an investor is entitled.

The main ways equity can be diluted are: the conversion of convertible debt or convertible preferred equity into stock, the exercise of equity options (more on this in a later chapter), and a simple issuance of new common stock.

24.18 Catalysts

Catalysts are specific events in the future of a company that stimulates the convergence of market price to intrinsic value. For event-driven investments, catalysts are the main basis of the thesis. Examples of potential catalysts are: new management, regulatory approval, emerging from a bankruptcy process, a series of positive earnings reports, an addition to an index, and more.

While important, catalysts are temporal and often short-term in nature. In the authors opinion, the greatest catalysts are: 1) an increase in the long-term cash flow of the business, 2) an increase in the sustainability of the long-term cash flow of the business, and 3) a *justified* increase in the markets *perception* of factors one and two. (i.e. the market waking up and realizing the potential or actualization of points one and two in a business the investor has already identified).

Remember, the determinant of the value of a business is the sustainability and growth of its long-term cash flow. The market might not appreciate the cash flow producing capability of a business in the short-term, but in the long-term, the market price of the business will track the sustainability and growth of cash flow.

24.19 Value Chain

The value chain is another concept developed by Michael Porter. It includes a chain of activities core to a generic business. When assessing competitive advantage, it is important to understand the generic value chain for the industry, and then the specific value chain for a given company. The goal of this analysis is to identify competitive advantages, or the lack thereof, internal to each of the activities in the value chain.

Value Chain

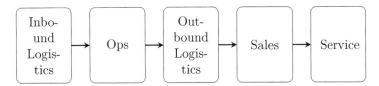

Below is a description of each of the relevant value chain activities:

- **Inbound Logistics** - this describes the receipt, management, and storing of supplies and inputs

- **Operations (Ops)** - this describes the processes that transform the supplies and inputs into the product the company sells

- **Outbound Logistics** - this describes the activities that deliver the completed product to the customer, such as distribution

- **Sales & Marketing** - this describes the activities associated with trying to convince customers to purchase the product

- **Service** - this describes the activities associated with trying to maintain the usefulness of the company's product post-sale, such as repair services and support

The components of the value chain are not, however, the only aspects of a business. A business' support activities enhance the activities of the value chain. The support activities include:

- **Procurement** - this describes the activity of purchasing key inputs and raw materials

- **Research and Development (R&D)** - this describes activities associated with developing new technologies for the firm

- **Human Resources (HR)** - this describes the activities associated with development, hiring, and employee compensation

- **Firm Infrastructure** - this describes the activities associated with maintaining the businesses infrastructure, such as finance and legal work

24.20 Mean Reversion

Mean reversion is the concept that prices, returns, growth, and other factors of a business eventually return to the mean of the market, the industry, or history. Mean reversion is a powerful concept. For example, a company that experiences supernormal sales growth relative to industry peers is likely to eventually "mean-revert" back to industry norms, unless a strong competitive advantage exists. Since strong competitive advantages are rare, the sales growth is more likely to mean-revert than be justified. The same concept applies to supernormal margins, returns, and valuations.

When the investor observes exceptional metrics in a business (such as sales growth, margins, or returns), he or she must ask: is this evidence of a real, un-reproducible competitive advantage? Or, is the observed result a statistical anomaly that will eventually mean-revert? Answering these questions requires a deep-dive into the company to determine whether a competitive advantage exists. If one does, the potential returns for the investor are great. If no durable competitive advantage can be identified to justify the supernormal metrics, the company is best avoided, since it will likely mean-revert.

24.21 Asset Coverage

In credit analysis, understanding asset coverage is particularly important. Asset coverage is the value of the underlying assets of the company, such as buildings, machinery, accounts receivable, and inventory, that can be converted into cash in the event the business goes really far south. Asset coverage is particularly important in bankruptcy and liquidation scenarios. Since credit analysis is focused on liquidity and downside protection (asset coverage), understanding the *true* value of the company's assets is important.

Remember, book value is not the same as market value. Furthermore, in a liquidation scenario, a company would be unlikely to get cash equal to the book value of its assets. The quickest shortcut to understand or analyze asset coverage is to use the equity value of the company as a measure of downside protection. Since equity is junior to all debt in the capital stack, the equity must be completely wiped out for the value of the debt to be impaired (in a bankruptcy scenario).

Another way to analyze asset coverage is to actually try to calculate the liquidation value of assets, typically by taking a healthy haircut to the given assets book value (depending on its liquidity). The liquidation value of accounts receivable often gets a 15-20% haircut to book value. Inventory gets a 30-35% haircut. PPE gets a 50-60% haircut. This gives one an idea of the cash the business can generate in a liquidation scenario.

Another way to analyze the assets of a business and asset coverage is to actually try to determine the market value of the company's assets. This works particularly well for properties the company owns. To do this, an investor can look at where the company's properties are located, and then look at the cost of similar properties on online real estate websites.

24.22   Access to Capital Markets

Access to capital markets refers to the ability of the company to raise debt or equity financing if needed. Access to capital markets depends on two main factors: 1) the company and 2) the market conditions.

If the company is hemorrhaging cash and has limited potential, access to capital markets will be difficult. Furthermore, if market conditions are terrible, such as they were during the 2008-09 financial crisis, access to capital markets will be limited.

Access to capital markets is particularly important for: 1) early-stage, cash flow negative businesses that are dependent on investor capital to survive, and 2) companies that raise debt without the intention of paying back the debt with their cash flow, instead fully intending to payback their debts through refinancing. When a company under description one fails to access capital markets when needed, it collapses and ceases to exist. When a company under description two fails to access capital markets when needed, it goes bankrupt. However, there are other situations where access to capital markets is important, the two described here are just the most critical for determining the longevity of the business.

25

Screening

25.1 Traditional Screens

Screening is the act of systematically narrowing the universe of companies an investor is considering. When he or she performs a screen, the investor restricts the universe of companies based on some criteria, such as valuation, market cap, industry, country, or price momentum. For example, just by considering only securities in the United States, the investor is screening. Some common screens:

- **Cash Flow/Earnings Based Value** - this screen aims to identify securities that are "cheap" relative to their cash flow or earnings. Some metrics used in this type of screen are: P/E, P/LFCF, EV/UFCF, EV/EBIT, and EV/EBITDA. There are many ways to define "cheap". Cheap could mean: the company is trading near its 52-week low, a lower metric relative to industry peers, a lower metric relative to the market as a whole, a lower metric relative to the company's own history, or just a numerically low metric.

- **Asset Based Value** - this screen aims to identify securities that are "cheap" relative to their earning assets less liabilities. The main metric used in this type of screen is P/(Book Value) or P/B. The same conversation on "cheapness" from the preceding bullet point applies to asset based value.

- **Momentum** - this screen aims to identify securities that are experiencing near-term upswings in price or trading volume. Some metrics used in this type of screen are: recent volume

relative to history and magnitude and frequency of recent
price changes relative to history.

- **Size** - this screen aims to identify securities of a specific size.
  There are several classifications for the size of a company
  based on its market cap. These are: nano-cap (under $50M),
  micro-cap ($50M-$300M), small-cap ($300M-$2B), mid-cap
  ($2B-$10B), large-cap ($10B-$200B), and mega-cap (over $200B).
  Beyond these classifications, another common metric for a
  company's size: its annual sales.

- **Geography** - this screen aims to identify securities based on
  geography. Common geographic screens are: United States
  exclusively; developed markets (includes the U.S., Canada,
  Western Europe, Australia, New Zealand, and others), and
  emerging markets (includes most of Asia, Africa, Eastern Europe, and South America).

- **Industry** - this screen aims to identify securities based on
  a specific industry. This screen is helpful for allowing the
  investor to narrow in on his or her "circle of competency", the
  business models and industries the investor knows something
  about.

- **Profitability** - this screen aims to identify securities based
  on a level of profitability. Common metrics for this screen are
  FCF margin, EBITDA margin, EBIT margin, and net income
  margin. Some investors require at least cash flow break even
  (FCF margin $>0\%$) in the companies they assess.

- **Returns** - this screen aims to identify securities based on a
  level of returns. Common metrics for this screen are ROIC,
  ROE, and ROA. These metrics are used by investors as a
  quick proxy for determining whether a business is "good."

- **Growth** - this screen aims to identify securities based on
  growth. Common metrics for this screen are: sales growth,
  FCF growth, EBITDA growth, EBIT growth, and net income
  growth. Common time frames to analyze growth over are:
  quarter over quarter (QoQ), year over year (YoY), 1-year,
  3-year, and 5-year.

- **Insider Activity** - this screen aims to identify securities
  based on the buying and selling activity of the management

team and board of directors of a company. Since the management team and the board of directors can buy and sell stock just like anyone else, it is considered a positive sign when these "insiders" are buying up stock in the market. Conversely, it is considered a negative sign when these "insiders" are selling stock in the market. The magnitude and number of people involved in insider buying and selling is important to analyze here. However, there are a lot of reasons for insiders to sell small portions of company stock, such as for tax purposes, so do not over analyze selling activity. But, there is really only one main reason an insider would buy stock.

- **News Activity** - this screen aims to identify securities based on the recent news or announcements of the company. This might include: articles, earnings releases, and press conferences.

- **Social Media Activity** - this screen aims to identify securities based on the social media activity of the company. A common metric for this screen is the momentum of social media mentions.

- **Combination** - this screen aims to identify securities based on two or more of the preceding screening strategies. Most investors use a combination screen, if they screen.

25.2 The Value of Screening

Screening is a controversial topic in many investing communities. Some believe it is a shortcut for hard-work. Others believe screening is a necessary evil to narrow down an insurmountable number of securities. Obviously, there is nothing *great* about leaving stones unturned. Still, it is impractical to perform deep due-diligence on every security.

For this reason, depending on the time constraints of the investor, screening is most likely necessary. However, as with all things in investing, heuristic-like simplifications, such as screening, should be taken with a grain-of-salt. The investor must be aware that his or her screens could be hiding gems.

In a universe of investors that mostly screens through the methods described in the preceding section, an investor could in theory add value by developing an unconventional proprietary screen-

ing and idea-sourcing process. The author will leave it to the reader
to contemplate what that could be.

Part VI

Value Investing

26

Value, Price, and Margin of Safety

"Confronted with a challenge to distill the secret of sound investment into three words, we venture the motto, margin of safety."

– Ben Graham

"All intelligent investing is value investing – acquiring more than you are paying for. You must value the business in order to value the stock."

– Charlie Munger

"The stock market is filled with individuals who know the price of everything, but the value of nothing."

– Phil Fisher

The core objective of value investing is to identify and invest in securities that are purchasable at a price below their intrinsic value. Price is the current market price of the financial instrument. Intrinsic value is a reasonable, rationale assessment of the actual worth of a security. The pragmatism of investing in a security that is trading at a discount to its intrinsic value is evident.

Would an investor ever willingly pay more to acquire a security than it is worth? Do investors ever completely ignore the concept of value? "Value agnostic" behavior actually dominates the capital markets, and is not consistent with the title of an investor. "Speculator" is a much more suitable title for a value agnostic participant in the securities markets.

The formal definition of a speculator is "a person who forms a theory or conjecture about a subject without firm evidence." This is the precise behavior consistent with a value agnostic capital market participant. Astute investing places the price paid in relation to intrinsic value at the forefront of the investing decision. Speculation places a lesser importance on price versus value, or, in many cases, ignores it completely. Therefore, speculators subscribe to the "greater-fool theory" – the notion that some "greater-fool" will come along and take away their already overpriced security at a higher price. While an optimistic notion, the greater-fool theory is no rational philosophical basis through which to grow or preserve the hard-earned capital of an individual, family, or client.

To identify as a value investor is to pursue bargain-priced securities. However, many individuals, finding the notion of value investing attractive and intuitive, adorn the title of value investor while ignoring the discipline and hard work requisite to successful value investing. As with all things, the practice of value investing is much easier said than done. Just as quickly as one individual legitimately subscribes to a value investing philosophy, one hundred more self-deceiving "value investors" subscribe to the latest Wall Street concoction, the latest momentum trend, or the latest promise of quick profits.

To understand where one lies on the speculator versus investor spectrum, he or she need look no further than an honest self-examination of ones own beliefs and historical decisions. Was price in relationship to value at the forefront of historical investing decisions? When considering future investment decisions, is the price/value relationship the chief concern? Answering these simple questions is not easy, though. As discussed previously, many a speculator happily wears the hat of investor while employing the thought process of a speculator.

If price versus value is at the forefront of the investing thought process, then an investor must be comfortable passing on an investment where value or its relationship with price is unclear. To not do so reverts back into the realm of speculation.

In previous chapters, we explored the concept of risk. Mitigating risk, or possible outcomes that would result in a permanent loss of capital, is the primary rationale for focusing on the price versus value relationship. A security that trades below its intrinsic value has some level of safety. This is called a *margin of safety*. The same security, trading further below its intrinsic value, has a greater *margin of safety*. There is a reason value investors call this concept a *margin of safety* and not *margin of potential return*. The reason is simple: value investors are focused on mitigating risk first. Value investors understand that the successful implementation of risk-averse investing will result in better risk-adjusted returns. While returns are important and essential to investing, they are secondary to risk-aversion as a rationale for demanding a margin of safety. Ensuring a healthy margin of safety is always the best way to mitigate risk. The value investor must be confident that, if risk is mitigated and silly mistakes avoided, the returns will come.

Another important take away from the margin of safety principle: as prices drop, the margin of safety inevitably widens. For this reason, the investor's conviction and desire to own a security should actually *increase* as the security price declines. This reasoning, though logically sound, is hard to implement, since many behavioral biases make it difficult to be a buyer when others are sellers.

A lot of attention has been given to the concept of intrinsic value. But how can one assess intrinsic value? Again, the answer is simple, but not easy. An investor can assess intrinsic value through a deep fundamental analysis of a company's operations. Until a business has been understood and the durability of any competitive advantages assessed, the investor can never hope to successfully ascribe a value to the business's worth. In a preceding section, we discussed the various technical tools and techniques that enable investors to value a business. With this in mind, it is essential to remind oneself that valuation is an art, not a science. Each number in a valuation model must be carefully decided to best reflect the economic reality and prospects of a business. Even then, the investors assessment or the number itself could prove horribly inaccurate, in fact, this is often the case. This is why demanding a margin of safety is so important. Without one, an investor leaves no wiggle room for any possible error in his or her assessment of the economic prospects of a business. Part of investing is admitting that one can and will be wrong. A margin of safety is the best hedge against the possibility of inaccurate judgment.

27

Price Movements and Market Efficiency

"When the price of a stock can be influenced by a 'herd' on Wall Street with prices set at the margin by the most emotional person, or the greediest person, or the most depressed person, it is hard to argue that the market always price rationally. In fact, market prices are frequently nonsensical."

– Warren Buffett

"The individual investor should act consistently as an investor and not as a speculator."

– Ben Graham

"Ships will sail around the world but the Flat Earth Society will flourish. There will continue to be wide discrepancies between price and value in the market place."

– Warren Buffett

An investor must inevitably interface with the capital markets to buy and sell securities. For this reason, it is essential the investor has a solid mental framework for thinking about market price fluctuations and their importance.

Many investors find it tempting to analyze security price movements on a daily basis. Not only do many people observe daily security movements, we actually have a strong tendency to try and provide rationales for or develop an understanding of daily price movements. This behavior makes the assumptions that 1) daily price movements can be understood and 2) understanding daily price movements is beneficial to the investing thought process. Value investors believe that point one is futile, which makes point two moot.

In fact, most value investors advocate completely detaching oneself from the daily market movement frenzy by not watching daily security price movements at all. An investor should be comfortable even if he or she could not see a price quote on the security for several months or years. This actually serves as a great measure of conviction. Beyond that, a focus on short-term price fluctuations actually encourages a number of detrimental behaviors we will elaborate on in later chapters.

An important, but obvious, realization about daily stock price movements is that they *must occur*. This decreases the significance of their occurrence. Furthermore, the capital markets are so complex and aggregate so many disjoint opinions and viewpoints on a security, that the investor cannot possibly hope to understand the true rationale for a security's daily price movement. There could be more than a thousand reasons why a stock price moves the way it does on a given day. Therefore, one of the greatest services an aspiring investor can do to his or her investing process is to detac from daily price movements. Not only does this liberate time to focus on more important, long-term questions, but it also reduces the impact of negative behavioral biases associated with frequently interfacing with the market.

All that being said, it is tempting to believe the financial news services can distill a company's 2% price move from yesterday into a single explanatory sentence. Enough people have been captivated and sold on this fallacious concept throughout history to enable short-term financial news services to outlast the test of time. But, this over-simplification of market forces drastically reduces the complexity of the capital markets, especially in the short-term.

A great framework for thinking about daily price movements is a concept coined by Ben Graham, called Mr. Market. Mr. Market is a moody fellow who will offer to buy and sell every security on a daily basis. His moods are not rooted in rationality. His moods are purely rooted in the whims of the day. Every day, Mr. Market comes and offers to buy a security from you for a given price. This day, he offers a slight premium to the preceding day. The next day, he offers a slight discount. The investor must always remember that the prices offered by Mr. Market are determined by his moods, which are inherently unpredictable. With such a man taking the other end of every trade, is there any value to trying to understand and analyze short-term price movements? Value investors contend that there is not.

So, where do price movements come into play, since obviously they matter to a successful investing process? The negligible importance of short-term price movements has already been established. Therefore, all that is left is a focus on long-term price movements.

So if Mr. Market determines short-term price movements, what or who determines long-term price movements? The answer is the price value relationship. Ultimately, in the long run, a business's market price will come to reflect the intrinsic value associated with the stability and realistic potential growth of that business's cash flow stream.

Many academic communities believe in a concept called efficient market theory (EMT). Under this theory, markets never present value opportunities. In the EMT, the current market price of a security aggregates all currently knowable information about a security, and therefore reflects its intrinsic value. The EMT is valuable to understand, even for a value investor, because under it the markets inevitably have some level of efficiency. In reality, the markets are quite efficient, which is one of the many aspects of investing that makes it difficult. However, a central tenet of value investing is that distortions between price and value can and will occur. These opportunities, while rare and difficult to find because of market efficiency, are a low-risk and rational way to procure a return from the capital markets.

While markets are usually efficient, they do exhibit inefficiency. And there are areas of the capital markets that are more inefficient than others. To name a few specific examples: smaller market cap stocks, complex situations (such as distressed debt), spin-offs, and index additions/removals often have a higher degree of inefficiency because of 1) the level of sophistication of the investor base, 2) the size of the investor base, or 3) the presence of motivated sellers.

28

Good Businesses

"Your goal as an investor should simply be to purchase, at a rational price, a part interest in an easily-understandable business whose earnings are virtually certain to be materially higher five, ten, and twenty years from now."

– Warren Buffett

"The number one idea is to view a stock as an ownership of the business and to judge the staying quality of the business in terms of its competitive advantage."

– Charlie Munger

"The key to investing is not assessing how much an industry is going to affect society, or how much it will grow, but rather determining the competitive advantage of any given company and, above all, the durability of that advantage."

– Warren Bufett

As we discuss more tenets of value investing, it is essential the reader not consider any one tenet in isolation. The "good businesses" concept must be considered in tandem with "Long-termism," the minimal importance of short-term price movements, the price value relationship, and the other tenets discussed in this part of the book.

A core belief of value investing is that great businesses are better than mediocre businesses. In the choice between a great business at a fair price and a fair business at a great price, a great business at a fair price is superior. When investing in stocks in particular, the investor must never forget they are buying partial ownership of an underlying business. Purchasing a great business will result in a great return for long-term stock investors. Purchasing a mediocre business will result in a mediocre return for stock investors.

Think about purchasing a standard household appliance. Say a coffee machine. Suppose coffee machine A costs $50 and produces great coffee for 5 years. Suppose coffee machine B costs $100 and produces great coffee for 15 years. In this scenario, the purchase of coffee machine B is clearly superior. If a consumer purchases coffee machine A, he/she must eventually purchase three different coffee machines the price of $50 over fifteen years to meet the value.

But what determines the value of an asset? As observed in this example, the durability of a long-term competitive advantage is often more important than the initial price paid.

What is taken for granted in the preceding analogy? We assumed the durability of the various coffee machines was completely knowable. In reality, especially when investing in assets such as stocks or bonds, assessing the durability or presence of a businesses competitive advantage is much more difficult. However, that does not mean the pursuit of doing so is futile. In fact, by referring to the famous quotes at the beginning of this chapter, the reader can discern that assessing competitive advantage and its durability is at the forefront of a sound value investing process.

That's all well and good. But why is it important to assess the presence and durability of a business's competitive advantage? The reason is simple – great businesses have durable competitive advantages. Why does a great business necessarily have to have a durable competitive advantage? Again, the reason is simple – both the stability and growth the long-term cash flow stream of a business are largely determined by the presence and durability of a competitive advantage. As a reminder, the chief determinant of the long-term value of a business is the stability and realized growth of its cash flow stream. Therefore, assessing competitive advantage is essential to assessing the quality of a business and its stock.

In the choice between great management and great business economics, great business economics is superior. Management is often temporal and subject to human mistakes. Business economics are the defining attributes of a business and the chief determinants of long-term cash flow. Unlike management, business economics are intrinsic to the business model and the competitive dynamics of the business and its industry. A great management team cannot transform a business with poor economics into a business with great economics. In this scenario, a great management team could only create a relatively competitive business within its industry that still has poor economics.

What if one finds a bad to mediocre business at a great price? Multiple perspectives on this exist within the value investing community. It is true that all assets have a price at which they are attractive investments. In certain areas of the financial markets, such as high-yield or distressed debt, this is often the case. The debt is high-yield or distressed for a reason – the soundness of the business is questioned by the markets. This being said, for an astute assessor of price versus value, there is opportunity to be had if the margin of safety is great enough. This is the premise of certain investors, notably, Howard Marks, who focuses on distressed debt scenarios. Other investors, such as Warren Buffett, focus their attention on trying to identify great businesses at a fair to great price. In fact, Buffett calls investing in bad to mediocre businesses at an attractive price "cigar-butt investing." He believes that investing in a mediocre business at an attractive price is analogous to identifying a half-lit cigar-butt on the ground and extracting one last puff before it dies out.

In the authors opinion, the importance of the quality of the business versus price depends on the type of security. For high-yield or distressed debt, a "cigar-butt" approach makes more sense, because the security itself is temporal and somewhat binary in nature (the interest and principal payments will either be paid or not). Beyond that, distressed debt investing can also have a significant "event-driven" or catalyst component, such as emergence from or settlement of a bankruptcy, that makes extracting that last puff a little more feasible. The ideal scenario in stock investing is to hold the stock of a great business indefinitely, as long as it stays great. Therefore, in the case of stocks, especially those without a specific catalyst, price has relatively less importance than the quality of the business in determining the long-term returns. From this analysis, we can see that the differences between the financial instruments themselves actually warrant a slightly different philosophical perspective. This is reflected in the actual philosophy employed by successful value investors of varying financial instrument focuses. This introduces an important concept: most great value investors develop their own specific flavor of value investing. The tenets discussed in this part of the book are just the roots and bedrock principles.

29

Long-termism

"If you aren't willing to own a stock for ten years, don't even think about owning it for ten minutes."

— Warren Buffett

"We don't get paid for activity, just for being right. As to how long we'll wait, we'll wait indefinitely."

— Warren Buffett

"In the short run, the market is a voting machine, but in the long run, it is a weighing machine."

— Ben Graham

It is regularly said that a long-term perspective is the single greatest competitive advantage that an investor can have in his or her intellectual arsenal. Why is this the case? For a competitive advantage to be present, the investor must operate, perceive, or think differently or superiorly than other investors. Is there anything unique about a long-term perspective? The answer is overwhelmingly yes.

Why are most investors short-term? Among many possible explanations, three are discussed here: economic, societal, and behavioral. First, investors have strong economic incentives to utilize a short-term perspective. Frankly, most, if not all, investors want to make money. However, most investors want to make money without having to bet on their ability to generate returns. Based on the fee structure of a hedge fund or mutual fund, what is the best way to make money without depending too much on one's returns or carried interest? By maintaining and growing AUM. What is the easiest way to maintain and grow AUM? By having capital agreement terms that limited partners like. What do limited partners often like? Liquidity: the ability to withdraw funds when performance is poor; and investment restrictions, the ability to restrict the asset classes that the fund invests in. What does this mean for capital agreement terms? Limited partners often desire a short lock-up period and investment restrictions. So by agreeing to a short lock-up period and restricting their investment universe, general partners can quickly grow AUM.

But that's only part of the issue. Remember that general partners both want to grow *and* maintain AUM. What is the best way to maintain AUM? By generating good returns within the time horizon of the lock-up period. The issue here, however, is that most general partners agree to a short-term lock-up period to grow AUM. Therefore, many general partners must focus on generating short-term returns or face capital withdrawals at the end of the lockup period. It becomes easier to see the difficulties in simultaneously growing and maintaining AUM when one considers the ability of the fund to generate even short-term returns is inhibited by the above-mentioned investment restrictions the general partners agreed on.

Value investors focus on returns and carried interest, not management fees. The best way to develop a returns oriented, long-term perspective is to patiently wait for limited partners who will provide long-term, unconstrained capital. A value investor strives to realize intrinsic value by pursuing the best risk/reward opportunities over a long time horizon. Remember: while short-term price fluctuations can deviate significantly from intrinsic value, in the long run, the market price will converge to meet intrinsic value. Sadly, the industry standard economic incentives and practices do not support this objective. Therefore, much of the investor community focuses on short-term results. Short-term results are much more difficult to successfully obtain because they depend on successfully timing the market, a tactic empirical research has shown to be very difficult, if not impossible. A long-term investor, however, need not time a thing. His or her ideal holding period of a great business is indefinite.

Several societal factors also influence the short-term nature of investors. Foremost that we live in a world centered on instant gratification. In fact, many of the "great" innovations of the past century pander to our desire for immediate satisfaction: fast food, one-click ordering, all of social media and its "liking" system, expedited delivery, text messaging, the list goes on. Without a doubt, there is utility to quick feedback and immediate gratification. However, it is naive to believe that a modern social structure, focused on short-term results and feedback, has not in some way influence the psychology and time horizon expectations of people and investors. When it comes to his or her investments, a value investor must be satisfied with delaying gratification, as demanded by a long-term horizon. Volatility complicates the equation even more. Markets rise and fall on a daily basis. So not only must the value investor delay gratification, he or she must do so in the face of down periods, trust in delayed end results.

The last factor heavily influencing the short-term disposition of investors is human nature itself. For most of our history, humans have *had* to focus on the short-term to survive. Up until around the 19th century, securing one's next meal was the chief subject of an individuals attention. For the first time in history, a portion of the modern, developed world has the incredible luxury of being capable of thinking with a long-term perspective. This does not mean it is easy to do so – our biological and evolutionary origins have conditioned us to think short. While it would be ideal if humans were able to completely overcome several millennium of behavioral development in just a century or two, it just is not scientifically feasible.

So unpacking the problem shows there are a number of factors adding to the proliferation of short-term thinking. As with anything, when all of the competition is doing one thing (short-term thinking), a competitive advantage can be developed by doing something else (long-term thinking). In this day and age, perhaps more than ever, it may pay to apply a long-term perspective to investments.

30

Contrarianism

"Be fearful when others are greedy, and greedy when others are fearful."

– Warren Buffett

"Value investing is at its core the marriage of a contrarian streak and a calculator."

– Seth Klarman

"First-level thinking says, 'I think the company's earnings will fall; sell.' Second-level thinking says, 'I think the company's earnings will fall less than people expect, and the pleasant surprise will lift the stock; buy.'"

– Howard Marks

In the dictionary, a contrarian is "a person who rejects popular opinion." A contrarian thinks differently than the crowd, and not necessarily for the sake of thinking differently, but because it helps produce above-average results. In a world where everyone drives in the right-hand lane, thinking differently and driving in the left-hand lane presents a huge opportunity.

Investing is *really* hard. If you do not appreciate this yet, then you have not been investing long enough. One of the most challenging components of investing stems from the complexity of current market price. The current market price for a security aggregates *all* the varying viewpoints and philosophies into one figure. This includes: day-traders, long-term value investors, long-term growth investors, short-term investors focused on earnings, technical traders, those who have no philosophy at all, and more.

In a preceding chapter, we discussed the occasional inefficiency of markets. While this is true, do not let this fact downplay
the normal efficiency of the markets. Generally the aggregated
viewpoint on a security is pretty accurate. So to really became
an advanced investor, one must look beyond the obvious, tier-one
thinking about a business or market. Why? Well, if something is
obvious to you, it is probably *obvious to everybody*, and *fully priced
into the current market price*. That sentence right there, well it is
one of the most important realizations to make about investing and
the markets.

Here is an example. Suppose the investor thinks a business has both strong and likely growth prospects – so long-term
cash flow will grow. Therefore, the investor thinks the stock is
a buy. However, the investor must stop and ask – who does *not*
already know that the business will have both strong and likely
growth prospects? If the growth is obvious, then other investors
will have already bid-up the price of the security in anticipation of
the growth, meaning the investment is not nearly as attractive as
it might seem based on a cursory thought. Instead, the investor
might think the growth is so obvious that the price is way bid-up.
Instead of buying, he/she sells on the premise that the realized
growth will be less than that priced into the security.

So how can an investor hope to make great profits if markets are this efficient? The answer is to think deeply, hard, and
differently. The main avenue to great profits as a value investor
is actually anticipating what *will* become obvious to investors *before* it is obvious to most investors. Put differently, the goal of the
value investor is to believe something no else yet believes. And to
be correct about the belief for successful value investing requires
being both contrarian and right. This can be *really hard* to do in
practice. To accomplish this, the investor must constantly ask the
question, "who doesn't already know this?" If a belief or perspective on a security is obvious, then it is almost assuredly priced in
already. We call this a value trap: a security that seems like a
value play, but is actually correctly priced or overpriced.

Value investors strive to identify situations where the economic or business reality/prospects materially differ from the markets perception. Or they aim to find securities that are irrationally
out-of-favor by the market.

To do this start looking at places in the market where securities *are* out-of-favor, then try to assess the rationality of the
markets perception. However, remember, the market is pretty right

most of the time, so going against the grain requires a deep level of conviction and fundamental research.

Where can the investor find out-of-favor securities? There are many answers. Securities currently at new 52-week lows. Companies that recently had an earnings miss. Companies trading at a discount to comparable companies. Spin-offs. Companies in or near restructuring processes. And industry laggards are all good places to identify out-of-favor securities.

Since value investors often like to look at out-of-favor securities, they regularly research stocks with low P/E ratios. The opposite of value investing is growth investing which looks at in-flavor securities. This means that growth investors regularly research stocks with high P/E ratios. Therefore, one of the most common "value" stock screens incorporates a low P/E ratio or low P/LFCF ratio. Stocks with low P/E ratios are often called value stocks. Stocks with high P/E ratios are often called growth stocks.

31

Adaptability

"Doubt is not a pleasant condition, but certainty is absurd."

– Voltaire

"It would be foolish, in forming our expectations, to attach great weight to matters which are very uncertain."
– John Maynard Keynes

"There is nothing wrong with changing a plan when the situation has changed."

– Seneca

As discussed previously, thinking and investing differently than the herd is a core concept of value investing. Value investors must apply skepticism to everything they encounter – including their own beliefs. A value investor must constantly ask the following questions. Why do I think this is the case? Have the facts materially changed enough to warrant a change in my perception? Who is the fool in this situation?

An amoeba is a unicellular organism that has no definite shape or dimension. An amoeba is physically fungible. A value investor must be an *intellectual* amoeba. A value investor must be as intellectually adaptable as an amoeba is physically maleable. There are a number of behavioral biases that make it difficult to change one's mind once it is made up. The value investor must strive to overcome these.

A value investor, by virtue of contrarianism, regularly bets against the crowd. However, this bet is not made blindly – it is based on a deep, rational assessment of the business's underlying facts and fundamentals. However, suppose the facts change as time passes. In this scenario, the investor may be tempted to hold on to previously held beliefs. This could prove to be a very costly intellectual mistake in the long run. For this reason, the value investor must adapt his or her perceptions to new information and update any investment thesis' accordingly.

32

Cycles

"The stock market is the story of cycles and of the human behavior that is responsible for overreactions in both directions."

– Seth Klarman

"But values aren't fixed; they move in response to changes in the economic environment. Thus, cyclical considerations influence an asset's current value. Value depends on earnings, for example, and earnings are shaped by the economic cycle and the price being charged for liquidity."

– Howard Marks

"The four most dangerous words in investing are: 'this time it's different.'"

– Sir John Templeton

Cycles are an inevitable part of investing. They are the ebb and flow of economic growth, productivity, and asset valuations. History has shown that almost all asset classes and economies prove cyclical. There are many theories regarding what causes cycles. The author believes the most plausible explanation is rooted in the behavior of investors. As discussed previously, investors are generally short-term. This applies both to forward thinking and to hindsight observation. Investors regularly forget the pain and mistakes of previous cycles, and begin to invest in dangerous, unsustainable ways. This creates a speculative "bubble" in which asset prices are not justified by asset values. Allured by quick profits, investors forget the lessons of the past and relax risk standards to partake in the latest investment phenomena.

A bubble might be specific to an entire market, such as the stock market as a whole, or just to a niche asset class. There are six main characteristics of cycles/bubbles: 1) They begin with actual investable opportunities – a truly innovative set of products, value-adding services, or underpriced financial assets. 2) In the euphoria of the economic and financial gain associated with the real, investable opportunity, investors and risk-takers begin to speculate and leverage their gains. Credit proliferates and the cost of liquidity decreases. 3) Due to the euphoria and leveraged investing, the price of investing in the original investable opportunity begins to exceed its value. This creates a valuation "bubble." 4) There is some tipping point – an earnings miss, a regulation change, a liquidity crisis – that causes investors to wake up and realize they made leveraged bets on overpriced assets, 5) The market becomes disgusted with the asset class or investable opportunity, valuations plummet, the cost of associated liquidity increases. 6) The process repeats itself.

It is common to read the preceding criteria regarding cycles/bubbles and begin to identify potential bubbles all over the place. The hardest and most complex part about bubbles: that step four is very difficult to predict. A common term for trying to predict when the step will occur is called "timing the market". Value investors believe that precisely timing the market is a largely futile endeavor, since history has shown this to be the case.

So if cycles/bubbles are inevitable, and timing the market is futile, what is the investor to do? First, an investor should try to have an understanding of historic bubbles, booms, busts, and crashes. This gives valuable insight into the nature/signs of investable opportunities, euphoria, and revulsion. Armed with an understanding of history, the investor is better equipped to not repeat the mistakes of the past. Second, precisely timing the market's revulsion is futile, but understanding where one is in the cycle, through pragmatic analysis and a knowledge of history, is not. By simply taking an honest look around, the astute investor can make more informed investment decisions through observing and avoiding the risky behavior seen in other investors.

What are some risky investor behaviors or indications of euphoria that can serve as a compass for navigating the current position in the cycle? There are dozens of answers to this question. But some specific signposts are:

- Risk-aversion is replaced by return-focused investing

- Credit and lending standards begin to relax – covenants become less restrictive, comparable yields decrease, getting access to syndicates deals becomes more competitive

- Valuations reach high levels relative to history with no justifiable reason

- Everyone is talking about the asset class or investable opportunity in question

- Your family members, not generally interested in investing, begin asking you questions about the asset class or investable opportunity in question

- The news headlines are full of information on the asset class or investable opportunity in question

- Lunch and dinner conversation with friends and colleagues is dominated by a discussion of the investable opportunity in question

An awareness, or lack thereof, of cycles causes some of the greatest opportunities for investor profit or loss. During a euphoric period, the investor must be diligent and in-control. Unrestrained investors will likely experience significant gains during this time. However, the losses associated with being heavily invested during the crash of a bubble can be detrimental to a portfolio, a reputation, and a career. Furthermore, an investor who is heavily invested during a euphoric period will also miss out on the opportunity to heavily invest following the crash. Remember, having cash to invest while everyone else in the world is selling represents one of the greatest investment opportunities for a value investor! Since price is the single most important factor in determining investment results, value investors are ecstatic during a crash, assuming they were prudent enough to hold cash in preparation for the fire-sale level prices.

33

Defensive Investing

"Rule #1: never lose money; Rule #2: never forget rule #1."

— Warren Buffett

"It is remarkable how much long-term advantage people like us have gotten by trying to be consistently not stupid, instead of trying to be very intelligent."

— Charlie Munger

"Value investing is risk aversion."

— Seth Klarman

At this point in the book, we have discussed risk-aversion, margin of safety, and other loss inhibiting concepts. These concepts are related to one core tenet of value investing: defensive investing.

Remember that the goal of the value investor is to minimize losses, not to maximize gains. In conversations with most investors, one will likely notice the top priority is making money quickly. The value investor thinks with the exact opposite mindset – not losing money, slowly.

Value investing is not sexy. There is nothing sexy about a patient, disciplined, risk-averse approach. Value investing is not a get rich quick scheme. However, as with most things in life, the "not sexy" approach is often most effective. Consider the areas of weight-loss/dieting, making good grades, starting a business, etc., the time-proven, optimal strategy to success in these areas is a patient, disciplined, risk-averse approach of consistently hitting singles rather than hoping for home-runs. The interesting thing is, most people know this. Most people know and believe in the long-term, patient, disciplined strategies of weight-loss, making good grades, or starting a business, they just choose not to implement them in their own lives. Let it be said that – this is a completely fine choice; and many people do not have the luxury to decide these things. However, for those pursuing long-term investment success, it is rational to pursue a time-proven, patient, disciplined, risk-averse strategy.

A value investor prefers a guaranteed, 10% return over a high-risk, 100% return. This describes the defensive investor mind-set. This is a rare approach. Most investors like the idea of doubling their money so much that they do not consider the pain of losing half their money during the investment decision. As with all things, when most people approach something one way, there is a competitive advantage in approaching it differently. Therefore, a defensive, risk-averse mindset is another competitive advantage in the value investors intellectual toolkit.

How can a value investor practically implement a defensive investing philosophy? First, the investor can demand a healthy margin of safety in his or her investments. Second, the investor can actively try to disprove their own thesis (this is called devil's advocacy) by constantly looking for dis-confirming evidence and asking – what can go wrong with this thesis as it stands? What assumptions are we making here that could go very differently in reality? What are we missing? What risks have we not considered? In credit investing, these questions are core to the investment process. In equity investing, investors are often so focused on upside that they fail to appropriately consider risk.

Defensive investing is important, as a single, careless, and aggressive mistake can undo an entire career of solid returns.

34

Simplicity

"Our job is to find a few intelligent things to do, not to keep up with every damn thing in the world."
 — Charlie Munger

"Keep things simple and don't swing for the fences. When promised quick profits, respond with a quick 'no'."
 — Warren Buffett

"Everything should be made as simple as possible, but not simpler."
 — Albert Einstein

It is easy to get overwhelmed by the world of investing and finance. Talk about a lot of information to process. However, more is not necessarily better. The simple solution is often best. Furthermore, the majority of useful information is procured in the initial stages of research. This is called the 80-20 information principle, by which 80% of useful information is acquired in the first 20% of time spent researching. Deep research is important, but deep research for the sake of deep research is not beneficial to arriving at great investment decisions.

It is hard to believe that investing is as simple as buying great businesses at a reasonable price and holding them for a long time. This solution appears too simple for our society and our minds, both of which are accustomed to complexity. By requiring complexity, many investors complicate their investment processes and distract their operations from the core questions that will determine whether the investment will be great. At the end of the day, if a business can consistently sell a widget at scale for more than it costs for a long time, the earnings of the business will march upwards and the stock of the business with it. Research that does not aim to assess whether a widget can be consistently sold for more than it costs at scale over a long time period is futile.

Why make investing more complicated than it needs to be? There is nothing new about valuing simplicity in problem solving. In the 14th century, an English theologian named William of Ockham created a problem-solving principle called Occam's razor. The principle states that among competing theories, the theory with the fewest assumptions is optimal, or, when there are two competing theories that make identical predictions about the future, the simpler one is better. Occam's razor: the simple solution is usually better.

The more assumptions an investor has to make, the more likely his or her thought process will be wrong in the long-term. Therefore, an investor should strive to make only *necessary* and prudent assumptions, while eliminating unnecessary research or theories. An investor need not keep track of every financial market or news stream in the world, he or she must simply identify a handful of great businesses and hold onto them over the long-term with a vice-grip.

35

Behavioral Biases

"We don't have to be smarter than the rest. We have to be more disciplined than the rest."
— Warren Buffett

"The hard part is discipline, patience, and judgment. Investors need discipline to avoid the many unattractive pitches that are thrown, patience to wait for the right pitch, and judgment to know when it is time to swing."
— Seth Klarman

"Further, security prices are greatly affected by investor behavior; thus we can be aided in investing safely by understanding where we stand in terms of the market cycle. What's going on in terms of investor psychology, and how does it tell us to act in the short run? We want to buy when prices seem attractive. But if investors are giddy and optimism is rampant, we have to consider whether a better buying opportunity might come along later."
— Howard Marks

There are dozens of books on the concepts covered in this chapter alone. In classic economic theory, humans are assumed to be completely rational actors devoid of emotion. A simple observation of society demonstrates this is not the case. Behavioral finance is the field that seeks to combine behavioral and cognitive theories with investing, economics, and finance to help understand the irrationality of human investment decisions. Behavioral finance is *incredibly* important. It is the chief reason people have difficulty successfully implementing a value investing philosophy. In this section, several behavioral biases are listed/discussed that directly affect investment decisions and thought processes. The goal of the disciplined, self-controlled investor is to overcome these biases and focus purely on the objective merits of an investment decision:

- **Recency Bias** – the tendency to focus only on recent history and recent past to forecast and predict future outcomes.

- **Hindsight Bias** – the tendency to explain-away phenomenon after they occur. This bias is the tendency, following the occurrence of an event, to describe and view the event as predictable.

- **Endowment Effect** – the tendency to mentally increase the perceived value and worth of assets and other belongings after they have been purchased. This bias results in the tendency to become attached to things we purchase or invest in.

- **Mental Accounting** – the tendency to separate money into various accounts based on several subjective criteria.

- **Overconfidence** – the tendency to exaggerate ones own abilities and knowledge.

- **Overreaction Bias** – the tendency to overreact and drastically change ones thinking or behavior when things go poorly.

- **Authority Bias** – the tendency to blindly listen to "authoritative" figures on various topics, such as investing talking heads on the financial news networks.

- **Scarcity Bias** – the tendency to ascribe more value to things that are scarce or rare.

- **Liking Bias** – the tendency to ascribe more value to things or people that we personally like.

- **Loss Aversion** – the tendency to avoid taking any risk at all, out of fear of things going poorly. Eventually, an investor must stomach the chance of loss.

- **Confirmation Bias** – the tendency to pursue and focus on information that confirms our beliefs or predispositions on a given topic.

- **Social Conformism** – the tendency to conform with the "herd" or consensus viewpoint. Few careers are sabotaged by social conformism, but no great careers are defined by doing what the rest of the herd does.

- **Anchoring** – the tendency to mentally attach to the first or earliest concepts introduced on a given topic. With sell-side analyst reports that give a target price for a stock, it is easy to anchor on the target price that they present. It is also easy to anchor on the current market price of a security as the primary determinant of value. Anchoring makes it difficult to separate price from value.

- **Optimism Bias** – the tendency to assume everything will go well.

- **Short-termism** – the tendency to focus on short-term events and instant gratification.

- **Planning Fallacy** – the reality that we have a difficult time predicting our own future behavior and the amount of time it will take us to do things.

- **Self-Attribution Bias** – the tendency to credit ones own abilities, talents, thoughts, decisions, and control when things go well.

- **Analysis Paralysis** – the tendency to become overwhelmed by the amount of information or possible complexity in an investment decision. The result of this overload is the inability to reach a confident decision.

- **Narrative Bias** – the tendency of humans to create and love stories, whether their own or others. Humans latch onto "story stocks", explain away phenomena *after* they occur, and often focus on the best story tellers in social/professional settings.

- **Abstraction Bias** – the difficulty of extrapolating smaller, building-block concepts into bigger ideas.

- **Greed and Fear Bias** – the tendency of ones emotions to move like a pendulum between two opposing forces, greed and fear, depending on the market context and dynamics.

- **Ignorance to Biases** – the belief/assumption that no behavioral biases apply to oneself. This is the most destructive behavioral bias, since an individual who struggles with this bias will struggle with them all. To be a great investor, one must first admit and *believe* that they are their own worst enemy. Not many people have the humility or self-awareness to do so. All great investors understand and work to control the biases described in this chapter.

36

Hard Work and Doing Due Diligence

"An investment operation is one which, upon thorough analysis, promises safety of principal and a satisfactory return. Operations not meeting these requirements are speculative."

– Ben Graham

"It is a capital mistake to theorise before one has data. Insensibly one begins to twist facts to suit theories, instead of theories to suit the facts."

– Sherlock Holmes

"Plough deep, while sluggards sleep, and you shall have corn to sell and keep. Work while it is called today, for you know not how much you may be hindered tomorrow. One today is worth two tomorrows, and never leave that till tomorrow, which you can do today."

– Benjamin Franklin

Due diligence in value investing is about uncovering the facts about a business and its industry in order to determine the sustainability and growth of long-term cash flow. This requires hard work. Remember, investing is simple in concept, but hard in implementation. A common goal of value investors is to understand a business better than anyone else. This often includes the people who actually manage and operate the business.

Answers to key questions regarding the sustainability and growth of long-term cash flow come much more easily once a business is understood deeply. Competitive advantage is easier to assess. The markets mis-perception is easier to interpret. All of the core tenets of value investing, such as contrarianism, a long-term perspective, and a margin of safety. become much more tangible when the investor successfully understands a business better than anyone else. Again, this requires a lot of hard, deep, and fundamental business analysis.

The rewards of hard work are well worth it. Significant monetary rewards will be realized if you can identify a business with the ability to sustain and grow cash flow for several years early on. Beyond this, when investing with a long-term horizon in a concentrated portfolio, the investor need only add one or two investments per year! Therefore, a long-term value investor has the luxury of being able to perform deep fundamental work on investments, since they only need to identify a handful of great companies per decade. This allows the depth and quality of fundamental research to increase exponentially. Most investors structure their investment process in a way that forces a shallow level of analysis, by using a short holding period and investing in many (>15-20) securities at once. This forces a high level of portfolio turnover, which means that many stocks have to be analyzed and added to the portfolio, which means an investment decision must be based on a shallower level of analysis.

It only takes a few great, decade-long investments to define an investment career (this being said, do not forget that it only takes one aggressive, imprudent investment to sabotage a career). Through deep fundamental research, an investor can "diligence away" a lot of risk, and identify asymmetric risk-reward opportunities that can provide lucrative monetary rewards for many years.

To successfully think and operate this way, an investor must structure his or her operations; diligence process; and, if possible, partnership in a way that is conducive to this way of thinking and research. To be a great investor requires an uncanny level of discipline throughout the investment process. However, to successfully exert discipline in the investment process, the investor must set him or herself up for thinking in an unencumbered, facts-oriented way at the inception of the firm. The second an investor accepts impatient, picky limited partner capital, the value investor loses the ability to implement a successful, long-term, disciplined thought process that is focused on hard, deep, fundamental research to uncover asymmetric risk-reward opportunities.

37

Professionalism

> *"It takes twenty years to build a reputation and five minutes to ruin it."*
>
> – Warren Buffett

> *"1) Don't sell anything you wouldn't buy yourself, 2) Don't work for anyone you don't respect, 3) Work only with people you enjoy."*
>
> – Charlie Munger

> *"Be so good they can't ignore you."*
>
> – Steve Martin

This chapter mainly applies to professional investors who invest largely with the money of others (though, in the author's opinion, it is essential that managing partners have some of their own money in the game to ensure aligned interests). Investment managers must be aware that their limited partners are their clients. As with any client relationship, the focus must be on the client. This being said, investment managers have the luxury of deciding who their clients are. Investment management is a unique space because the client relationship is more of a partnership. Therefore, investment managers should not accept capital from anyone – they should only accept capital that allows them to invest in a prudent, unconstrained manner. Having a real partnership, with shared goals, philosophies, and aspirations, is essential to successful long-term investing. This is much easier said than done. The investment manager must pass on dozens of potential limited partners because of this restrictive criteria.

Once limited partner relationships are established, the investment manager must approach that relationship with professionalism. A focus on the clients' needs is essential to successful long-term partnerships. This is why it is so important to align goals, values, and philosophies in the partnership – it will make focusing on your clients wants and needs identical to focusing on your own wants and needs.

Professionalism and high ethical standards are essential to any service based industry, or almost any business for that matter. A value investor understands this. A value investor understands that limited partners have a massive array of potential investment managers that they could invest in. For this reason, it is an honor and a privilege to be the recipient of aligned limited partner capital. That capital, and the people behind it, must be treated with the utmost respect. This enhances the investment managers own reputation, making future, aligned limited partner capital raises easier. More importantly, it is ethically sound to treat clients with respect and honesty and to manage their capital with integrity and a diligent effort.

38

Circle of Competence

*"You don't need to be an expert in order to achieve sat-
isfactory investment returns. But if you aren't, you must
recognize your limitations and follow a course certain to
work reasonably well."*
                                            – Warren Buffett

"Know what you own, and know why you own it."
                                            – Peter Lynch

"Risk comes from not knowing what you're doing."
                                            – Warren Buffett

Successful investors must know: 1) why they are investing,
2) how to philosophically think about investing, 3) how they are
investing, 4) how to interpret and assess potential investments, and
5) what they are investing in. This goal of this book is to equip
an investor with an understanding of concepts one through four,
which are essential to any investor's toolkit. The best way to develop concept five is to actually research businesses and industries.
By combining all five concepts, the investor develops a *circle of
competence* around a given business model, business type, or industry classification.

By employing the first four concepts on a variety of businesses, the investor will begin to understand concept five at a
deeper level. This is the arc of developing a circle of competence.
A circle of competence is simply an area of the investing universe
that the investor knows something about, and is, with hope, relatively skilled at assessing. This might be as broad as an industry,
such as biotechnology, or as granular as a specific type of business,

such as car classified businesses.

A value investor must understand and assess his or her own circle of competence. Many investors strive to be generalists (invest in any industry) without taking the time to actually deeply understand the companies and businesses they invest in. It is risky business to invest outside of one's circle of competence. Avoiding an honest self-assessment of one's own circle of competence is even riskier. Almost all investors have an understanding of concepts one, three, and four. Fewer investors have a deep understanding of or sound framework for concept two. Even fewer investors can combine concepts all four to develop a deep understanding of concept five for a variety of investments.

The only way to really develop a strong circle of competence is to spend a lot of time, years really, immersing oneself in deep research on a given type of business or industry. Even then, the investor will regularly be wrong and have to adapt viewpoints. However, the intellectual and monetary rewards of establishing a circle of competence are significant. Overtime, once a circle of competence is established, the investor will begin to recognize patterns in the markets and in successful investments. This simplifies the diligence process and allows the investor to hone in on the critical questions quickly.

Until a circle of competence is established, an investor should focus on businesses they know and understand. These businesses are most likely ones they have personal exposure to. Overtime, by following these understood businesses and researching additional businesses and industries when given the opportunity, the investor can invest within his or her circle of competence while expanding it.

Some investors intentionally restrict their circle of competence. This is a completely viable strategy, and empirical research actually suggests this can be more effective. The basis of this strategy: why know a little about a lot of things, when it is possible to be an expert on a narrow area of the investment universe and outperform in that area? Since it is risky to invest in areas that the investor knows little about, this is a practical and realistic approach. For investors that strive to be generalists, an extra level of diligence and effort is required to develop competence and pattern recognition in a broad variety of business models and industries.

39

Time Well Spent

"Most of what we say and do is not essential. If you can eliminate it, you'll have more time, and more tranquility. Ask yourself at every moment, 'is this necessary?'"
– Marcus Aurelius

"Part of having uncommon sense, I think, is being able to tune out folly, as distinguished from recognizing wisdom. You've got whole categories of things you just bat away so your brain isn't cluttered with them. That way, you're better able to pick up a few sensible things to do."
– Charles Munger

"We constantly ask: 'what should we work on today?' We keep calling and talking. We keep gathering information. You never have perfect information. So you work, work, and work...how you fill your inbox is very important."
– Seth Klarman

As an investor performing deep fundamental research, it is tempting to try and answer every possible question about a company. However, a value investor must remember: the determinant of the long-term value of a business is the sustainability and growth of long-term cash flow. Therefore, questions that do not help assess the sustainability and growth of long-term cash flow are not important. In fact, it is often better to stop and consider what questions are important, before trying to answer any at all.

To illustrate this point, consider the following thought experiment. Suppose an investor is able to identify nine possible questions that relate to a business. However, unbeknown to the

investor, only the answers to questions two and seven will determine the sustainability and growth of long-term cash flow. If the
investor divides research time evenly between the nine questions,
then only 2/9 of the research time will be spent trying to answer
the important questions. The diagram below illustrates this scenario.

Time Spent Researching a Company

Time Spent Answering Questions

Now, imagine that another investor spends a large chunk of
time, let's say the first third of his research time for the investment,
contemplating which questions are important to the sustainability
and growth of long-term cash flow, rather than blindly trying to
answer all nine possible questions. Suppose the investor is able
to narrow down the universe of questions to three core questions.
Furthermore, the investor is actually wrong about question five's
level of importance, but correct about question two and seven. The
diagram below illustrates this scenario.

Time Spent Researching a Company

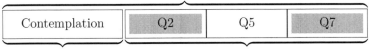

What is the question?   Time Spent Answering Questions

Based on the assumptions of this thought experiment, by
simply contemplating the importance of possible questions with
some level of accuracy, the investor can greatly increase the time
spent actually answering important questions. In this example, the
investor who spent time contemplating actually increased the time
spent answering important questions by 100% to 4/9 of the time.

This thought experiment aims to exhibit that an investor
who asks and answers "what is the question" with some degree
of success can drastically simplify the research process and reduce
clutter, all while spending more time answering important questions. Obviously, this thought experiment assumes many things
that make this analysis work. Most likely, the most important
assumption is the investor's level of effectiveness at accurately narrowing the universe of questions through contemplation. In reality,
an investor's ability to accurately narrow the universe of questions
through contemplation is completely dependent on the investor.

40

In-a-Nutshell

> *"While some might mistakenly consider value investing a mechanical tool for identifying bargains, it is actually a comprehensive investment philosophy that emphasizes the need to perform in-depth fundamental analysis, pursue long-term investment results, limit risk, and resist crowd psychology"*
>
> – Seth Klarman

In Part VI of this book, most of the core tenets of the philosophical framework of value investing have been discussed. In conclusion, the various tenets will be listed and summarized in this chapter for ease of reference and memory.

- **Margin of Safety** – an objective of value investing is to identify bargain-priced securities through deep fundamental analysis. Bargain-priced securities have an intrinsic value sufficiently below price to ensure a margin of safety in the investment. This helps to mitigate risk and protect the investor's downside if the thesis proves wrong.

- **Price Movements** – daily price movements are inevitable, and the value investor must aim to ignore these. Focusing on daily price movements encourages short-term behavior and active trading, both of which can be detrimental to an investor's success.

- **Good Businesses** – a great business at a good price is better than a good business at a great price. The sustainability and realized growth of long-term cash flow are the ultimate determinants of the long-term value of a business. Durable competitive advantages result in a recurring cash flow stream.

- **Long-termism** – a long-term perspective is one of the greatest competitive advantages an investor can have. In the long run, price will converge to intrinsic value. The value investor must patiently wait for this convergence, even if the road is bumpy.

- **Contrarianism** – an investor must have a great deal of respect for market efficiency and the current market price of a security. However, markets do have inefficiencies. To believe that the current market price is wrong, an investor must think differently and at a deeper level than the market. This is called contrarianism. However, to experience success as a contrarian, the value investor must also be correct. This requirement of being both contrarian and right makes investing very difficult.

- **Adaptability** – as the facts materially change, a value investor must be willing to modify his/her viewpoints and thesis.

- **Cycles** – markets are inevitably cyclical. It is difficult to time cycles, but there are characteristics to cycles that are common and often identifiable. History is important. Timing the market is futile, but an astute investor can look for signposts to determine the current position in the cycle.

- **Defensive Investing** – the primary goal of the value investor is to mitigate risk and losses by avoiding silly mistakes. The focus is on consistently hitting singles, not high risk home runs.

- **Simplicity** – the world of investing and finance is complex. The value investor must strive to reduce this complexity as much as possible, while not sacrificing information that is critical to assessing the long-term cash flow prospects of a business.

- **Behavioral Biases** – humans are not devoid of emotion and flaws. In fact, this is far from the truth. Behavioral biases define our thought processes and investment decisions. A value investor must accept and control this inevitable component of investing psychology.

- **Doing Due Diligence** – nothing great comes easy. Value investors work hard to understand businesses better than other people. The goal is to identify asymmetric risk/reward investment opportunities that the market is missing. This is not easy and requires deep fundamental analysis

- **Professionalism** – a professional value investor treats his limited partners and co-workers with an incredible level of respect. This is monetarily wise and it is the right thing to do.

- **Circle of Competence** – an investor has pockets of the investing universe that he or she knows something about. This is called the investor's circle of competence. A value investor understands his or her own circle of competence, only investing within that circle of competence. Furthermore, value investors strive to grow their circle of competence through deep fundamental research of new businesses and industries. Value investors understand their limitations, though, while often trying to improve their circle of competence.

- **Time Well Spent** – a value investor is constantly assessing whether time is being well spent. Rather than blindly answering every possible question about a business, the value investor focuses on identifying and answering the questions that relate to the long-term cash flow producing capability of a business.

Part VII

Private Equity

41

Leveraged Buyout Basics

41.1 Introduction

At this point, the reader has covered, and with hope understood, almost all of the core concepts of this book. We have worked up from a basic understanding of the goals of investing, to finding information on companies, to analyzing the financial statements and information of companies, to comprehending capital structure, to actually valuing and modeling a business, to assessing fundamental aspects of a business, and to presenting a philosophical framework through which to employ these tools. This is no small feat. Few investors take the time to deeply understand the concepts presented thus far. Consequently, they often wear the hat of an investor while having the perspective of a speculator.

In Part VII, knowledge of all the preceding concepts culminates in the practice of private investing. Private equity (and credit) is the most technically challenging topic covered in the book up to this point. A strong understanding of Parts II, III, and IV is essential to the next two chapters.

Is private investing better than public investing? It depends on the investor. The two investing styles have many differences, but at the same time, many similarities. For all sound investing, in public or private markets, the thought processes discussed in Part V and much of Part VI are critical. These are concepts that are vital to any investment process where the company is at the core of the analysis.

So, what are the differences between private and public investing? The main differences: liquidity; price availability; idea generation; and, in the case of buyout private equity, actual ownership and operation of the business. All of these differences impact the investing mentality and process:

- **Liquidity** - in public investing, contingent on market conditions and the size of the investors position, the investor can usually trade in or out of a position in a day or within a week or two. Public markets are very liquid relative to private markets. The market for trading entire companies and private placements is much more illiquid. Put differently, connecting a buyer with a seller in private markets is much more difficult.

  How does this impact the investing process? First, it requires private investors think with a long-term perspective or risk floundering. Second, it requires that private investors have more conviction in their thesis since any investment is almost guaranteed to be a much longer-term commitment (granted, this is not necessarily true, depending on the temperament of a comparable public investor).

- **Price Availability** - in public investing, the investor can track his profit and loss (P&L) record on a daily basis. Every single day, the public investor knows exactly how much money he made or lost. This difference, considered in tandem with the availability of liquidity in public markets, has powerful implications for the psychological differences between private and public investing.

  How does this impact the investing process? First, it means that public investors are much more susceptible to certain behavioral biases (covered in Chapter 35), such as action bias, short-termism, and anchoring. Second, it means that the price versus value relationship is harder to determine in private investing, since price is not nearly as available (this does not apply for the buyout of public companies or private placements in public companies).

- **Idea Generation** - in public investing, the universe of investable companies is limited to those who have publicly traded securities. In private investing, the universe of investable companies is *any* company in existence (contingent on the operators of the company wanting to raise capital or sell the company). This is a huge difference. This can make generating ideas in private investing overwhelming, since any company is a candidate. Furthermore, it also means that private investors have to sift through (and with hope avoid) a lot of bad companies.

How does this impact the investing process? First, deal sourcing and finding potential investments is a huge component of private investing. Second, when *good* (whether in reality or by perception) companies are identified, a lot of private investors want a stake in the deal. For this reason, relationships and networks among private investors are *very* important. They enable the formation of *syndicates* around certain deals. Granted, syndicates are formed for many other reasons, such as to help mitigate portfolio exposure to a single investment.

- **Ownership and Operation** - in public investing, the investor is fairly detached from the operations of a business (except in the rare case of activism). The investor takes a view based on the long-term cash producing capability of the current business as it stands (or will be), purchases a stake in the security of interest, and then 1) waits for the thesis to be realized, 2) monitors the progress of the company to determine whether the economic reality has materially deviated from the thesis, 3) liquidates his position if economic reality materially deviates from the thesis or intrinsic value is reflected in the market price.

  In private investing, buyout private equity in particular, the investor becomes the owner of the business. Therefore, the investor is entitled to do pretty much whatever he or she wants with the business. Examples include: firing large portions of staff, putting a new management team in place, improving corporate governance, establishing better cost controls and procedures, improving product pricing decision making, leveraging the capital structure, utilizing the acquired company's cash flow to "roll-up" other companies, and more.

  How does this impact the investing process? First, the buyout private equity investor can attempt to address any significant risks, such as a bad management team, that the public investor has no control over. This can make attractive to buyout private equity investors investments that are unattractive to public investors. Second, the buyout private equity investor (and the firm's analysts) must often perform extensive record-keeping and administrative activities related to the acquired company, since the investor owns the company and has full access to its financial and operational data.

Having described some of the key differences between public and private investing, let us dive into the details. In the first two chapters we will focus on (the main activity referred to when the term "private equity" is used in industry) and related private credit. Then growth equity and venture capital will be briefly discussed.

41.2   What is a Leveraged Buyout?

In a sentence, a leveraged buyout (LBO) is the purchase of an entire company using significant leverage (debt) to reduce the equity contribution and magnify the returns to equity. With the exception of early-stage companies, a company generally produces some cash flow stream. The premise/goals of an LBO are:

1. Acquire a company's entire cash flow stream by purchasing the entire company using a significant amount of debt

2. Use a portion of the cash flow stream to make interest payments and pay-down the debt

3. Stabilize or grow the cash flow stream

4. Exit the business with an equity value that is premium to the equity value at the time of purchase

In this chapter, we will explore all of the conceptual content related to the preceding four steps. In the next chapter, we will walk through an example of a financial model (LBO model) that models the preceding four steps.

The premise/goals of an LBO, as described by the previous four steps, likely raise some questions, such as: who are the participants? How is step 1 actually structured? Why is debt used in step 1? What type of company might make a good LBO candidate for successfully accomplishing steps 2 and 3? How can step 3 be accomplished? How can the investor "exit" the company, as described in step 4? Also from step 4, what determines whether the equity value at exit is premium to the equity value at entry? How is the success of an LBO measured? Is there a simple way to model this process? All of these questions will be addressed by the end of this chapter.

41.3 Price of Purchase

The price paid upfront to acquire a company is a critical factor in determining the success of the buyout. The price paid is an important determinant of the transaction/deal structure as well. We have actually already covered the formula for the cost of purchasing a business. Remember, enterprise value is analogous to the cost of actually purchasing a business. When purchasing a business, the acquirer: 1) buys-out the full capital stack, including equity, preferred equity, and debt, 2) receives the cash of the acquired business (which effectively reduces the purchase price), and 3) buys-out other debt-like obligations such as minority interest and unfunded pension liabilities. From these facts, the enterprise value of a business can be calculated as:

Enterprise Value (EV) = Equity Value + Debt + Preferred Equity - Cash + Minority Interest + Unfunded Pension Liabilities

Enterprise value is *almost* the price paid for a business in an LBO. In an LBO, the acquirer usually hires investment bankers to facilitate and advise the process. Investment bankers charge fees that must be paid by the acquirer. Furthermore, expenses related to raising debt financing for the LBO often arise. Therefore, the total purchase price in an LBO is:

Purchase Price = Enterprise Value (EV) + Deal Related Expenses

The total purchase price listed above is often referred to as *uses of funds*. This is because the capital invested by the equity and debt investors in an LBO will be *used* to pay the purchase price for the business being acquired.

However, we have overlooked an important detail: determining the equity value. For a public company, the equity value is the number of fully-diluted shares outstanding, times the share price plus some control premium. Determining the equity value of a private company is a little more difficult. There are a few ways to try and approximate the equity value of a private company, such as by looking at precedent transactions of similar companies or by looking at the equity value of comparable public companies.

Ultimately, the chief determinant of equity value and purchase price is *value*. An acquirer will pay a price up to the intrinsic value of the business (with a control premium factored in) and no more. It is the job of the acquirer to assess intrinsic value. In reality, the acquirer will only pay a price that is a healthy discount to their assessment of intrinsic value to ensure a margin of safety. Just like in public investing, the price paid upfront is the chief determinant of returns.

However, an acquisition is not that simple. The acquirer has its own assessment of intrinsic value and a price that he or she is willing to pay for the business. The goal of the acquirer is to minimize the price paid in order to maximize total potential return. However, the owners of the business also have their own assessment of intrinsic value and a price that they are willing to accept for the business in order to maximize their total potential return. These conflicting interests can make the negotiations surrounding a potential acquisition very difficult. In some cases, no deal is struck purely on the basis of price. For a deal to go through, both parties have to be satisfied with the transaction price. This is also true for transactions in public markets, but much less relevant or noticeable because of the liquidity in public markets.

How is the *expensiveness* of the purchase price assessed? The term expensive is relative to the acquirer's assessment of intrinsic value. This being said, the industry standard metric for measuring the expensiveness of acquiring a business is EV/EBITDA. Remember, the industry considers EBITDA the best short-hand proxy for a business's cash flow. Therefore, the price of a deal is measured relative to the established cash flow producing capability of the business. The average LBO EV/EBITDA multiple at close is between 5-10x depending on the economic conditions. Naturally, as the perceived stability and potential growth of a company's cash flow stream increases, the EV/EBITDA transaction multiple also increases. Conversely, as the perceived stability and potential growth of a company's cash flow stream decreases, the EV/EBITDA transaction multiple also decreases.

41.4   Capital Stack Review

We have just spent quite a bit of time talking about how much an acquirer pays for a business. As a reminder, this is called the *uses of funds*. But where does this money come from? What are the *sources of funds*? In short: equity and debt investments from investors. Remember, when acquiring a business, the acquirer must completely buyout the old capital structure. Therefore, the acquirer can (and must) place an entirely new capital structure on the acquired business.

The components of the new capital structure are under the discretion of the acquirer, who generally wants to maximize the tolerable usage of leverage (debt) since this magnifies the returns to the equity. Counterbalancing the leverage-maximizing goal of the equity investors is the discretion of debt investors. The sole focus of debt investors is getting their money back plus interest. Debt investors will only agree to a certain level of leverage, beyond which, they will either 1) demand a higher potential return or 2) not invest. Fortunately for equity holders who desire a lot of leverage, a company's capital structure comes with many flavors. Therefore, when one group of debt investors chooses option 2, another group of debt investors will choose option 1. To exemplify this point, let us bring back our old friend, the capital stack:

Highest seniority, lowest risk, lowest return

> **Senior Secured Debt**
> 20-30% of LBO capital stack
> 2-6% targeted returns

> **Senior Unsecured Debt**
> 10-20% of LBO capital stack
> 6-12% targeted returns

> **Mezzanine Debt**
> 0-10% of LBO capital stack
> 12-15% targeted returns

> **Preferred Equity**
> 0-10% of LBO capital stack
> 15-20% targeted returns

> **Common Equity**
> 30-50% of LBO capital stack
> 20%+ targeted returns

Lowest seniority, highest risk, highest return

The nature of the capital stack is well-suited for leverage-maximizing equity investors. As one group of debt investors reaches their risk tolerance, another group of more risk tolerant debt investors will invest in a more junior portion of the capital stack in exchange for a higher prospective return. It is almost as if the modern capital stack was designed for the purpose of enabling leverage-maximization in LBOs (it was). The capital stack in an LBO allows investors of all risk-reward profiles to take part in the transaction and invest in the acquired business. Due to this, debt regularly funds a very significant portion of the acquisition funds (sources of funds) in an LBO. From the preceding diagram, we can see that common equity usually takes up 30-50% of the capital stack, meaning that debt regularly makes up 50-70%.

41.5   The Participants

At this point, we have discussed the technicalities and dynamics surrounding an LBO transaction. An LBO transaction has two counterbalancing legs: *uses of funds*, the funds associated with the buying out of the acquired company's old capital structure plus deal related expenses, and *sources of funds*, the investor capital that actually funds the transaction and makes up the acquired company's new capital structure. With this in mind, this section will actually describe all the *possible* participants in a leveraged buyout.

- **Sponsor -** the sponsor (or "financial sponsor") is the private equity firm that actually sources, initiates, and executes the purchase. The sponsor contributes the equity portion of the capital structure (remember, the target company is acquired with both debt and equity).

- **Syndicate Members -** if the sponsor wants to reduce their portfolio exposure to the investment, maintain good relations with other private equity firms, or just get help paying for and running the target, the sponsor can ask other private equity firms to split the equity tranche with them. This is called "forming a syndicate." Creditors can also create syndicates and split a tranche amongst many investors.

- **Target -** the target is the company that is potentially will be or is being acquired. Later on in this chapter, attention will be given to the characteristics of a good target LBO candidate.

- **Management** - the management team of the target is an important player in an LBO. They negotiate the purchase price, along with help from the board of directors. Most sponsors like management to have a chunk of equity in the company post acquisition to align incentives. Sponsors will either give management a small portion of the equity tranche or allow management to buy-in to the tranche and co-invest with the sponsor. A management buyout is when the management team initiates and pursues an acquisition of the company that they manage.

- **Secured Creditors** - at the top of the capital stack are secured creditors. These are the investors with the lowest risk tolerance, and the commensurately lowest return. Secured creditors have a first lien on the company's assets. The specific secured credit instruments are generally: the revolver, TLAs, and some TLBs, provide mostly by commercial banks but some institutional investors as well. These are usually private instruments.

- **Senior Creditors** - senior, unsecured creditors are below the secured creditors and usually have a second lien on the company's assets. The specific senior credit instrument is likely TLBs provided by some higher-return focused commercial banks and institutional investors. The debt in this portion of the capital stack is often privately placed.

- **Bond Creditors** - as a reminder, bonds are the publicly traded debt portion of the capital stack and are generally junior to the private instruments. Bonds usually have a second or third lien on the assets of the company. Bond creditors in an LBO receive a fairly high coupon. In the capital stack diagram on the preceding pages, bonds might fall in the senior unsecured or mezzanine portion of the capital stack.

- **Mezzanine Investors** - mezzanine investments are generally tailor-made and often come with an "equity kicker" to juice upside potential. Mezzanine investments make up a small portion of the capital stack, are highly negotiated, and come with high return potential. For the sake of this discussion, preferred equity is lumped in with mezzanine debt as a portion of the capital stack.

- **Investment Banks** - as mentioned previously, investment banks are usually hired to serve as advisers and facilitators of the transaction. Investment banks are usually paid fees based on the total closing amount of the deal, so their incentive is to make sure the deal closes.

41.6   Sources of Returns in LBOs

There are two ways that LBOs generate return for equity investors: enterprise value expansion and deleveraging. There are two ways for enterprise value expansion to occur as well: multiple expansion and EBITDA growth. The reasons that these various mechanisms generate returns to equity are discussed in this section. On the credit side, the source of return is simple to explain: creditors receive compensation in the form of interest expense, and, hopefully their money back at maturity.

The first way that LBOs generate returns for equity investors is through enterprise value expansion. Before diving in, let us establish that there are four main discrete time periods over the course of an LBO: 1) sourcing, due-diligence, and deal-prep; 2) the actual execution of the deal; 3) the holding period (usually 3-7 years); and 4) the eventual exit or sale of the company. Ultimately, the returns to the equity investors are determined by the price paid at point two and the price exited at in point four. So, in a discussion on returns, we need only focus on the enterprise value (and its components) at the time of purchase and at the time of sale.

It is intuitive that an increase in enterprise value (or enterprise value expansion) over the course of the holding period would result in returns to equity investors. But, there are actually two different ways enterprise value expansion can occur: multiple expansion and EBITDA improvements.

Remember, LBO deals are assessed on an EV/EBITDA basis, that is, the purchase or sale price is considered relative to the cash flow producing capability of the firm. The EV/EBITDA multiple at purchase is called the purchase multiple and the EV/EBITDA multiple at sale is called the sale multiple. Multiple expansion is when the sale multiple is greater than the purchase multiple. Why would this grow equity value? Consider a company that produces $100 in EBITDA. The company is purchased for 10x EBITDA using a 50% debt (5x EBITDA), 50% equity mix (5x EBITDA). Therefore, $500 of debt is used and $500 of equity is used to purchase the business for $1000. But what happens if the sale multiple is higher, let's say, 13x (assuming constant EBITDA and no paying-down of debt)?

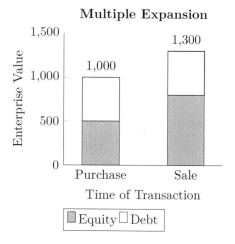

Multiple Expansion

In the diagram to above, based on this scenario, a 13x exit multiple on $100 of EBITDA corresponds to an enterprise value of $1300. But debt does not grow on its own, so the $500 of debt at purchase still totals $500 of debt at sale (since we assumed no deleveraging). Since enterprise value grew due to multiple expansion, and since debt did not change, the equity captures all the growth in enterprise value, as exhibited in the preceding diagram. Therefore, the equity value at exit is $800 versus an equity contribution of $500 at entry. This is a 60% total return to equity over the holding period.

At this point, it is helpful to discuss the value of leverage. In the scenario just discussed, we assumed a 50% debt, 50% equity mix. Now imagine the exact same scenario financed with 100% equity ($1000 of equity at purchase). Just as before, enterprise value expands to 13x EBITDA or $1300 at exit. This results in an equity value of $1300. Notice, relative to the initial equity contribution, this only produces a 30% return. Compare that with the 60% return generated under the same scenario with a 50% debt, 50% equity blend, and one can begin to understand the powerful return enhancing effects of leverage.

Here's the phenomenon we've observed here: since the use of leverage reduces the initial equity contribution, an absolute dollar increase in equity value will produce a much greater return, relative to the initial equity contribution, due to the use of leverage. Put differently, a simple return formula is: (equity value at exit)/(equity value at entry) - 1. If equity value at exit increases by a fixed amount (relative to equity value at entry), the % return will be greater as the equity value at entry decreases. Leverage reduces the equity value of entry, therefore magnifying the % return to equity for a fixed increase in equity value at exit (relative to equity value at entry).

Now, we can return to the discussion on enterprise value expansion. Enterprise value expansion through multiple expansion was just covered. The other way for enterprise value expansion to occur is through EBITDA improvements. Again, assume that a $100 EBITDA business is purchased with a 50% debt, 50% equity mix at a 10x EBITDA multiple for a total purchase price of $1000. Suppose the EBITDA multiple at exit is still 10x. But, EBITDA increases to $120.

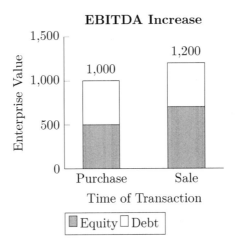

The diagram above exhibits this scenario. The increase in EBITDA to $120, even with the exit multiple held constant at 10x, results in an increase of enterprise value to $1200. Similar to the last example, since no debt was paid-back, debt is constant at $500. Therefore, equity value grows from $500 at purchase to $700 at exit.

There is one other mechanism that generates equity returns in an LBO: deleveraging or paying-down debt. In isolation, debt pay-backs do not grow enterprise value. But, debt pay-backs do grow equity value's share of the enterprise value. To illustrate this,

consider the following example. Just as with preceding examples, a
$100 EBITDA business is bought for a 10x EBITDA multiple with
50% debt and 50% equity. Over the holding period, the company
is able to generate sufficient cash flow to pay-down $200 of debt
by exit. Therefore, $300 of debt remains at exit. EBITDA at exit
is still $100. The exit multiple is also 10x. Therefore, enterprise
value at exit is still $1000.

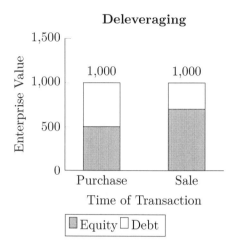

The diagram above exhibits this scenario. Notice that even
though enterprise value is constant between purchase and sale, the
equity value grew because of the lower debt total. This exhibits
that equity value increases as the company's capital structure becomes less leveraged. Put differently, equity value captures the
reduction in debt.

The various mechanisms that generate equity returns in an
LBO have been discussed so far, including enterprise value expansion through multiple expansion, enterprise value expansion
through EBITDA improvements, and equity value expansion through
deleveraging. However, we have assumed these various mechanisms
occur in isolation. In reality, all three mechanisms play a role in
determining the final return to equity.

Assume again that a company is purchased at a 10x EBITDA
multiple, with $100 EBITDA, and a 50% debt/50% equity mix.
Over the course of the holding period, EBITDA increases to $110
and the company is able to generate sufficient cash flow to pay-
down $200 of debt. At exit, the company is able to sell the business

at an 11x EBITDA multiple.

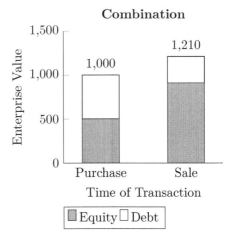

In this scenario, exhibited in the preceding diagram, enterprise value expands to $1210 due to the combination of the EBITDA increase and the multiple expansion. The debt total is reduced to $300 due to deleveraging. Therefore, equity value is $910.

A lot of attention has been given to the mechanics of LBO returns. But, the key factors determining whether multiple expansion, EBITDA improvements, and deleveraging actually occur over the holding period have not been discussed. Some of these factors are reviewed briefly here:

- **Multiple Expansion** - market conditions, improvements in the company's competitive position, sales growth, profitability improvements, new growth opportunities

- **EBITDA Improvements** - cost cuts, sales growth, profitability improvements, operational improvements, implementing industry best practices

- **Deleveraging** - production of sufficient levered free cash flow to fund debt pay-down

Now, having presented the mechanics of LBO returns and the factors that determine whether the company can actually take advantage of these mechanics, it is valuable to discuss the pre-acquisition characteristics of a company that make for attractive LBO targets.

41.7 Good LBO Candidates

Not all companies are good LBO targets. The due-diligence process, pre-acquisition, focuses on identifying companies that can sustain high levels of leverage, stabilize and improve cash production, improve competitive position, and grow the business. With these objectives in mind, the characteristics of a good LBO candidate are fairly intuitive:

- **Significant, Sustainable Cash Flow** - as the reader has probably noticed, cash flow is very important to a successful LBO. Cash flow is required to service the interest payments on the debt and make debt repayments. Without cash flow, an LBO would be impossible, since the post-acquisition company would be unable to service interest payments and enter bankruptcy.

  Beyond this, the cash flow stream of a good LBO target must be sustainable. There are many reasons for this. First, the target's post-acquisition capital structure is largely determined by the cash flow producing capability of the business at the time of acquisition. Therefore, a deterioration in the cash flow of the business during the holding period could result in the business being "over-leveraged" relative to its cash flow producing capability, which is risky. Second, the exit price is usually determined as a multiple of cash flow or EBITDA, so a deterioration in cash flow production would inhibit returns. In fact, a deterioration in cash flow could also result in multiple contraction (a reduction in the cash flow multiple), so returns could be inhibited through two mechanisms.

  To assess the sustainability of cash flow, recurring revenue, customer concentration, product or service quality, and customer retention are very important. All of these metrics give visibility into the future cash flow producing capability of the firm.

- **Low Capital Intensity** - capital intensity generally refers to the level of capital expenditures required to maintain or grow cash flow. Low capital intensity is a positive. Less capital expenditures means more cash flow for deleveraging. Beyond that, high capital intensity firms have less flexibility in regards to capital allocation since the nature of their business demands that a significant portion of cash flow is allocated to capital expenditures.

Capital intensity is generally inherent to the industry. Firms with heavy machinery and intricate or expensive production processes are much more capital intensive than subscription software businesses.

- **Cost Cut Potential -** many businesses, especially private firms owned by families, have a lot of inefficiencies in areas such as: corporate governance, cost optimization, employee count, and supply chain/value chain management. The presence of these inefficiencies means that cost cuts are possible. Cost cuts are super valuable for a few reasons: the associated increase in EBITDA increases the exit price and the associated increase in cash flow during the holding period improves debt repayment capability.

- **Established Competitive Advantages -** as has been discussed extensively, the primary determine of durable long-term cash flow is the presence of a competitive advantage. Therefore, since cash is king, an LBO target should have established competitive advantages.

- **Growth Opportunities -** growth opportunities are valuable since sales growth results in additional EBITDA and cash flow, both of which are essential to a successful exit and deleveraging.

- **Asset Coverage -** a significant amount of asset coverage reduces the interest expense on the debt of the target post-acquisition. This is because the company can grant several, valuable liens on the assets of the business, which reduces the riskiness of the debt and the interest rate as well. Since a reduction in interest expense results in more levered free cash flow, asset coverage indirectly improves deleveraging capability.

41.8   Post Buyout Considerations

In the preceding section, six attributes of good LBO targets were discussed: cash flow, capital intensity, cost cuts, competitive advantage, growth opportunities, and asset coverage. Following the buyout, the sponsor's goal is to develop, maintain, or grow these characteristics in their portfolio companies. There are several ways a sponsor might do this: selling underperforming or unprofitable assets, implementing industry standard cost control practices, implementing better corporate governance, implementing better pricing protocol, focusing on key business lines, pursuing growth opportunities, growing brand recognition, improving sales operations, enhancing existing customer relationships, releasing new products and services, rolling up other similar companies with synergies, and more.

41.9 Types of Exit

The goal of an LBO is to generate a return for the sponsor over the holding period and at exit. In this section, we explore the tangible ways that a private equity firm can accomplish this. There are two ways to actually exit the investment and effectively end the holding period: 1) sell the business to another private equity firm or strategic acquirer (another business) or 2) take the company public in an initial public offering (IPO) and liquidate the stake over time in the public markets. Beyond this, there are two additional ways private equity firms can juice up returns without actually exiting the business: 1) a leveraged recapitalization or 2) a below par debt repurchase.

- **Sale -** this is the first of two ways that a private equity firm can exit a portfolio company. This is simply a sale of the business to another party. The sponsor can sell the business either to another private equity firm or to a strategic acquirer (another business). Generally, strategic acquirers will pay more for the same business because they capture the economic impact of synergies, whereas private equity firms do not get synergies when acquiring a business.

- **Initial Public Offering (IPO) -** the second way that a private equity firm can exit a portfolio company is through an initial public offering (IPO). The sponsor can take the company public and then sell its stake in the public markets over time.

- **Dividend Recapitalization -** a dividend recapitalization is not an actual exit. The sponsor will still own the target following a dividend recapitalization. A dividend recapitalization is simply raising additional debt to pay a special dividend to the equity holders. If an LBO is going particularly

well over the holding period, the sponsor might juice their returns by taking on new debt (after having deleveraged a lot)
and using the proceeds from the debt to pay a large dividend
to the equity holders.

- **Buying Debt at a Discount** - sometimes, over the course
  of the holding period, the credit quality (or the markets perception of the credit quality) of the portfolio company can
  deteriorate. This will be reflected in the market price of the
  bonds. Just like a business can buy its own stock in the
  public markets, it can also buy its own debt in the public
  markets. If the debt is trading at 80, a decent discount, the
  company can buy back the debt in the public markets and
  remove a dollar of debt for only eighty cents. Buying debt at
  a discount in this manner can be a great allocation of capital since it instantly generates a positive return on capital
  invested.

41.10   Internal Rate of Return (IRR)

All the conceptual content surrounding an LBO has been
covered except for one important topic: internal rate of return
(IRR), the primary method for assessing the prospective and realized success of an LBO. IRR is the annualized rate of return for a
given set of cash flows over a period of time. For calculating IRR,
IRR is simply the discount rate (r) that satisfies the following formula (using a holding period of five years):

$$-CF_0 + \frac{CF_1}{(1+r)} + \frac{CF_2}{(1+r)^2} + \frac{CF_3}{(1+r)^3} + \frac{CF_4}{(1+r)^4} + \frac{CF_5}{(1+r)^5} = 0$$

This is the same formula used to solve for the yield-to-
maturity of a bond. CF_0 is the equity contribution (not the entire
price paid) when the target is acquired. CF_1 through CF_5 are the
cash flows to the equity sponsors over the course of the holding
period and at exit that could come from: dividends or the equity
value at the time of sale.

To give an example, suppose that a company is purchased in
time period 0 with an equity contribution of $300. Over the course
of the holding period, the sponsor pays itself a special dividend of
$100 in year 3. At exit, in year 5, the company sells the business
with an equity value of $600 (return to section 43.6 for a reminder
on the different mechanisms that can expand equity value over the

course of the holding period). Plugging this cash flow profile into the IRR formula from above:

$$-\$300 + \frac{\$0}{(1+r)} + \frac{\$0}{(1+r)^2} + \frac{\$100}{(1+r)^3} + \frac{\$0}{(1+r)^4} + \frac{\$600}{(1+r)^5} = 0$$

Solving for r, the IRR on this cash flow profile is 19.91%. This means the annualized return on the investment is 19.91%. Private equity firms usually target a prospective IRR of 15-20%+ depending on market conditions. When assessing a potential deal, private equity firms will analyze how IRR changes depending on various operational and financing scenarios. Private equity firms demand a high IRR to ensure a margin of safety in case the future progresses differently than expected.

Most public equity investors would be satisfied with a prospective IRR on an investment of 10-15%. Why do private equity investors demand a premium to this level? There are many possible answers for this, but some possible ones are: a liquidity premium, a premium for actually operating the business, and a premium for buying a highly levered equity (that is inherently riskier).

41.11   Paper LBO

Finally, we are ready to start exploring how to model an LBO. There is a shorthand method for modeling an LBO called a paper LBO model, which is covered in this section. The next chapter covers LBO modeling in detail. In LBO modeling, there are four main steps to model: 1) the entry transaction, 2) the holding period, 3) the exit transaction, and 4) a returns analysis (usually using IRR).

Company Z Entry Transaction		
Entry Multiple		6.0x
Entry EBITDA		$40
Purchase Price		$240
Debt	50%	$120
Equity	50%	$120
Total	100%	$240

Table 41.2: Paper LBO Assumptions

Company Z Assumptions					
			Projection Period		
Year	2018E	2019E	2020E	2021E	2022E
Sales Growth	NA	10%	10%	10%	10%
EBITDA Margin	40%	40%	40%	40%	40%
DA (% of sales)	5%	5%	5%	5%	5%
Interest Rate (% of debt)	10%	10%	10%	10%	10%
Tax Rate (% of PBT)	40%	40%	40%	40%	40%
CapEx (% of sales)	10%	10%	10%	10%	10%
Change in WC (% of sales)	2%	2%	2%	2%	2%

Table 41.3: Paper LBO Income Statement

Company Z Income Statement					
		Projection Period			
Year	2018E	2019E	2020E	2021E	2022E
Sales	$100	$110	$121	$133	$146
EBITDA	$40	$44	$48	$53	$59
Less: DA	$5	$6	$6	$7	$7
EBIT	$35	$39	$42	$47	$51
Less: Interest	$12	$12	$12	$12	$12
EBT	$23	$27	$30	$35	$39
Less: Taxes	$9	$11	$12	$14	$16
Net Income	$14	$16	$18	$21	$24

Table 41.4: Paper LBO Free Cash Flow Calculation

Company Z Free Cash Flow					
	Projection Period				
Year	**2018E**	**2019E**	**2020E**	**2021E**	**2022E**
Net Income	$14	$16	$18	$21	$24
Plus: DA	$5	$6	$6	$7	$7
Less: CapEx	$10	$11	$12	$13	$15
Less: Change in WC	$2	$2	$2	$3	$3
FCF	$7	$8	$10	$11	$13

Company Z Exit Transaction	
Exit Multiple	6.0x
Exit EBITDA	$59
Exit Price	$351
Beginning Debt	$120
Cumulative FCF	$49
End Debt	$71
Beginning Equity Value	$281
End Equity Value	$120
IRR	18.5%

42

Leveraged Buyout Walk Through

42.1 Introduction

An actual leveraged buyout model (LBO) is much more complicated than a paper LBO model. There are many reasons for this. First, a full leveraged buyout model captures the balance sheet impacts of the actual transaction. Second, most full LBO models assume that excess cash will be used to pay back debt (this is called a cash flow sweep), rather than stockpiled. This makes the modeling of interest expense and debt much more complicated. Third, a full LBO model performs detailed returns analysis based on a variety of exit conditions. Finally, a full LBO model allows for robust analysis of various operating scenarios, financing scenarios, credit statistics, and possible future financing decisions (such as dividend recaps).

A leveraged buyout model is basically a very detailed three-statement model, with some nuances at the beginning to capture the impact of the actual transaction. This discussion assumes that the modeler is building a cash flow sweep model. The main steps to an LBO model are: sources and uses, balance sheet adjustments, building a three statement model to determine the amount of cash from operating and investing activities that can be allocated to debt repayment, building a debt schedule that determines interest expense and actual debt repayment (the cash flow sweep), linking interest expense to the income statement to create a circular model, and then calculating returns to equity based on certain exit assumptions. A sophisticated LBO model will have more than this, including: a revenue projection model, several operating scenarios and assumptions, several deal financing scenarios, credit analysis, and a toggle for turning off the cash flow sweep.

42.2   Sources and Uses

As a reminder, from the previous chapter, sources of funds are the various types of investor capital that fund the acquisition of the target. Since the cash the company has on hand reduces enterprise value, the current cash balance of the company is also a source of funds. The uses of funds relate to the buying out of the target's old capital structure. This includes existing debt and equity. There are also fees associated with the transaction (for hiring investment bankers and for establishing credit agreements) that are a use of funds.

The total sources of funds must always equal the total uses of funds. This intuitively makes sense. If this was not the case, some party would be paying too little or too much, and the transaction would not be balanced. The uses of funds are easy to determine based on the values of the target's current capital structure components. The sources of funds are more variable, because there are hundreds of different capital structures that the sponsor can place on the post-acquisition company. For this reason, sophisticated LBO models consider several mutually exclusive post-acquisition capital structures.

Generally, the sponsor wants to maximize leverage, until creditors eventually stop lending. Therefore, the debt quantum that the sponsor is able to raise is largely determined by current capital market dynamics. Because of this, the equity contribution that the sponsor provides is more flexible relative to the potential debt amounts and serves as the "plug" or the balancing factor that guarantees the total sources and total uses balance. Put differently, the sponsor must provide in equity whatever it cannot raise in debt.

42.3   Balance Sheet Adjustments

Now, once the sources and uses are determined, the balance sheet of the company must be adjusted to reflect the new capital structure and transaction adjustments, the loss of cash, the creation of goodwill, and the capitalization of financing fees. The main adjustments are:

- **Cash Adjustment** - to the extent that the targets existing cash was utilized to fund the acquisition, it must be deducted from the previous cash balance.

- **Capital Structure Adjustment** - the old capital structure of the company was removed, and a new capital structure put in place. Therefore, the old capital structure must be removed from the balance sheet and the new capital structure added to the balance sheet. This means: removing the historical long-term debt(s), removing the historical equity accounts, adding the new long-term debt(s), and adding the equity contribution as the new book value of the company's common stock.

- **Capitalization of Fees** - rather than expensing the fees, modelers usually add these to the balance sheet as a capitalized asset that will be amortized overtime.

- **Goodwill Creation** - as a reminder, goodwill is the price paid for the equity of a company in excess of the book value of the company's equity. Goodwill serves as the "plug" that will guarantee the balance sheet, post transaction adjustments, will still balance. To calculate the added goodwill amount, the modeler subtracts the book value of the *old* equity accounts from the equity value paid in the uses of funds section.

42.4 Determining Cash Flow Available for Debt Repayment

At this point, the impacts of the transaction should be fully reflected in the company's balance sheet. The balance sheet, in the post adjustment time period, should be balanced. The next step is to build a three-statement model to determine cash flow from operations and cash flow from investing activities.

As with the three-statement model discussed in a previous chapter, it is wise to develop income statement, balance sheet, and cash flow statement assumptions in advance of the actual calculation of the income statement, balance sheet, and cash flow statement line items. The key income statement assumptions are: sales growth rate, COGS, SG&A, tax rate, and dividend payout ratio. The key balance sheet assumptions are: DSO, DIH, other current assets, DPO, other current liabilities, other long-term assets, and other long-term liabilities. The key cash flow statement assumptions are: capital expenditures, depreciation, amortization, amortization of capitalized fees, and acquisitions.

Once these assumptions are filled out, the modeler can build the income statement with interest expense left blank. Then, the current assets, current liabilities, other long-term assets, and other long-term liabilities can be calculated. Next, cash flow from operations and cash flow from investing activities can be filled out. Then, PPE can be linked to capital expenditures and depreciation on the cash flow statement to calculate PPE in all time periods. Goodwill is linked to amortization on the cash flow statement. Financing expenses are linked to the amortization of financing fees on the cash flow statement. Retained earnings is linked to net income on the income statement.

With the majority of the three statement model complete, the only items left to fill out on the balance sheet are: cash, revolver, and the long-term debt items. The only items left to fill out on the income statement is the various interest expenses. The only items left to fill out on the cash flow statement is in the cash flow from financing activities section.

42.5   Debt Schedule and Cash Flow Sweep

The reader has probably noticed that the only remaining sections of the model are related to debt. At this point, we are ready to construct the debt schedule to: determine debt pay-down capability, determine the amount of cash allocated to debt pay-down, and determine interest expense. This will allow us to fill out the remaining sections of the three statement model including: debt balances on the balance sheet, cash payments towards debt on the financing section of the cash flow statement, cash balance on the balance sheet, and interest expense on the income statement.

Before building the debt schedule, let us remind ourselves that the interest rate on loans and floating rate debt instruments are determined as a spread off LIBOR. Therefore, the modeler must forecast LIBOR into the projection period. This is the first step of building the debt schedule.

Next, the modeler must determine the amount of discretionary cash flow that the company can allocate towards debt repayment. This is simple to calculate based on the model built thus far: simply add CFO to CFI to determine how much cash flow is available for financing activities. CFO + CFI equals the cash available for *mandatory* debt repayment. Remember, loans and other debt instruments often have a required annual amortization amount that must be paid. All required amortization payments must be made before discretionary debt pay-down is determined.

To determine mandatory debt payments, it is essential at

this point to build a debt waterfall. A debt waterfall contains the key money terms for the various debt instruments in the capital structure and allows the modeler to determine all the essential information over the projection period for a given debt instrument. The instruments in a debt waterfall are ordered by seniority, with the revolver at the top, term loans next, and bonds/subordinated debts at the bottom. A debt waterfall contains the following information for *each* debt instrument (including the revolver): the name of the instrument, the pricing (interest rate) on the debt, the annual amortization rate, the maturity, and the principal amount. This information is fixed and inherent to the debt instrument, so it does not change over the course of the projection period. However, each debt instrument does have a few line items that do change over the course of the projection period. These must be included in the debt waterfall. For each instrument, these include: the debt balance at the beginning of the period (BOP), mandatory repayments, optional repayments, any new debt issuance, the debt balance at the end of the period (EOP), the interest rate (for floating rate instruments), and the interest expense.

Once the shell of the debt waterfall is created, the modeler can fill out the fixed characteristics of each instrument, such as instrument name, pricing, amortization rate, maturity, and principal. The debt balance in the first year of the projection period equals the principal amount. The required amortization figure equals the principal amount times the amortization rate for all time periods. The debt balance at BOP equals the debt balance at EOP from the preceding time period. By filling out this information, the modeler can calculate the mandatory repayment, debt balance BOP, debt balance EOP, and interest rate for each instrument over all time periods in the projection period. The only line item left blank at this point is optional repayment. The revolver is a tricky debt instrument, and has some unique features, so the revolver BOP and EOP balances should also be blank.

Now, the mandatory debt repayment amount for each instrument has been calculated. Therefore, we can subtract the total mandatory debt repayment from the previously calculated figure, cash available for mandatory debt repayment (CFO + CFI). The result is: cash available for *optional* debt repayment. What happens if cash available for debt repayment is less than mandatory repayment? The revolver gets drawn.

From here, the cash flow sweep begins, since we assume that all discretionary cash (cash available for optional debt repayment) will go towards paying down debt. Cash available for optional repayment is used to pay down the debt instruments at the top of the debt waterfall first. When cash available for optional repayment is negative, the revolver should get drawn. When cash available for optional debt repayment is negative, debt should get paid back in the order of the debt waterfall. This means, the revolver is paid back first (if it has a positive balance). Then, any cash beyond that which paid down the revolver goes towards paying down the next junior instrument. Once a debt instrument is fully repaid, excess cash goes towards paying down the next level of the debt waterfall. By calculating this figure for the optional repayment amount of every debt instrument, at this point, the BOP and EOP debt balances should be correctly calculated.

Finally, the modeler is prepared to calculate interest expense. To do this, multiply the interest rate for a given projection period year by the average of the BOP and EOP debt balance for that instrument. At this point, the debt schedule is complete.

The modeler can now link the key components of the debt schedule to the various line items in the other three statements. First, the EOP debt balance for each instrument, including the revolver, is linked to the respective long-term debt line item on the balance sheet. Next, the modeler links the net issuance (since the revolver can be a source of cash) figure from the revolver to the cash flow statement. Then, by summing all optional and mandatory debt repayments, the modeler can calculate the total cash spent on debt repayment and link this to the cash flow statement. Then, the dividends line item on the financing section of the cash flow statement can be linked to dividends from the income statement. With the cash from financing activities section complete, the net change in cash can be calculated by summing CFO, CFI, and CFF. This enables the calculation of the cash balance in each time period, which can then be linked to the balance sheet. In a cash flow sweep model, the cash flow balance will generally equal $0 or some other minimum cash balance set by the modeler, since all discretionary cash is going towards debt repayment. At this point, the balance sheet should be balanced in all time periods. Finally, interest expense on the debt schedule is linked to the empty interest expense section on the income statement. This produces a circular reference and generally reduces the amount of debt repayment that occurs in the model. The three-statement model is now complete, and the balance sheet should still be balanced in all time periods.

42.6   Calculating Returns

With the three-statement model complete, the modeler is prepared to analyze the prospective returns of different exit scenarios using IRR. To do this, the modeler must calculate the enterprise value at exit, for a given EBITDA level, based on an assumed exit multiple. The EBITDA level for a given year is easy to determine by adding EBIT from the income statement to D&A from the cash flow statement. The exit multiple is a very important assumption, and is determined by the modeler's assessment of future market conditions and the future financial and competitive strength of the firm. The multiple paid for the company is also a good guide for a reasonable exit multiple.

Once the prospective enterprise value is calculated for each possible exit year in the projection period, the predicted net long-term debt amount associated with that specific exit year is subtracted to determine equity value at exit. The combination of the equity value at exit and dividends over the holding period makeup the cash flows to the equity holders. The initial cash outflow by the equity investors is the equity contribution from the sources of funds section. By combining all the equity cash flows for a given exit year, the prospective IRR is easily calculated, based on the model's assumptions and an assumed exit year.

In a more complex LBO, the modeler might assess prospective returns using: a full revenue projection model, multiple different sets of operating assumptions for the three statement model, multiple different financing scenarios and capital structures, and a credit analysis to understand the risk of bankruptcy in the proposed investment.

42.7   What About Debt?

For debt investors to assess the investment, the model is built the exact same way. To assess the credit worthiness of the prospective deal, the credit investor uses a credit analysis that focuses on the business's leverage levels relative to cash flow and the ability of the business to safely make interest payments.

To determine the prospective IRR for the debt instruments, the modeler builds out the cash flows associated with a given debt instrument, similarly to the way equity cash flows were determined. The cash flows associated with a given debt instrument are: the initial investment, the interest payments, and any principal repayments. These numbers are easily found on the debt schedule.

42.8   Reference Model

In the next pages, a reference model is included that demonstrates the modeling techniques and tools described in this chapter.

Equity Value Calculation

FDSO	100
Share Price (with control premium)	$15
Equity Value	$1500
Net Income	$105
P/E	14.3x

Purchase Multiple

EBITDA	$300
Equity Value	$1500
Debt	$450
Cash	$50
Enterprise Value	$1900
EV/EBITDA	6.3x

Sources

Source	Pricing	% of Funds	Amount
TLA	L+3.5%	35%	$700
TLB	L+6.0%	18%	$350
Bonds	10%	10%	$200
Cash on Hand		3%	$50
Equity Portion		35%	$700
Total Sources		100%	$2000

Uses

Use	% of Uses	Amount
Equity Value	75%	$1500
Current TLA	15%	$300
Current TLB	0%	$0
Current Bonds	8%	$150
Fees	2%	$50
Total Uses	100%	$2000

Forecasted Income Statement Assumptions

Year	Historic 2017A	2018E	2019E	2020E	2021E	2022E
Sales Growth Rate	NA	5%	5%	5%	5%	5%
COGS (% of sales)	60%	60%	60%	60%	60%	60%
SG&A (% of sales)	30%	30%	30%	30%	30%	30%
Tax Rate (% of PBT)	40%	40%	40%	40%	40%	40%
Payout Ratio (% of NI)	0%	0%	0%	0%	0%	0%

| | Forecasted Income Statement | | | | | | |
| | Historic | Projection Period | | | | | |
Year	2017A	2018E	2019E	2020E	2021E	2022E
Sales	$2000	$2100	$2205	$2315	$2431	$2553
COGS	$1200	$1260	$1323	$1389	$1459	$1532
Gross Profit	$800	$840	$882	$926	$972	$1021
SG&A	$600	$630	$662	$695	$729	$766
EBIT	$200	$210	$221	$232	$243	$255
Interest Expense:						
Revolver	$0	$2	$2	$0	$0	$0
TLA	$10	$38	$39	$37	$32	$26
TLB	$0	$28	$28	$28	$28	$28
Bonds	$15	$13	$5	$5	$5	$5
Profit Before Tax	$175	$129	$146	$161	$178	$196
Tax Provision	$70	$52	$58	$64	$71	$79
Net Income	$105	$78	$88	$97	$107	$118
Dividends	$0	$0	$0	$0	$0	$0

Forecasted Balance Sheet

Year	Historic 2017A	Adjustments +	Adjustments -	2017PF	2018E	2019E	2020E	2021E	2022E
						Projection Period			
Cash	$50		($50)	$0	$0	$0	$0	$0	$0
Accounts Receivable	$200			$200	$210	$221	$232	$243	$255
Inventory	$300			$300	$315	$331	$347	$365	$383
Prepaid Expenses	$100			$100	$105	$110	$116	$122	$128
Current Assets	$650			$600	$630	$662	$695	$729	$766
LT Assets:									
PPE	$1000			$1000	$1021	$1043	$1066	$1091	$1116
Goodwill	$200	$450		$650	$608	$564	$518	$469	$418
Financing Exp.	$0	$50		$50	$45	$40	$35	$30	$25
Other LTA	$100			$100	$105	$110	$116	$122	$128
Total Assets	$1950			$2400	$2409	$2419	$2429	$2440	$2452
Revolver	$0			$0	$75	$0	$0	$0	$0
Accounts Payable	$300			$300	$315	$331	$347	$365	$383
Other CL	$100			$100	$105	$110	$116	$122	$128
Current Liabilities	$400			$400	$495	$441	$463	$486	$511
LT Liabilities:									

Long-term Debt:									
TLA	$300	$700	($300)	$700	$693	$675	$572	$459	$335
TLB	$0	$350		$350	$341	$333	$324	$315	$306
Bonds	$150	$200	($150)	$200	$50	$50	$50	$50	$50
Total LT Debt	$450			$1250	$1084	$1057	$946	$824	$691
Other LTL	$50			$50	$53	$55	$58	$61	$64
Total Liabilities	$900			$1700	$1631	$1553	$1467	$1371	$1266
Equity Accounts:									
Common Stock	$100	$700	($100)	$700	$700	$700	$700	$700	$700
Retained Earnings	$950		($950)	$0	$78	$165	$262	$369	$487
Equity	$1050			$700	$778	$865	$962	$1069	$1187
Total L + E	$1950			$2400	$2409	$2419	$2429	$2440	$2452
Balance Check	*0.000*			*0.000*	*0.000*	*0.000*	*0.000*	*0.000*	*0.000*

Forecasted Balance Sheet Assumptions

Year	Historic	Projection Period				
	2017A	2018E	2019E	2020E	2021E	2022E
DSO	36.5	36.5	36.5	36.5	36.5	36.5
DIH	91.3	91.3	91.3	91.3	91.3	91.3
Prepaid Expenses (% of sales)	5%	5%	5%	5%	5%	5%
Other LTA (% of sales)	5%	5%	5%	5%	5%	5%
DPO	91.3	91.3	91.3	91.3	91.3	91.3
Other Current Liabilities (% of sales)	5%	5%	5%	5%	5%	5%
Other LTL (% of sales)	2.5%	2.5%	2.5%	2.5%	2.5%	2.5%

Forecasted Cash Flow Statement Assumptions

Year	Projection Period				
	2018E	2019E	2020E	2021E	2022E
Depreciation (% of sales)	3%	3%	3%	3%	3%
Amortization (% of sales)	2%	2%	2%	2%	2%
Amortization of Financing Fees ($ amount)	$5	$5	$5	$5	$5
CapEx (% of sales)	4%	4%	4%	4%	4%
Acquisitions (dollar amount)	$0	$0	$0	$0	$0

Forecasted Cash Flow Statement

Year	Projection Period				
	2018E	2019E	2020E	2021E	2022E
CFO:					
Net Income	$78	$88	$97	$107	$118
+ Depreciation	$63	$66	$69	$73	$77
+ Amortization	$42	$44	$46	$49	$51
+ Amortization of Financing Fees	$5	$5	$5	$5	$5
Changes in Current Assets (Inc.)/Dec.:					
Accounts Receivable	($10)	($11)	($11)	($12)	($12)
Inventory	($15)	($16)	($17)	($17)	($18)
Prepaid Expenses	($5)	($5)	($6)	($6)	($6)
Changes in Current Liabilities Inc./(Dec.):					
Accounts Payable	$15	$16	$17	$17	$18
Other CL	$5	$5	$6	$6	$6
Changes in LTA or LTL:					
OLTA	($5)	($5)	($6)	($6)	($6)
OLTL	$3	$3	$3	$3	$3
CFO	$175	$190	$204	$219	$235

CFI:					
Capital Expenditures	($84)	($88)	($93)	($97)	($102)
Acquisitions	$0	$0	$0	$0	$0
CFI	($84)	($88)	($93)	($97)	($102)
CFF:					
Revolver Issuance/(Repayment)	$75	($75)	$0	$0	$0
Debt Repayment	($166)	($27)	($111)	($122)	($133)
Dividends	$0	$0	$0	$0	$0
CFF	($91)	($102)	($111)	($122)	($133)
Cash BOP	$0	$0	$0	$0	$0
Net Change In Cash	$0	$0	$0	$0	$0
Cash EOP	$0	$0	$0	$0	$0

Forecasted Debt Schedule

		Projection Period				
		2018E	2019E	2020E	2021E	2022E
LIBOR Curve		2.00%	2.25%	2.50%	2.75%	3.00%
CFO		$175	$190	$204	$219	$235
CFI		($84)	($88)	($93)	($97)	($102)
Cash Available for Mandatory Repayment		$91	$102	$111	$122	$133
Mandatory Debt Repayment + Dividends		($166)	($16)	($16)	($16)	($16)
Cash Available for Optional Repayment		($75)	$86	$95	$106	$117
Instrument:	Revolver					
Pricing:	L+3.50%	Balance BOP	$0	$75	$0	$0	$0
Amortization:	0%	Net Issuance	$75	($75)	$0	$0	$0
Maturity:	7 years	Balance EOP	$75	$0	$0	$0	$0
		Interest Rate	5.50%	5.75%	6.00%	6.25%	6.50%
		Interest Exp.	$2	$2	$0	$0	$0
Instrument:	TLA	Balance BOP	$700	$693	$675	$572	$459
Pricing:	L+3.50%	Mand. Repay	($7)	($7)	($7)	($7)	($7)
Amortization:	1%	Opt. Repay	$0	($11)	($95)	($106)	($117)
Maturity:	6 years	Balance EOP	$693	$675	$572	$459	$335
Principal:	$700					

		5.50%	5.75%	6.00%	6.25%	6.50%
	Interest Rate	5.50%	5.75%	6.00%	6.25%	6.50%
	Interest Exp.	$38	$39	$37	$32	$26
Instrument:	TLB					
Pricing:	L+6.00%					
Amortization:	2.5%					
Maturity:	7 years					
Principal:	$350					
	Balance BOP	$350	$341	$333	$324	$315
	Mand. Repay	($9)	($9)	($9)	($9)	($9)
	Opt. Repay	$0	$0	$0	$0	$0
	Balance EOP	$341	$333	$324	$315	$306
	Interest Rate	8.0%	8.25%	8.50%	8.75%	9.00%
	Interest Exp.	$28	$28	$28	$28	$28
Instrument:	Bonds					
Pricing:	10.00%					
Amortization:	0%					
Maturity:	8 years					
Principal:	$200					
	Balance BOP	$200	$50	$50	$50	$50
	Opt. Repay	($150)	$0	$0	$0	$0
	Balance EOP	$50	$50	$50	$50	$50
	Interest Rate	10.00%	10.00%	10.00%	10.00%	10.00%
	Interest Exp.	$13	$5	$5	$5	$5

Returns Analysis

	IRR	Purchase	Projection Period				
		Purchase	2018E	2019E	2020E	2021E	2022E
EBITDA			$320	$336	$352	$370	$388
Exit Multiple			6.5x	6.5x	6.5x	6.5x	6.5x
Exit EV			$2080	$2182	$2290	$2403	$2521
Long-term Debt			$1084	$1057	$946	$824	$691
Equity Value			$996	$1125	$1344	$1578	$1830
Dividends			$0	$0	$0	$0	$0
2018 Exit CFs	IRR: 42.3%	($700)	$996				
2019 Exit CFs	IRR: 26.8%	($700)	$0	$1125			
2020 Exit CFs	IRR: 24.3%	($700)	$0	$0	$1344		
2021 Exit CFs	IRR: 22.5%	($700)	$0	$0	$0	$1578	
2022 Exit CFs	IRR: 21.2%	($700)	$0	$0	$0	$0	$1830

43

Other Types of Private Equity

43.1 Growth Equity

In growth equity, the investment firm takes a *minority*, non-controlling stake in the business. This is very different than LBO activity, in which the investment firm takes control of the business. Because the growth equity firm does not actually control the business, a strong *partnership* between the growth equity firm and the company is critical. Since the growth equity firm is dependent on the existing management (and in many cases, management is dependent on growth equity capital to execute their strategy), establishing a partnership between the two parties is critical to the success of the strategy.

A focus of growth equity firms and investments, as the name implies, is growth. Since a growth equity investor does not generate returns through leverage, like buyout activity, it is critical for the company to move to a new stage of operational success (e.g. improve sales, improve EBITDA, improve competitive position, etc.) so that the value of the minority equity stake increases over the holding period.

Typically, the capital provided by growth equity firms is used to fund a specific growth initiative or investable opportunity, such as a roll-up strategy (the acquisition of several smaller, similar businesses) or expansion into a new geography, which will hopefully produce growth for the company. Another common objective of growth equity capital is to provide the founders, owners, or former investors (such as earlier stage venture capital investors) with a liquidity event.

43.2   Venture Capital

Venture capital funds also take minority equity positions in very early stage companies. Early stage companies are usually cash flow negative and often pre-revenue. Because of the early stage nature of the target companies, venture capital investments are high risk and have a high potential reward if the company is successful.

Venture capital is raised in discrete investment rounds. By staging the investment process, venture capital funds can see that a firm makes operational progress before deploying more capital into the company. This makes the venture capital firm more willing to deploy capital early as well, since they can commit a small amount, see how the company develops, and then deploy more if they continue to be excited about the opportunity.

Venture capital funds usually have a specific industry or business focus. Venture capital firms usually specialize in seed, early, mid, or late stage investments, all within the realm of early stage businesses.

Venture capital is a fairly niche industry relative to other investment functions in terms of AUM. For this reason, key venture capital concepts such as the venture capital method, a specific valuation method utilized in the venture capital, and the major term sheet provisions (a term sheet is the investment document between a venture capital firm and a start-up that details the valuation, share price, liquidation preferences, etc.) between start-ups and investors will not be covered in this book.

Part VIII

Advanced/Selected Topics

44

Distressed Investing

44.1 Chapter 7 versus Chapter 11

Financial distress is when a company is unable to, or has difficulty, paying off its financial obligations to creditors. When a company defaults on an interest or principal payment (or knows that it will), the business undergoes either a Chapter 11 financial restructuring process or a Chapter 7 liquidation process. Both Chapter 11 and Chapter 7 are legal processes managed by legal courts in the United States. Therefore, Chapter 11 and Chapter 7 are as much a legal process as they are a financial restructuring process.

When a company "enters bankruptcy", the beginning of the Chapter 11 process is usually underway. Financial distress arises because the assets of a business were not sufficient to meet or cover the liabilities. Put differently, the liabilities were larger than the assets, essentially resulting in negative equity value. Note, the preceding discussion refers to the economic value of assets and liabilities, not the book value, which must always balance by the balance sheet equation.

The goal of the Chapter 11 bankruptcy/restructuring process is simple: restructure and reduce the size of the liability side of the balance sheet of the balance sheet. Effectively, the capital structure of the business is shifted around, some securities are often wiped out or eliminated, and the size, scope, and expensiveness of debt are usually reduced. The goal of Chapter 11 is to create an economically feasible entity that can remain a going-concern by drastically improving its ability to meet financial obligations. At the same time, Chapter 11 also has the goal of maximizing the value paid out to the various investors in the capital structure in an absolute priority order based on the seniority and security of the financial instruments in the capital structure. If it is unlikely the company will be able to remain a going-concern, even after Chapter 11, or if the value to investors would be better in a liquidation, then the assets of the company are liquidated instead (Chapter 7) and the cash produced is paid out to the various investors in the capital structure in the same absolute priority order.

It is important to realize that bankruptcy *can be* a positive for a company since it enables the renegotiation of contracts and a more feasible capital structure. This being said, bankruptcy has significant costs, both direct and indirect. Bankruptcy is usually best avoided at all costs. However, when necessary, bankruptcy can be an essential process for allowing a business to remain a going-concern. In the public perception, bankruptcy is often considered the end of a company – this is actually the exact opposite of what bankruptcy is. Bankruptcy is a new, more economically feasible beginning for a business, with a hefty price tag.

44.2   Causes of Financial Distress

In this section, some causes of financial distress are discussed:

- **Poor Operating Performance** – sometimes, a business simply does much worse than creditors expect. Obviously, creditors will lend to a business within their risk tolerance. However, almost all creditors expect to get paid back. Therefore, if the company enters Chapter 11 or Chapter 7, something materially impacted the cash flow producing capability of the business. Some possible factors are: deterioration of customer relationships, increased competitive pressures, the turning of the economic cycle for the worst, loss of key customers, or increased costs.

- **Lack of Access to Capital Markets** – often, debt is raised with the expectation that it will be refinanced at maturity rather than paid back through the cash flow of the firm. This is completely fine, if the company has access to capital markets when it needs to refinance. Access to capital markets can lock up based on the expectations surrounding the firm or the market. If this is the case, a firm might be forced to enter bankruptcy to restructure those liabilities since it cannot and was not expecting to have to pay them with cash flow.

44.3 Valuation and Exiting Restructuring

In a restructuring, the various constituents of the capital structure are divided into classes. For the sake of this discussion, we will assume Company Z has three classes in its capital structure: secured creditors who have a claim of $100, unsecured creditors who have a claim of $100, and equity investors who have a claim of $200. Cash on the balance sheet is then $0. Suppose Company Z has $50 of EBITDA. Therefore, the total claim value over EBITDA is 8.0x and the business was levered 4.0x.

The goal of every class is to maximize their total value received. Since secured creditors are the least likely to get wiped out, their focus is on maximizing the staying power of the post-reorganized entity. Equity holders, on the other hand, just want to receive *something* so they are not left completely empty handed (which is often the case). Therefore, the goal of equity holders is to maximize the projected value of the future going-concern in the bankruptcy negotiations.

Remember that Company Z has three classes of financial claims: secured creditors, unsecured creditors, and equity holders. When a bankruptcy resolution plan is proposed, a class receiving its claim in full ($100 in the case of secured creditors) is automatically said to "approve" the plan. A class receiving nothing (often the equity holders) is automatically said to "disapprove" the plan. The class that receives a partial satisfaction of its claim is called the fulcrum security. The fulcrum security class approves the plan if 1/2 in number and 2/3 in amount of the fulcrum security investors vote in support of the plan. If a plan fails to be confirmed by the fulcrum security, the judge can "cram-down" a plan as long as at least one voting class approves of the plan.

To value the business in a restructuring process, investment bankers and the various stakeholders first work to determine a prospective adjusted EBITDA figure. Often times, underperforming or less profitable assets are sold in a restructuring process. Going forward, prospective EBITDA can therefore change significantly. For the sake of the example, suppose the adjusted EBITDA of Company Z is $40. Investment bankers and the various stakeholders must also decide what the business is worth as a multiple of adjusted EBITDA. After considering the weakened competitive position and low growth potential of the business, the EV/EBITDA multiple is determined to be 4.0x. The entire enterprise is then worth $160. But remember how the secured creditors had a $100 claim, the unsecured creditors had a $100 claim, and the equity holders had a $200 claim? Total claims are $400. Since the enterprise is only worth $160 following the restructuring, the equity holders are completely wiped out (as is often the case) and the unsecured creditors are the fulcrum security. Lastly, the investment bankers and various stakeholders must decide a leverage level that the business can support. For Company Z, they decide on 3.0x debt/EBITDA or $120 of debt. Since company has an EV of $160 and debt of $120, the post reorganization equity value is $40. Beyond this, suppose the $120 of debt is broken up into $60 of secured credit and $60 of unsecured credit.

After all this is determined, one can assess what each class receives under the law of absolute priority. The original secured creditors, who had a claim of $100, receive $60 of secured credit and $40 of secured credit, completely recovering their value. The original unsecured creditors, who had a claim of $100 junior to the secured creditors, receive $20 of unsecured credit and $40 (or 100%) of the post-reorganization equity, recovering 60% of their claim. The former equity holders are completely wiped out and receive nothing.

44.4   Points on Distressed Investing

When it becomes reasonably possible that a company will enter bankruptcy, the various debts of the business will likely trade at a discount. The secured credits will trade at a moderate discount, and the unsecured credits will often trade at a deep discount. This means that the yield on these debt instruments is relatively high. Therefore, an investor might analyze the financial and competitive situation of the business and determine that bankruptcy is less likely than the market is pricing, and buy the securities of the business assuming a bankruptcy will be avoided. If these situations are identified correctly, investors can receive equity-like returns. Conversely, an investor might short the securities of the business if he or she believes bankruptcy is more likely than the market is pricing in. This is one form of distressed investing.

In the preceding example with Company Z, the unsecured creditors became the sole owners of the reorganized business. If an investor believes bankruptcy could or will happen, investors might try to predict which security will be the fulcrum security by valuing the business themselves before bankruptcy and determining what each class of claims will likely receive. Investors could then buy a huge portion of the anticipated fulcrum security at a deep discount (with Company Z this was the unsecured credits) before the restructuring process in anticipation of receiving the post-reorganization equities. This is a relatively cheap way to become a controlling owner of a business. So, you see, in some cases distressed investors actually want the post-reorganization securities and will invest on this basis.

Most distressed investors will analyze their potential returns in both scenarios: the assumed occurrence or the assumed no occurrence of bankruptcy. Then, based on the investors perception of the probability of each outcome, he or she will determine whether the risk/reward profile of the prospective investment is attractive.

Much more can be said about distressed investing. This discussion aims to only provide a cursory introduction to the concepts and thought processes common to the practice.

45

Macroeconomic Considerations

45.1 Interest Rates

The central bank of a country decides the short-term rate at which commercial banks can lend to each other. The central bank of a country also has the ability to purchase securities in the open market, such as bonds, artificially inflating the price and reducing the yield of the bonds. This is called open market operations. Through these two mechanisms, a central bank can exert moderate control over the interest rates for safe government securities. Most credit instruments are considered in relation to these safe government securities. Therefore, the government can influence the yields or attractiveness of a wide variety of credit instruments.

Beyond this, when interest rates are low, two important things can happen. First, because the cost of liquidity (money) is low when interest rates are low, businesses and enterprises have the ability to lever up cheaply. This can induce credit euphoria, which can be risky in the long run and result in credit crunches. Second, low interest rates can result in a lot of money flooding the stock market, perhaps creating over-valuations. This occurs because most investors are chasing return. When yields are low, let's say 2.5% or less on long-term government bonds, the attractiveness of investing in bonds is low. Effectively, a 2.5% interest rate is the same as buying a security with a 40 P/E ratio. Therefore, when the average P/E ratio of the S&P is about 15 throughout history, a low interest rate environment can result in a strong investor preference for stocks, since they are often "cheaper" relative to low yielding debt securities.

The yield curve is the graph of the interest rates for government securities at different maturities. Generally, the yield curve is upward sloping, meaning that investors want to be compensated more for taking longer risks, which makes intuitive sense.

45.2   Inflation

Inflation is the general increase in the prices of goods over-time. Macroeconomists and most central banks believe there is a strong relationship between inflation and interest rates. It is hard to ascertain whether this is true, since economists cannot ever prove causal relationships, because financial history never presents a counter-factual (what would have happened if something did not happen). Due to this belief that inflation and interest rates are linked, central banks try to control the level of inflation through interest rates. The inflation rate that the United States targets is 2%. The general belief is that a slightly positive inflation rate is ideal since it results in increasing prices, which incentivizes consumer spending now. If inflation was a significantly positive number, consumer wages would not keep up with price increases. If inflation was a negative number (deflation), consumers would have an incentive to save rather than spend. This could harm the businesses in an economy.

Inflation is basically a hidden or often forgotten tax. Over-time, the spending power of dollars tends to decrease due to inflation. Therefore, some investors make strides to protect against inflation. Debt instruments are ineffective for inflation protection since their income stream is purely in nominal terms and not inflation adjusted terms. There is a special type of debt instrument called treasury inflation protected securities (TIPS) that are sold by the United States government. These are debt instruments in which the principal of the instrument increases with inflation. Stocks are considered another way to protect against inflation. The general belief is that the revenue side of a business grows faster due to inflation than the cost side, resulting in a degree of inflationary protection from stocks.

45.3   Exchange Rates

A currency is the form/type of money used by a country or group of countries. For example, the United States utilizes the United States Dollar (USD) and the European Union utilizes the Euro. Most currencies are "floating rate" which means that they vary in value relative to other currencies. The specific value or conversion rate between one currency and another is called the exchange rate. The market in which exchange rates are traded is called the foreign exchange (ForEx) market. The ForEx market never closes. There are dozens of factors that would make one currency more desirable than another, such as political stability, interest rates, and economic opportunity. When investing in international stocks, exchanges, or markets, the investor must be aware of exchange rate risk. Often times, international investors will try to hedge exchange rate risk through special derivatives. These derivatives and hedging techniques are beyond the scope of this book. Still, an awareness of these tools is valuable.

46

Stock Options

46.1 Stock Option Basics

Options are a type of *derivative*. A derivative is a security or agreement between two parties that derives value from a separate underlying security (such as a stock) or a group of assets (such as an index). The value of a derivative depends on the value of these underlying assets. The most common underlying assets are stocks, bonds, indexes, and commodities. Options and derivatives are a broad and complex topic. There are hundreds of books on stock options alone. In this book, only stock options are briefly discussed.

There are two types of stock options: call options and put options. In a sentence, a call option is the *right* to buy a stock at a specific price at or before a specific date. A put option is the *right* to sell (short) a stock at a specific price at or before a specific date. There is a lot packed into this one sentence definition, so let us define some key terms that relate to it:

- **Buyer** – the individual or entity that actually purchases the right to buy (call)/sell (put) a stock at a specific price at or before a specific date. The buyer is said to be "long" the call or put.

- **Writer** – the individual or entity that sells the rights to the buyer to buy (call)/sell (put) a stock at a specific price at or before a specific date. Therefore, the writer is obligated to sell (call)/buy (put) the stock to/from the buyer at the *strike price* if the buyer chooses to exercise the option at or before *expiry*. For this reason, the buyer of the option has *optionality* and the writer of the option has no optionality. The writer is said to be "short" the call or put.

- **Spot Price** – the spot price is the current price of the underlying stock.

- **Strike Price** – the strike price is the price at which the writer must sell (call)/buy (put) the stock to/from the buyer if the buyer chooses to exercise the option at or before *expiry*.

- **Exercise** – when the buyer of the option chooses to force the writer to sell (call)/buy (put) to/from the buyer at or before expiry.

- **Expiry** – the time/date at which the optionality of the buyer expires and the option contract between the buyer and writer terminates.

- **Time to Expiry** – the remaining amount of time until expiry.

- **Optionality** – the right of the buyer of the option to exercise the option at the strike price before expiry. The writer of the option sells optionality to the buyer for a *premium*.

- **Price or Premium** – the upfront cost that the writer charges the buyer for entering into the option contract. Since the writer is selling optionality to the buyer, the buyer must pay upfront for this optionality, since optionality is valuable. The writer is compensated for selling optionality through the premium. Since options are traded over an exchange like a stock, the price of an option changes over time until it expires.

- **In-the-Money (ITM)** – when the spot price is significantly above (call)/below (put) the strike price before expiry. For example, suppose a call option has a strike price of $45 and the spot price is $50 with a time to expiry of one year. In this scenario, the buyer of the call option has the right to exercise the option and force the writer to sell the stock to the buyer at $45. Since the stock is currently worth $50 in the market, the buyer could then sell the stock for $50 and make $5. In this scenario, the option is in-the-money (ITM).

- **Out-of-the-Money (OTM)** – when the spot price is significantly below (call)/above (put) the strike price before expiry.

- **At-the-Money (ATM)** – when the spot price is right around the strike price before expiry.

- **Covered Call** – when the writer of a call option also already owns the underlying stock. Therefore, if the buyer of the call option chooses to exercise the option, the writer can simply give the buyer the underlying stock that he already owns. The underlying stock functions as perfect collateral.

Having established some basic terms and concepts associated with stock options, it is helpful to generalize the two main factors that determine a stock option's premium. These are moneyness and time value. Moneyness refers to how "in-the-money" (ITM) an option is. As a stock option becomes more ITM (or less OTM), the premium or price of the option increases. As a stock option becomes less ITM (or more OTM), the premium or price of the option decreases. Also remember that the writer of an option is selling optionality to the buyer. Optionality only has value to the extent that there is *time remaining* in the option contract to utilize the optionality. Therefore, the other determinant of an options price or premium is time value – the value associated with the optionality. As time passes, time value deteriorates, since there is less time to utilize the embedded optionality in an options contract. Therefore, time value decays over the life of an option and eventually becomes worthless at expiry, at which point the buyer of the option no longer has optionality, and the option contract no longer has time value.

When dealing with "vanilla" options (calls and puts), the investor has four possible trades: long/buy a call, sell/short/write a call, long/buy a put, and sell/short/write a put. These four trades are viable and can be effective in isolation. However, options get really interesting when these four trades are combined to design more complex payoff scenarios. This will be covered later in this chapter.

Why are options used at all? The main reasons are financial leverage and risk mitigation. Suppose the investor is bullish on a stock and believes its price will increase overtime. When buying the stock, an investor must pay the entire current stock price to express that view. When buying a call option, an investor will pay a fraction of the current stock price to express that view. If the investor ends up being correct and the stock price does appreciate, then the percent return associated with being correct will be greater if an option was purchased rather than a stock. This is

because the investor has to put less money upfront to express the
view in the case of the option, which magnifies returns if the thesis
plays out. It also magnifies losses if the thesis does not play out
(the option expires OTM) since the investor will lose 100% of the
premium paid. This is the concept of financial leverage.

Options are also used to mitigate risk and hedge. If an investor is long a stock and its price drops 50%, the investor loses
50%. If an investor is long a call option and the stock/underlying
price drops 50%, the most the investor can lose is the premium
paid. This mitigates downside risk. Options are also used to coun-
terbalance positions and hedge. For example, an investor might go
long a stock and also go long a put. In this scenario, the investor
caps his or her downside risk since the put will start to be ITM
as the value of the stock declines, if it declines. Therefore, for the
cost of the premium, the investor mitigates downside risk while
capturing all the potential upside in the stock.

46.2   Stock Option Payoff Diagrams

A payoff diagram is a way to visualize the profit and loss
of a financial asset as the spot price changes. The y-axis of a
payoff diagram is the profit or loss (P&L) of the security. The
x-axis of a payoff diagram is the spot price. In this section, we will
review the payoff diagrams of stocks, calls, puts, and some possible
combinations of these.

First, consider the payoff diagram of a stock bought for $25.
The P&L is $0 when the spot price is the same as the purchase
price – $25. The payoff diagram of being long a stock is a line with
a slope of 1 and an x-intercept at the purchase price. The graph
below shows an example:

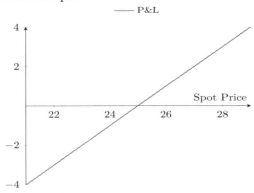

The payoff diagram of being short a stock is just the opposite. It is a line with a slope of -1 and an x-intercept at the sale price. In the example below, assume that the sale price is $25. This introduces an important rule of thumb: to convert the payoff diagram of being long a set of securities to the payoff diagram of being short the same set of securities, simply reflect the payoff diagram over the x-axis.

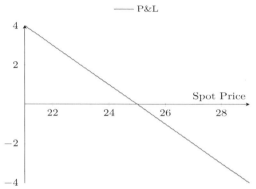

Now, consider the payoff diagram of being long a call option right at expiry. Above the strike price, a call option has the payoff diagram of being long a stock. However, the entire graph is shifted down by the premium paid. Said option has no "moneyness" when spot is below the strike price. Therefore, when spot is below the strike price, the option is worthless and the investor loses the entire premium paid without making any money from moneyness. The diagram below is an example of a long call payoff diagram at expiry with a strike price of $25 and an upfront premium of $1.

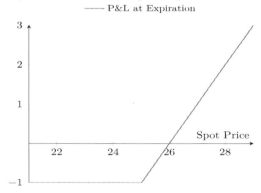

If the investor writes or sells the call, the payoff diagram simply flips over the x-axis. Therefore, the writer collects the premium and then begins to lose money as spot increases above the strike. The diagram below is an example of a short call payoff diagram at expiry with a strike price of $25 and an upfront premium of $1.

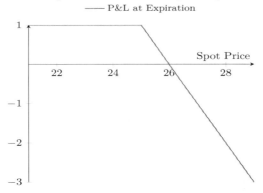

The buyer of a put option has the right to sell a stock at the strike price at or before expiry at the cost of the premium. Therefore, the long put payoff diagram looks like the payoff diagram of being short a stock when spot is below the strike price. However, the entire graph is shifted down by the premium paid. When spot is above strike, exercising the option is worthless and the investor loses the entire premium. The diagram below is an example of a long put payoff diagram at expiry with a strike price of $25 and an upfront premium of $1.

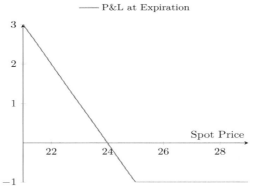

When selling or writing a put, the writer gives away the right to the buyer to force the writer to buy the underlying at the strike price. Therefore, when the spot price is below the strike price, the buyer will not exercise the option, since the buyer could make more money selling a share in the market. For this reason, the writer collects all the premium when the spot price is above the strike price. Below the strike price, the payoff diagram looks like that of a long stock, since the writer will be forced to go long the stock when spot is at or below the strike price. The diagram below is an example of a short put payoff diagram at expiry with a strike price of $25 and an upfront premium of $1.

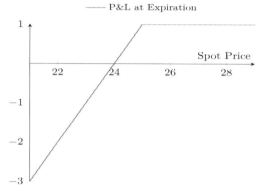

So far we have only considered buying and selling one put or call at a time. What if the investor makes multiple trades at once? It is actually fairly simple to combine individual payoff diagrams. To do this, simply add the y-component of each individual payoff diagram for a given spot price. Using this rule of thumb, observe the following diagram below. The diagram below is the payoff diagram of a long call with a strike of $24 for $2 at expiry combined with the payoff diagram of a short call with a strike of $26 for $1 at expiry. This is called a *bull call spread*. In fact, this is the basic shape of any payoff diagram in which a call is purchased at a lower strike and another call is sold at a higher strike.

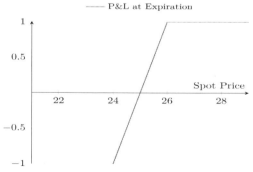

What if the investor wants to short the call spread? This is called a *bear call spread*. To do this, the investor simply makes the opposite trade for each trade in the entire play. So, the investor would sell the lower strike call and buy the higher strike call. The example diagram below shows a call with a strike of $24 sold for $2 and a call with a strike of $26 bought for $1.

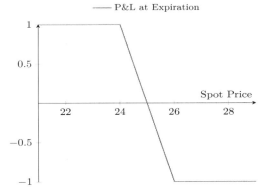

What about puts? Suppose the investor buys a put and call at the same strike price. This is called a *straddle*. The example diagram below is the payoff diagram of a long call at a $25 strike for $1 with a long put at a $25 strike for $1. Put differently, this is the payoff diagram of a long straddle centered at $25.

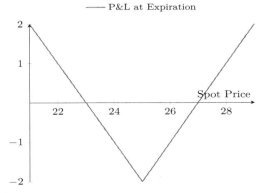

A strangle is similar to a straddle. In a long strangle, a put is purchased at a lower strike than the purchased call. The example diagram below shows a long strangle. In this strangle, the investor is long a \$24 strike put for \$1 and long a \$26 strike call for \$1.

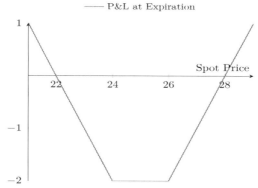

In this chapter, we have completed a very elementary introduction to stock options, associated terms, and payoff diagrams.
With hope, the reader now better understands concepts such as employee stock options and warrants, which are basically long-dated
call options with some nuance differences. For those intrigued by
this discussion, there are a few resources in the References section
at the end of this book that provide a more thorough introduction
to options and other derivatives.

47

Unique Industries

47.1 Biotechnology

Biotechnology is an incredible industry. Biotechnology is a specific subset of the healthcare space. Biotechnology is the industry responsible for producing new and novel drug therapies. This is no simple process. In fact, it is very complex. In the United States, to produce and market a new drug therapy to consumers, a prospective drug therapy must undergo multiple phases of clinical testing to validate the safety and efficacy of the potential drug therapy. The Federal Drug Administration (FDA) then evaluates the clinical data and will approve or deny the drug for commercial sale in the United States.

The clinical testing process generally takes 5-10 years and costs tens to hundreds of millions of dollars. The astute reader has noticed something important – biotechnology companies that do not have an FDA approved product do not have any revenue or cash flow for the entire developmental time period. So who pays for the development of these potential drug therapies? Investors!

Since early-stage biotechnology companies have no cash flow, a lot of the thought processes and techniques covered in this book are useless. Instead of cash flow, early-stage biotechnology investors focus on the quality, depth, and breadth of the clinical data and the underlying science driving the clinical results. The risks are high in biotechnology investing; the industry is very volatile, since a bad clinical trial result can cause a company's valuation to plummet. But, the rewards to astute, disciplined, and careful investors are significant.

If a biotechnology company successfully receives FDA approval for a new drug therapy, the economics of commercialization are generally very promising for a few reasons. First, the first company with an approved product for treating a disease usually receives a government sanctioned monopoly for many years. This gives investors an incentive to invest in these companies, otherwise competition would immediately erode the monetary rewards of innovation. Second, individuals that the therapy is intended for usually want or need the therapy, which makes selling the product easier. Since the post-approval economics are promising, most investors focus their attention on analyzing the pre-approval clinical data to try and foreshadow which drugs will successfully receive FDA approval.

Biotechnology is unique from an investing perspective. Biotechnology also serves a critical role in society. Biotechnology and its regulatory structure fuel effective and safe therapeutic innovation that improves life quality and longevity for millions of people across the globe.

47.2   Financial Companies

Financial companies, such as banks, investment banks, insurance companies, and asset managers, are also very unique. Almost every type of financial company has a specific set of financial ratios for analysis. For example, banks have additional financial ratios that analyze loan delinquency, loan quality, and capital quality. When performing a financial analysis on any financial company, it is important to understand the industry standard metrics for that given type of financial company and to employ them in the analysis.

Lastly, the book value of assets and liabilities for a financial company is significantly more accurate. Due to this, the book value of equity for a financials business is much more accurate relative to other industries. In most industries, valuation ratios such as P/E, P/LFCF, and EV/EBITDA are utilized since earnings and cash flow are a more reliable measure of the businesses worth. Since book value is much more accurate for financial companies, the valuation of financial companies is generally assessed on a P/B or (Market Cap)/(Book Value) basis. Furthermore, return on equity (rather than ROIC) is the go-to return metric for financial companies since the book value of equity is much more reliable.

48

Other Topics

48.1 Taxation

Taxes are an important consideration for investors. Income streams from securities such as interest payments and dividend payments are usually taxed as ordinary income. The price appreciation of securities is taxed at the capital gains rate. The capital gains rate for an individual is based on two things: the holding period of the security and the income tax bracket of the individual. The capital gains rate is reasonably lower than the income tax rate of the individual. If an individual holds a security for more than a year, the gains, upon exiting the position, will be taxed at the long-term capital gains rate which is lower than the short-term capital gains rate. The lower long-term capital gains rate aims to encourage long-term investing. Capital gains tax is determined by the entry and exit price of a security position. Therefore, no capital gains tax arises until a security is sold at a gain.

Through special investment vehicles, such as an IRA, individual investors can invest with tax immunity. This is fantastic for wealth creation. An investor should always put their highest conviction trades in his or her tax-free account. The government limits the amount of money that an individual can put in an IRA per year. However, with consistent IRA deposits and the power of compound interest, an IRA can become quite large over time. For individuals interested in investing, opening an IRA is generally the best way to start. However, there are a few different types of IRAs, so this endeavor requires a little bit of research to determine the IRA structure that is optimal for one's wants and needs.

48.2   Short Selling Mechanics

Short selling, or betting on the price of a security going down – has been referred to frequently in the book. However, we have not discussed the actual mechanics and processes surrounding a short sell. Let's demystify it now.

A broker holds many securities on behalf of its clients. For example, all of a broker's clients combined might own 1000 shares of AAPL stock. However, the broker is responsible for holding those shares. Therefore, a broker has 1000 shares of AAPL stock sitting idly. What could the broker do with these idle AAPL shares? Lend them out! This is precisely how a short sell works.

Another investor might want to bet on the price of AAPL stock going down. This other investor contacts a broker currently holding 1000 shares of idle AAPL stock. Then, the broker can lend the investor some of these idle shares. As with any loan, the investor must repay principal and pay interest. The principal is the actual shares. The interest fee is a cash expense over the life of the loan that increases as more investors are borrowing the same stock from the same broker. Once the stock is borrowed, the investor immediately sells the stock and receives cash for the stock sale. Therefore, if the stock price decreases, the investor can re-buy the same stock, pay back the loan principal with shares, and collect the difference between the cash received at sale and the cash spent at repurchase. This is the process of a short sale.

To provide a tangible example, suppose the current price of AAPL stock is $130. An investor short sells a share of the stock at the current price with a 2% interest rate per year. Therefore, the investor owes the broker a share of AAPL stock and interest over the life of the short. The investor receives $130 cash for selling the borrowed stock. A year later, AAPL stock is $120. The investor repurchases the AAPL stock at this price, returns the borrowed share to the broker, and collects $10. However, the investor also had to pay $2.60 in interest expense. Therefore, the investor made $7.40 of profit.

Shorts have infinite downside and limited upside, so they must be handled with significant care. Most investors advise against shorting a stock simply because it is overvalued. Generally, the best shorts have a specific catalyst that will cause the price to decline significantly and in a timely manner.

48.3   Activism

Activism is a special type of investing in which investors aim to purchase a large chunk of a company's stock to secure representation on the board of directors and influence the company's operations. Activist investors try to identify businesses that are under-performing relative to their potential, and need a strategic overhaul. Activism is all about concentrated and high potential reward investments. Not many investors are activists since it requires a huge capital commitment into one position. Activism, which is very difficult and complicated to execute, is a rare art form.

49

Getting in the Game

A brokerage account is similar to a bank account. This is the account through which an individual can trade in public securities such as stocks, bonds, and options. This section reviews some important considerations when opening your first brokerage account:

- **Company Reputation** – the company that one opens a brokerage account with is very important. Generally, this is a very long-term commitment, so it is nothing to take lightly. Just like with a bank account, it is a liability to keep money with a company with a bad reputation. Lower quality companies will often try to entice potential customers with low fees. It is important to do some research before opening a brokerage account. Find a brokerage account that fits your needs and desires. Ultimately, it is recommended an investor open a brokerage account with a reputable and widely known company.

- **Transaction Costs** – all brokerages charge money for trades made. For small trades, brokerage firms usually charge a fixed fee. For larger trades, the fee begins to scale with the size of the trade. Transaction costs add up! In a $1000 trade, a $5 fixed fee is fairly common. Therefore, after entering and exiting the position, the investor is already down 1%. It is important to be aware of transactions costs and their impact on returns. The best way to mitigate transaction costs is to trade less by investing with a long-term perspective.

- **Mobile Support** – we live in a mobile world. It is very valuable to have a brokerage with mobile support. However, the

ability to trade and follow stocks on a mobile device man-
dates that the investor maintain even stricter discipline to
think with a long-term perspective and resist the effect of
short-term price movements.

- **Minimum Capital Requirement** – many brokerages have
  a many capital commitment. This is important to be aware
  of before opening a brokerage account.

- **Securities Available** – most brokerages do not provide access to every security in the investing universe. Options access, certain debt instruments, and international investing
  access can be hard to come by. It is important to know what
  securities you will actually be able to trade with your brokerage account.

- **Educational Support** – some brokerages will provide extensive training on the software and interface. This can be
  helpful for getting up to speed with the services and functionality of the brokerage and its software.

- **Research** – some brokerages will provide research on stocks,
  bonds, and other securities. This can be helpful. But remember an astute investor must arrive at his or her own conclu-
  sions and opinions!

50

What Is Next?

So, you've read this book, and opened a brokerage account, what is next? The journey is just beginning! Experience is the single best way to get better at investing. Start by doing some research using the tools and techniques discussed in this book. If you find a security that appears under-priced, make a modest investment in it. most important, document *why* you think this security is a viable investment. This allows you to analyze and improve your investment process over time.

As you gain more experience, your circle of competence will grow. Your understanding of the tools and techniques in this book will grow as well. While this will make you a more articulate investor, do not let it lull you into a false sense of confidence. Never forget the lessons in Part VI of this book. These are lessons to learn and live by. If you stay honest with your abilities, disciplined with your behavior, and prudent with your judgments, investing success will likely come.

The pursuit of becoming a great investor is a lifelong journey filled with research, reading, conversation, and hard work. All of the world's most successful investors will tell you there is no "get-rich-quick-scheme" in the world of investing, despite the general publics fascination with this concept. Congratulations on making it this far and best of luck with your investing endeavors.

Bibliography

- Alice Schroeder. The Snowball. Bantam, 2009.

- Andrew Chisholm. An Introduction to Capital Markets. Wiley, 2002.

- Aswath Damodaran. The Little Book of Valuation. Wiley, 2011.

- Avinash Dixit. Thinking Strategically. W. W. Norton & Company, 1993.

- Benjamin Franklin. The Autobiography of Benjamin Franklin. Dover Publications, 1996.

- Benjamin Graham. Security Analysis. McGraw-Hill Education, 2008.

- Benjamin Graham. The Intelligent Investor. Harper Business, 2006.

- Bruce Greenwald. Value Investing. Wiley, 2004.

- Christopher Browne. The Little Book of Value Investing. Wiley, 2006.

- Claudia Zeisberger. Mastering Private Equity. Wiley, 2004.

- Dan Ariely. Predictably Irrational. Harper Perennial, 2010.

- Daniel Kahneman. Thinking Fast and Slow. Farrar, Straus, and Giroux, 2013.

- David Stowell. Investment Banks, Hedge Funds, and Private Equity. Academic Press, 2012.

- David Young. Corporate Financial Reporting and Analysis. Wiley, 2013.

- Frank Fabozzi. The Handbook of Fixed Income Securities. Wiley, 2012.

- Howard Marks. The Most Important Thing. Columbia University Press, 2013.

- James Montier. The Little Book of Behavioral Investing. Wiley, 2010.

- James Montier. Value Investing. Wiley, 2009.

- Jason Zweig. The Little Book of Safe Money. Wiley, 2009.

- Jeffrey Hirsch. The Little Book of Stock Market cycles. Wiley, 2012.

- Jeffrey Hood. Inefficient Market Theory. Jeffrey Hood, 2014.

- Jeffrey Hooke. Security Analysis and Business Valuation. Wiley, 2010.

- Joel Greenblatt. The Little Book That Still Beats the Market. Wiley, 2010.

- John Bogle. The Little Book of Common Sense Investing. Wiley, 2007.

- John Mauldin. Bull's Eye Investing. Wiley, 2004.

- Joshua Rosenbaum & Joshua Pearl. Investment Banking. Wiley, 2013.

- Martin Whitman. Distress Investing. Wiley, 2009.

- Max Bazerman. Judgment in Managerial Decision Making. Wiley, 2008.

- McKinsey & Company. Value. Wiley, 2010.

- Michael Belucci. The LSTA's Complete Credit Agreement Guide. McGraw-Hill Education, 2016.

- Michael Porter. Competitive Advantage. Free Press, 1998.

- Michael Porter. Competitive Strategy. Free Press, 1998.

- Nassim Taleb. Black Swan. Random House Trade Paperbacks, 2010.

- Nassim Taleb. Fooled by Randomness. Random House Trade Paperbacks, 2005.

- Nate Silver. The Signal and the Noise. Penguin Books, 2015.

- Pat Dorsey. The Little Book That Builds Wealth. Wiley, 2008.

- Paul Asquith. Lessons in Corporate Finance. Wiley, 2016.

- Philip Fisher. Common Stocks and Uncommon Profits. Wiley, 2003.

- Preston McAfee. Competitive Solutions. Princeton University Press, 2005.

- Richard Brealey, Stewart Myers, & Franklin Allen. Principles of Corporate Finance. McGraw-Hill Education, 2016.

- Robert Bruner. Applied Mergers and Acquisitions. Wiley, 2017.

- Robert Cialdini. Influence. Harper Business, 2006.

- Robert Kricheff. A Pragmatist's Guide to Leveraged Finance. FT Press, 2012.

- Seth Klarman. Margin of Safety. HarperCollins, 1991.

- Sheldon Natenberg. Option Volatility and Pricing. McGraw-Hill Publishing, 1994.

- Stephen Moyer. Distressed Debt Analysis. J. Ross Publishing, 2004.

- Thomas Ittelson. Financial Statements. Career Press, 2009.

- Thomas Sowell. Basic Economics. Basic Books, 2014.

- Warren Buffett. The Essays of Warren Buffett. Carolina Academic Press, 2015.

- William Maxwell. Leveraged Financial Markets. McGraw-Hill Education, 2010.

Glossary

- **10-K** – the annual report of a publicly traded business.

- **10-Q** – the quarterly report of a publicly traded business.

- **8-K** – the special event report of a publicly traded business.

- **Access to Capital Markets** – the ability of a firm to raise debt or equity in the capital markets.

- **Activism** – buying a significant equity stake in a business with the objective of getting some form of control (board seat) and dictating the operations and strategy of the business.

- **Adaptability** – the value investing principle of updating ones thesis and opinions based on rationality and facts.

- **Alternative Data** – unique sources of data such as credit card data, social media data, web scraped data.

- **Asset Coverage** – the value of the assets of a business (inventory, accounts receivable, PPE) that serves as downside protection in case things go south. Particularly important for credit analysis.

- **Assets** – things that a firm owns or expects to become or produce cash in the future.

- **Balance Sheet** – one of the three financial statements. Exhibits what a company has (assets) versus what it owes (liabilities). The difference is the book value of shareholder's equity.

- **Balance Sheet Equation** – the equation that indicates the balance sheet was appropriately prepared; Assets = Liabilities + Equity.

- **Behavioral Biases** – the innate human tendencies that make acting with rationality at all times difficult.

- **Board of Directors** – the governing body of a business; represent the shareholders; decide the management team and maintain other important protocols and procedures.

- **Bond** – a publicly traded debt instrument. They usually have a fixed rate coupon, longer maturity, and junior to bank debt. A bond trading below par is at a discount and has a higher yield than the coupon. A bond trading above par is at a premium and has a lower yield than the coupon.

- **Business Overview** – the section of a 10-K or 10-Q that reviews the core operations and characteristics of the business.

- **Buy-side** – the portion of the professional investing universe that buys and invests in securities to generate a return.

- **Call Option** – the right to buy a stock at a given price within a certain time period.

- **Capital Allocation** – the cash allocation policy that a business utilizes.

- **Capital Structure** – the mix of debt and equity that a business utilizes.

- **Cash Conversion Cycle** – the period in days that it takes inventory purchased on credit to actually be converted to cash. The formula is CCC = DSO + DIH - DPO.

- **Cash Flow from Operating Activities** – appears on the cash flow statement. The amount of cash generated from actual business operations.

- **Cash Flow Statement** – one of the three financial statements; reconciles the changes to the businesses cash account on the balance sheet.

- **Catalyst** – a specific event or potential occurrence that will help price converge to intrinsic value.

- **Changes in Working Capital** – a component of all the cash flow formulas; captures the cash impact of changes in current assets and liabilities.

- **Chapter 11** – the formal bankruptcy process. Entered into when a company fails to make an interest or principal payment or fails to satisfy a covenant. The objective of Chapter 11 is to restructure a businesses capital structure and liabilities to enable it to remain a going- concern.

- **Chapter 7** – the formal liquidation process.

- **Circle of Competence** – a value investing principle; the area of the investment universe that an investor knows something about.

- **Commercial Banks** – the most senior lenders in the capital structure. Generally, they provide short-term bank loans and revolvers.

- **Comparable Companies Analysis** – a relative valuation methodology that depends on the calculation of industry average valuation multiples to value a specific business.

- **Contrarianism** – a value investing principle; the concept that outsized and safe financial returns require differentiated thinking.

- **Convertible Debt** – debt in which the holder has the ability to receive a principal repayment in either cash or shares of the issuer's stock.

- **Cost Advantages** – structural advantages to a businesses operations or processes that enable cheaper production of the same or similar product/service as competitors.

- **Cost of Debt** – the percent cost associated with debt financing for a business. The required rate of return of debt investors.

- **Cost of Equity** – the percent cost associated with equity financing for a business. The required rate of return of equity investors. Usually calculated using the capital asset pricing model.

- **Costs of Financial Distress** – the direct and indirect costs of going through a Chapter 11 restructuring process.

- **Covenant** – provisions in a credit agreement that mandate what the issuer can do, cannot do, and must do over the life of the credit investment.

- **Credit Rating Agency** – professional agency that rates the credit quality of a business.

- **Customer Concentration** – the level of revenue concentrated in a small subset of customers.

- **Customer Retention** – the ability of a business to keep customers coming back to the product or service.

- **Cycles** – the ebb and flow of the economy, credit, valuations, and businesses.

- **Days Inventory Held** – the days that it takes for inventory to be sold.

- **Days Payables Outstanding** – the days that it takes for accounts payable to be paid back.

- **Days Sales Outstanding** – the days that it takes for accounts receivable to be paid.

- **Defensive Investing** – a value investing principle; the concept that an investor should focus on protecting downside before considering potential return.

- **Depreciation and Amortization** – the non-cash expense associated with the gradual wear and tear of physical property (depreciation) and the reduced value of intangible assets overtime (amortization).

- **Discounted Cash Flow Analysis** – a cash flow based valuation technique. The primary method for business valuation. Determines intrinsic value.

- **Due Diligence** – the process of researching and assessing a business or security for potential investment.

- **Earnings Transcript** – the written record of a public business's earnings call.

- **EBIT** – earnings before interest and tax. Operating income. Appears on the income statement. A proxy for cash flow.

- **EBITDA** – Earnings before interest, tax, depreciation, and amortization. Operating income plus depreciation and amortization. The main proxy for cash flow.

- **Efficiency Ratios** − financial ratios that measure how efficiently assets are used in generating cash and sales.

- **Endowment** − the investment organization that manages a university's money. Generally long-term, patient, institutional capital. Regular serve as limited partners.

- **Enterprise Value** − the cost to buy an entire business. The value of a business including the claims of all parties in the capital structure. A measure of business value independent of financing decisions.

- **Equity Multiple** − a financial multiple that only considers the value and claims of equity holders.

- **Equity Value** − the value of just the equity portion of the capital structure. Also called market cap for public companies.

- **Exchange** − the entity through which securities are actually traded.

- **Exit Multiple Method** − one of two common methods for determining terminal value in a discounted cash flow analysis. This method assumes that the business is sold at some exit multiple of EBIT or EBITDA at the end of the projection period.

- **Financial Statements** − the statements through which a business shows its financial situation and results to interested parties. There are three financial statements − income statement, balance sheet, and cash flow statement. The financial statements are prepared according to the generally accepted account principles (GAAP).

- **Firmwide Multiple** − a financial multiple that considers the value and claims of all constituents of the capital structure including equity and debt holders.

- **Generic Strategies** − the basic strategies that a business can adopt. The main two are: product differentiation or price advantage.

- **Good Businesses** − businesses that have durable competitive advantages to ensure sustainable and growing long-term cash flow.

- **Growth Equity** – a type of private equity that makes a minority equity investment to a growing business. The capital is usually used to fund a specific growth initiative for the business, such as a roll-up strategy, geographic expansion, or new product release.

- **Hedge Fund** – a flexible, largely unregulated investment vehicle. Consists of limited partners (capital providers) and general partners (investment managers). General partners are compensated with the 2 and 20 fee structure – this includes a 2% management fee on AUM and a 20% incentive fee on returns.

- **Income Statement** – one of the three financial statements; exhibits how much money came in (revenue), expenses associated with that revenue (operating expenses), capital structure expenses (interest expense), and taxes. Ultimately results in net income, the bottom line, or earnings. This is different than cash flow.

- **Industry Reports** – reports that provide information on a specific industry.

- **Inflation** – the increase in prices of goods overtime. In the United States, the targeted inflation rate is 2%.

- **Insurance Company** – a special type of investment company or limited partner that invests using the float produced by unpaid insurance claims.

- **Intangible Assets** – the non-physical assets of a company, such as brand or customer relationships.

- **Interest Expense** – the expense associated with debt.

- **Investment Bank** – a financial intermediary that provides many valuable services, such as investment banking, asset management, and sales and trading. Investment banks are the main party involved with the sell-side.

- **Investor Presentation** – a presentation prepared by a business for presenting strategy, financial results, and management results. Usually available on the investor relations section of a public company's website.

- **Leveraged Buyout** – the acquisition of a business utilizing a significant portion of debt or leverage.

- **Levered Free Cash Flow** – cash flow to equity holders; free cash flow to firm minus interest expense.

- **Liabilities** – the financial obligations of a firm.

- **Liquidity Ratios** – ratios that measure the ability of a firm to produce cash.

- **Loan** – a private debt instrument. Generally floating rate, longer term, and covenant heavy. Often provided by commercial banks and specialized hedge funds.

- **Long-termism** – a value investing principle. The concept that a long-term investing perspective is superior, safer, and more effective.

- **Management** – the group of individuals who make the operational and financial decisions regarding a business.

- **Management's Discussion and Analysis** – a section of a 10-K or 10-Q in which management discusses the strategy, results, and prospects of the business.

- **Margin of Safety** – a value investing principle. The concept that an investor should aim to pay less than intrinsic value for a security, with a healthy discrepancy between price and intrinsic value.

- **Mean Reversion** – the concept that most things revert to average level.

- **Net Income** – the bottom-line of the income statement. Also called earnings. The primary focus of most sell-side analysts.

- **Network Effects** – the phenomenon by which the value proposition of a business's products/services actually increases with the number of users.

- **Operating Expenses** – the expenses associated with producing revenue.

- **Operating Leverage** – the amount of sales growth that translates to EBIT growth. Determined by the fixed versus variable cost structure of a firm.

- **Operating Metrics** – the core revenue/cash producing units of a business.

- **Payoff Diagram** – a diagram that shows the P&L of a security based on the spot price.

- **Pension Fund** – a special type of investment operation that invests money on behalf of future retirees. Often serves as a limited partner.

- **Perpetuity Method** – one of two methods for determining terminal value in a discounted cash flow analysis. Assumes that cash flow will grow at some rate into perpetuity to determine a perpetuity value that is then discounted back to present time.

- **PIK Debt** – debt in which the interest expense is paid by increasing outstanding principal rather cash payments. PIK debt actually increases cash flow prior to maturity because of the tax shields. Usually very junior in the capital stack.

- **Porter's Five Forces** – a framework for analyzing the competitiveness and attractiveness of an industry.

- **Precedent Transactions Analysis** – a relative valuation method based on historical multiples paid for comparable businesses.

- **Preferred Equity** – a junior portion of the capital stack that has characteristics of both debt and equity. Generally, preferred equity has a face value and pays accumulating dividends, similar to debt. However, preferred equity holders also regularly get board representation and voting rights, similar to equity. Some preferred equity securities also have the ability to convert into common equity.

- **Present Value** – the value of a future cash flow discounted to the present time frame using some discount rate.

- **Price Movements** – a value investing principle; the concept that short-term price fluctuations are a distraction and are of little importance to the long-term value of a business or security.

- **Private Equity Fund** – a firm that engages in leveraged buyout activity.

- **Product Quality** – the level of quality of a business's products or services. This is an intangible asset and is a source of competitive advantage.

- **Professionalism** – a value investing principle; the belief that an investment manager must ask with integrity and respect when investing with other people's capital.

- **Profit Margins** – the percent of sales converted to profit, for a given profit metric.

- **Put Option** – the right to sell a stock at a specific price within a certain time period.

- **Return Ratios** – financial ratios that measure the ability of capital investments to produce financial returns.

- **Revenue** – the top-line of the income statement; represents the total amount of money that came into the business over the fiscal period.

- **Revenue Projection Model** – a component of a three statement model, DCF, or LBO model that predicts the revenue of a business. A RPM is either bottom-up (based on operating metrics) or top-down (based on market share and market size).

- **Revolver** – a line of credit for a business. Generally provided by commercial banks. Basically a big credit card for a business.

- **Risk** – the range of possible negative outcomes that can but will not necessarily happen.

- **Scalability** – the ability of a business to scale attractive unit economics across many units.

- **Seasonality** – the variability in a company's cash flows and revenue due to the seasons.

- **Security** – a financial instrument through which investors hope to receive some form of monetary compensation from over time.

- **Sell-side** – the participants in the investing profession that provide services to the buy-side.

- **Sell-side Research** – market research that comes from sell-side research analysts.

- **Seniority** – the priority of repayment of a security within the capital stack. A more senior security is paid back first. As seniority increases, potential return decreases. Debt is more senior than equity.

- **Shareholder's Equity** – the book value of equity on the balance sheet. The difference between assets and liabilities.

- **Short Selling** – the act of borrowing securities from a brokerage firm that holds the securities of many investors, selling those securities, and promising to return those securities in the future. Over the borrowing period, there is an interest cost associated with the security loan.

- **Signaling** – the phenomenon by which management communicates its expectations indirectly through financial decisions. Relevant because of information asymmetry between insiders and investors.

- **Simplicity** – a value investing principle. The belief that things should be as simple as possible, but not simpler.

- **Size Advantages** – the concept that businesses with larger scale operations have inherent operations and improved bargaining leverage.

- **Solvency Ratios** – financial ratios that measure the cash flow producing ability of a firm relative to leverage levels.

- **Structural Subordination** – the concept that debt at the operating company level is structurally senior to debt at the holding company level.

- **Sum-of-the-Parts** – a valuation approach by which several dissimilar businesses are valued independently and aggregated to determined a combined value.

- **Switching Costs** – the costs and difficulties associated with a business's customers switching products or services.

- **SWOT Analysis** – an analysis of the strengths, weaknesses, opportunities, and threats of a business.

- **Tax Expense** – the expense paid to the government based on the income produced by the business after operating expenses and interest expenses are paid.

- **Tax Shields** – the concept that interest expense is tax deductible, moderately offsetting the monetary cost of interest expense.

- **Terminal Value** – the value of the cash flows beyond the projection period in a discounted cash flow analysis.

- **Three Statement Modeling** – a model that aims to forecast and recreate the three financial statements of a business over a projection period.

- **Time Value of Money** – the concept that money now is worth more than the same amount of money in the future.

- **Time Well Spent** – a value investing principle. The concept that time should be spent answering core, relevant questions.

- **Total Addressable Market** – the total potential annual sales of an industry at maturity.

- **Total Return Investing** – an investing approach in which the targeted source of returns is through security price appreciation.

- **Unit Economics** – the profitability and return of a business on an operating unit level.

- **Unlevered Free Cash Flow** – cash flow to the entire firm, including interest expense.

- **Value Chain** – the various value creating activities of a standard business.

- **Value Investing** – an investing philosophy centered on long-term returns, discipline, risk mitigation, and identifying bargain priced securities.

- **Venture Capital** – a niche type of private equity. The goal of venture capital is to identify a small number of companies very early on that will provide massive returns to investors.

- **WACC** – the cost of capital of a company's entire capital structure. Weights and combines the costs of debt and equity. Used as the discount rate in a discounted cash flow analysis.

- **Warrants** – long-dated call options issued by a company for their own stock.

- **Yield Investing** – an investing approach in which the targeted source of returns is through income (dividends, interest payments, etc.).

Index

Made in the USA
Coppell, TX
01 April 2020